ANATOMY
OF WALES

ANATOMY OF WALES

editor

R. BRINLEY JONES

72 - 170887

© 1972
ISBN 0 903453 00 2
Published by Gwerin Publications, Peterston-super-Ely, Glamorgan, Wales
Printed by D. Brown & Sons Limited, Cowbridge, Glamorgan

CONTENTS

EDITOR'S PREFACE

The Oxford English Dictionary has among other definitions of 'Anatomy' one which is "the science of the structure of organized bodies" and another which is "a living being reduced to skin and bone". It was with the former definition in mind that I set out to collect material for this volume.

There have been other anatomies, *The Anatomy of Abuses* (1583) by Philip Stubbes, *Anatomy of Absurdity* (1589) by Thomas Nash, *The Anatomy of Melancholy* (1621) by Robert Burton and *Anatomy of Britain* (1962) and *Anatomy of Britain Today* (1965), both by Anthony Sampson—to mention some. This Anatomy owes nothing to any of them. It owes more to the painting "The Anatomy Lesson" by Rembrandt, a painting that taught me a good deal about perspective, many years ago now. For this collection of essays, I invited a dozen friends to look from their particular vantage points and to view Wales; their mandate was to view it through the perspective of history. Within that brief they have had complete freedom of treatment. It seems to me that the picture *in toto* is much more pleasing and hopeful than "The Anatomy Lesson" by Rembrandt.

This is not a complete Anatomy, as many will readily recognize. There could well have been essays on Sport, on Agriculture, on Architecture—the list is limitless; it is an eclectic Anatomy and I hope that my selection will go some way towards a better understanding of Wales and the Welsh.

The book has depended much on the kindness of friends and I record, with gratitude, the willingness and co-operation of all the contributors. I am obligated to Sir Goronwy Daniel, not only for his readiness to write the Foreword but also for other valuable suggestions. I must also thank my wife for much patience, encouragement and help over very many months. The publishers and the printers have been helpful at every stage; I know only too well how difficult their tasks can be.

R. Brinley Jones

May 1972

ix

FOREWORD

It is easy to describe a country in a way that might befit a year book or an encyclopaedia but difficult to illuminate it in a way that conveys its individuality and character. Thus we can readily say that Wales covers an area of some 8,000 square miles (of which about a quarter is over 1,000 feet above sea level) and that it has a population of 2·8 million. And we can also point out that this area of land makes Wales twice the size of Lebanon and half that of Switzerland, while the population equates us with Uruguay or New Zealand. But although this and similar information about our rocks and soils, our climate and vegetation, our industries and public services is significant, it far from suffices to give an understanding of Wales.

Other keys to understanding are provided by history—keys which open many different doors and yet do not enable us to see more than a part of what lies within and nothing of what lies beyond. Thus history can show in Wales an example of one of the striking features of human history—namely, the way in which peoples keep their sense of separate identity over long periods of time even though they lose their economic and political independence. It can show the story of the resistance and subsequent adaptation of Celtic peoples to the Roman invasion, their resistance to the Anglo-Saxon newcomers and creation of islands of Christian civilisation in the Dark Ages, their conquest by the Normans and absorption by the Tudors into the realm of England and their continuing efforts over the four following centuries to preserve their culture and tradition and to manifest a separate identity. History can also reveal something of the technological and other springs of successive industrial revolutions and the profound effects of these on our economic and social structure. It can describe some of the changes in our scientific, religious and political thought and literary and artistic efforts. And yet what it permits us to understand of all these matters is limited and we are left with unanswered questions about changing attitudes and problems and the forces that are now working to shape our future.

It may well be that full understanding is unattainable and that many of the most important questions are unanswerable. A country, like man himself, is an indivisible whole of such complexity that no single writer or group of writers can hope to understand it fully. Just as physics and chemistry, anatomy and physiology, psychiatry and psychology are needed to understand the individual and yet fail to understand him wholly, so the learning of the geographer and the historian, the economist and sociologist, the educationalist, the artist and the philosopher are needed to explain a nation and their joint efforts are likely to have only limited success in doing that and to fail altogether when it comes to prognostication.

But although success is sure to be incomplete, the effort to deepen understanding of Wales and its people remains worthwhile and this work by Dr. Brinley Jones and his colleagues, all of them experts in their fields, will certainly be so judged. From their twelve essays the reader may come to appreciate at least a little more fully than before what lies behind our Soars and Tabernacles, our Sunday schools and University, the gymanfa ganu and the eisteddfod; he will come to understand a little better the miner and the steelworker and the significance of the short-of-breath, blue-scarred men now to be found producing micro-circuits; he will get more meaning out of Dylan and Gwenallt; he will see more clearly what lies behind equal validity and road signs, and the significance of the Secretary of State and of Emlyn and George and Gwynfor.

No one can write without reflecting something of his personal sympathies and these twelve writers are all the better for the sympathetic understanding which they show for their subjects. One of our greatest living writers has a poem which starts with the line 'Beth yw'r ots gennyf i am Gymru?' (What care I about Wales?) He goes on to give some good reasons for disconcern but then after his muse has taken him back to his native vale he realises that the claims on him of his own land are not to be resisted:—

> "Ac mi glywaf grafangau Cymru'n dirdynnu fy mron.
> Duw a'm gwaredo, ni allaf ddianc rhag hon."

The twelve who have written these chapters do care about Wales and because of that as well as their learning I believe they will succeed in making their Welsh readers care a little more and help to make other readers understand us a little better.

GORONWY DANIEL

WALES: A
GEOGRAPHICAL PROFILE

F. V. EMERY

I

THE geographical spirit has flourished in Wales, in response to the early (and continuing) excellence in teaching Geography at the national university. Even so, as a term 'the geography of Wales' could mean quite different things to different people, and for this reason we should make plain at the outset that two distinct but related themes will be followed in this chapter. The first is to distinguish the main geographical environments that we may experience within Wales. The second, in respect of the belief that geographers should help people to understand how their surroundings have come into being, illustrates some of the main influences at work in the Welsh countryside since about 1800.

These two aspects by no means exhaust the studies with which Welsh geographers are preoccupied. Other well-trodden directions where research continues include the prehistoric and proto-historic antecedents of culture areas and cultural movements; the palaeo-ecology of upland Wales; the systematic analysis of Welsh towns and cities; or the framework for regional economic and social planning.[1] As may be inferred from this selection, the tree of geographical knowledge is currently expanding itself with as many branches as the monkey-puzzle or Chilean pine (*Araucaria imbricata*), which was planted so enthusiastically in the gardens of Victorian Wales.

THE GEOGRAPHICAL ENVIRONMENTS OF WALES

Although there is a tendency for the geographical regions that may be identified in Wales to proliferate—the standard text-book for instance has nine regions, 'real entities in the geographical sense', 'well established in the minds of their inhabitants'—we can be content with four principal expressions of the geographical environment. The first to command our attention should be *Upland Wales*, for this is the cardinal feature of a country that stands apart from England by virtue of its assemblage of mountains, hills and valleys. Indeed, its earliest demarcation by Offa's Dyke (the course of which was followed remarkably closely by the political lines that have come down to us from the sixteenth century) was attributed to what Fox called 'natural causes'. The Dyke marked an abrupt change in physical characteristics along the

[1] See, for instance, E. G. Bowen, *Saints, Seaways and Settlements*, 1969; R. T. Smith and J. A. Taylor, 'The post-glacial development of vegetation and soils in North Cardiganshire', *Transactions of the Institute of British Geographers*, 48, 1969, p. 75; G. Manners (ed.) *South Wales in the Sixties: studies in industrial geography*, 1964; H. Carter, *The growth of the Welsh city system*, 1969; H. Carter and Wayne Davies, *Urban Essays*, 1970.

2

outcrop of resistant Palaeozoic rocks, which 'forms in fact a natural frontier'. Where this was clear-cut, in the Berwyns and Clwydian hills, external influences were kept out, but further south, 'the broken character of the Palaeozoic frontier' allowed early Mercian settlement to infiltrate along the Wye valley into the Cambrian massif.

Upland Wales is now the least habitable sector of the country, a region of difficulty set aside for reasons of hostile, restrictive climate, unrewarding soils, and comparative remoteness. It represents, in Bowen's words, 'the core of the Principality in the physical sense', and he outlined it by the association of three sets of natural phenomena, all extremes: areas where the land stands higher than 700 feet above sea level, where the mean annual rainfall is more than 60 inches, and where coarse grasses (*nardus, molinia*) cover large tracts of open moorland. Essentially this is an environment of upland plateaux with a growing season that is late, slow and short-lived. A series of gently undulating, open summit levels has been identified, such as that found on Epynt in mid-Wales, sloping only from 1,500 to 1,200 feet over a distance of 15 miles. Above these high plateaux (the topmost of them attains 2,000 feet) tower the really rugged mountain peaks, from Snowdonia to the Brecon Beacons, reaching 3,000 feet and more, pitted with lakes and seamed by deep valleys that still bear the imprint of Quaternary glaciation.

The nature of the upland climate is familiar enough in general outline, notably the excessive, persistent rainfall and low sunshine totals, but it was not until 1958-60 that we had a set of reliable climatic figures actually recorded in the Welsh uplands. They reveal some striking facts about conditions there, at Fan Frynych near Sennybridge, the recording station lying 2,000 feet above sea level and overlooked by the Brecon Beacons and Fforest Fawr. The loss of temperature with increasing altitude was worked out as 1°F for every 250 feet (sharper than the standard rate of 1° for 300 feet), but in the spring season even this was exaggerated to 1° for 235 feet. In other words, the contrast between temperatures on the uplands and at sea level is most acute in the critical season when plant growth should be under way: the April mean temperature at Fan Frynych was 42·3°F, while at Swansea it was 50·3°F. The 1959 rainfall reached a total of 75 inches, in 1960 it was 106 inches, but at least as significant in an ecological sense was the high incidence of humidity, with the air near to or at saturation point: relative humidities of 90 per cent and over were experienced for a period of eight months of each year. For these reasons, together with the cool summers (the highest summer mean temperature was 56·7°F in August 1959) and the damaging effects of strong winds over the open plateaux, we find here some of the most severely depressed intensities of plant growth in the British Isles.

Add to these climatic inhibitions the incidence of archaic rocks throughout Upland Wales, poor in minerals and bases, often with impeded drainage due to the scouring or dumping effects of glaciation, and it is not surprising that the moorland grasses are so poor, or that peat bogs form both in undrained

3

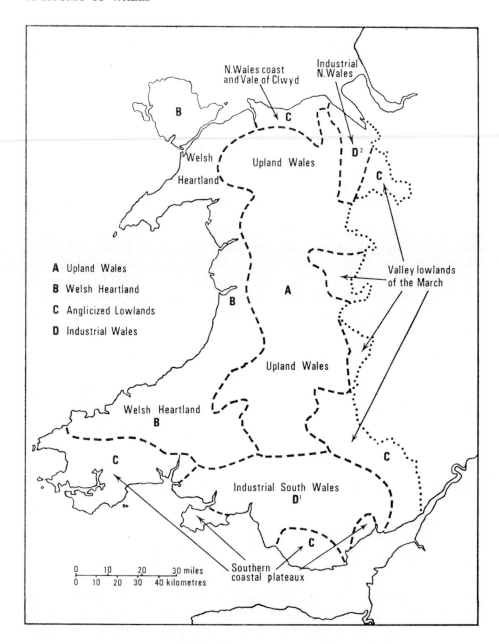

Wales: Geographical Environments

Maps printed on pages 4, 6 and 13 reproduced by permission of the Longman Group Limited

hollows at low levels and as blanket bogs on higher ground. But we should remember that the uplands were wooded until about 3,000 B.C., when the nutrient status of their soils had declined to a critical point; thereafter a series of changes in temperature and humidity led to a gradual floral transition to heathland. Grazing by the flocks and herds of Bronze and Iron Age peoples also played its part in creating open moorlands.

Upland Wales is a region of extremes, easy to define and delineate in terms of natural phenomena, but we can supplement its 'area variation' in relief, climate and so on by others of a more social and communal kind. In particular it is a thinly populated part of the country, much of it quite uninhabited; it has suffered serious losses of population; but among those people who still live there the Welsh language is a vigorous part of their way of life. Demographic and linguistic values of this kind are essential to distinguishing the second environment, the *Welsh Heartland*. A strong degree of Welshness persists into this part of the country, but it is reinforced by a high density of population (by Welsh standards), most of the people being engaged in the more prosperous pastoral and mixed farming that becomes possible on the coastal lowlands of western Wales. The extent and characteristics of this true 'Pays de Galles' were outlined by Bowen on the basis of statistics of population and ability to speak Welsh as given by the 1951 census, although it was plain to see on a map (Fig. 48) in his *Wales: a study in geography and history* (1941), where he used the 1931 figures.

The Welsh Heartland is characterised by population levels of more than 50 persons per square mile, with more than 80 per cent of the people able to speak Welsh, and (at least until very recently) a fairly stable demographic status, without the serious loss of rural population experienced in Upland Wales. The Heartland possesses two nuclei: one lies in the north-west, including Anglesey, coastal Arfon, Llŷn and Merioneth; the other is in the south-west, comprising most of Cardiganshire and Carmarthenshire, with north Pembrokeshire. A peripheral zone, where Welsh-speakers are still + 80 per cent but with population densities of less than 50, barely succeeds in joining the two core areas. The dividing line between such highly Welsh concentrations and areas with far lower values (under 30 per cent) has been very abrupt on each of the linguistic maps drawn from the censuses of 1931, 1951 and 1961; there is little in the way of a buffer between the extremes of Welshness and anglicisation, only the narrowest of transitional belts. This is true not only in the thinly-populated margins between the Welsh Heartland and Upland Wales, but also in the contrasts between a Welsh-speaking industrial *paysage* in the Llanelli-Rhydaman hinterland with the anglicised districts of Swansea and Gower.

The strength of the Heartland is proportional, of course, not absolute. Parishes in Llŷn may have linguistic values of over 90 per cent, but the actual numbers of Welsh speakers in Anglesey, Merioneth, Cardigan and Carmarthen taken together are little more than the 216,000 who lived in Glamorgan (1961),

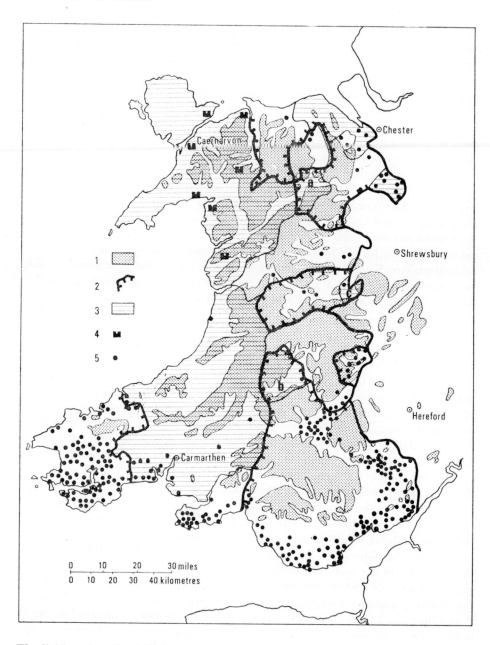

The division of medieval Wales

with a proportion of only 17 per cent in that populous county. The coming of industrial towns in Wales has meant, as a rule, the weakening of spoken Welsh, although the survival of what might be termed a 'culture area' in the Heartland reflects other factors in the pace and direction of anglicisation, such as simply increasing distance westwards from England, the sheltering effect of Upland Wales, the varying degree of alienation of land from the Anglo-Norman conquest onwards. Environmentally at the present time there is a positive advantage here on account of its westerly maritime location, which makes it have an early and protracted growing season, and so forms a favoured mild habitat for grass and crops. One method of measuring 'regional warmth' of this sort is by accumulated temperatures, and on the maps of such values the coastal lowlands, valleys and low plateaux of the Heartland show up as having more than 2,500 day degrees per annum—the second highest category in England and Wales. This advantage has a bearing on agrarian life, and especially on the bias towards dairy farming for the production of liquid milk. Undoubtedly this has helped to support a relatively high level of rural population, both on the farms and on the collecting and distribution sides, notably since the appearance of the Milk Marketing Board in the 1930s.

A distinctive sequence of landscape-making may be discovered in this environment, one fruitful starting point being its close association with the Crown lands in Wales as they stood in 1284. These were the private domains of Edward I, most of them conquered in the wars of 1277 and 1282-3. As the

---

The division of medieval Wales

Explanation of the symbols used on the map :

1. Land above 800 feet.

2. Territory conquered and occupied by Anglo-Normans, 1100.

3. Crown lands in Wales, 1284: the private domains of Edward I, most of them conquered in the wars of 1277 and 1282-3. They included the shires of Flint, Anglesey, Caernarvon and Merioneth; the counties of Cardigan and Carmarthen; and the royal lordships of Emlyn, Builth and Montgomery, *a*, *b*, and *c* on the map.

4. Castles built or strengthened by Edward I in northwestern Wales.

5 Manorial settlement in Wales *c*. 1300: each dot marks a manor that had a territorial basis of arable and other land held on feudal lines; there could be several villages and hamlets in each manor.

The early Anglo-Norman conquests together with the manorial estates in being by 1300 express the situation of Outer Wales and the Englishries of the March, especially in the south and east of the country. Inner Wales, 'Wales Proper', lay in what had become the principalities of northern and western Wales, in the hands of Edward I by 1284.

(Based on plates 30, 45 and 47 in William Rees, *An Historical Atlas of Wales*, Cardiff, 1951.)

tribal principalities of northern and western Wales they had been *Pura Wallia*, 'Wales Proper', representing that Inner Wales which looked to itself culturally, resisted external influences, and still remains strongly Welsh. One feature of it is the appearance (after many complex stages of development) of a landscape in which the single scattered farmstead is dominant. Its dispersed pattern of settlement is now one of the stumbling blocks to modern attempts to improve rural standards of living. Because the population is spread thinly and evenly at so many points in the countryside, it is more expensive to provide the community with services like a piped water supply or better roads. Economically the problem expresses itself as that of a large number of small farms; of 47,000 farms in Wales as many as 39,000 work less than 100 acres of land.

A third environment may be found in the *Anglicised Lowlands*. They fall into place as the coastal or valley lowlands that fringe the northern, southern and eastern margins of the country, carrying again a high density of population (300 to 400 persons to the square mile in some rural areas). Their demographic status is positive, even to the extent of clear gains in numbers of people in the period 1961-71, e.g. up by 38·2 per cent in Chepstow R.D., 29·7 per cent in Gower, 17·3 per cent in Castlemartin. But the characteristic that sets them apart most convincingly is their extreme anglicisation, for since the census figures first became available for determining the strength of spoken Welsh in 1931 these lowlands have been in the lowest brackets, some parts having fewer than 10 per cent of their population as Welsh speakers.

In the valleys of the Marches borderland, together with the southern coastal plateaux, their anglicisation is of long standing. It began on a substantial scale with the Anglo-Norman incursions of the late eleventh and early twelfth century, which in itself was a powerful formative phase in the historical geography of Wales, because the new land settlement was initiated in those lowland areas of greatest suitability to arable systems of agriculture. So obvious were their resources that they were developed by means of 'colonisation' from the English estates of those magnates by whom they were acquired. Pembrokeshire south of the *landsker*, Gower, the Vale of Glamorgan and coastal Gwent all underwent such conversion into alien *paysages*. Among their site advantages were a geological foundation of limestones, rare in Wales, covered with well-drained, light loam soils which are in sharp contrast with the waterlogged heavy clays found beyond their margins on the Coal Measures shales and grits. Further, their good soils lie on generally level surfaces, easy to cultivate, especially the flat coastal plateaux at 200 and 400 feet that terminate abruptly in splendid ranks of high sea-cliffs.

The outcome in these Anglicised Lowlands was the creation of a distinctive kind of man-made countryside, traceable alike in its placenames, farming villages pitched around castle, church or green, rectilinear field systems of open texture, and imposing demesne farms. Always the natural avenues through which innovations have entered Wales, these areas of scenic individuality are now reinforced by a modernised agriculture, as their large and regular farm-field structure, combined with easy accessibility to markets, accommodates the advance of mixed farming, dairying and even horticulture.

Alongside such developments as the production of early potatoes in the long growing seasons of Pembrokeshire and Gower, we find the coastal districts also experiencing a massive expansion in catering for various forms of tourism and the 'summer visitors'. This in itself brought anglicisation to the North Wales coast when the Chester-Holyhead railway opened it to the Lancashire towns after 1848. Here, too, we find amenities for seaside recreation which in the long term have buttressed the holiday towns of Llandudno, Colwyn Bay and Rhyl (the second of which grew in population by 9·9 per cent between 1961 and 1971, compared with a growth rate of 3 per cent for the whole of Wales), as well as many satellite resorts.

And so we are left, finally, with *Industrial Wales*, as self-evident in its way as the Upland environment. True to the geographical fragmentation that seems to be inescapable in Wales, it is split between the twin coalfields of South Wales and the Cheshire borders, their proportions being those of Goliath to David. Most Welshmen have their homes here: out of a national total of 2·72 million people the counties of Glamorgan and Monmouth—comprising the industrial foundation of the country—alone have 1·7 million between them. Densities become so congested they are best expressed in terms of persons per acre, notably in the urbanized systems enshrining the cities and towns from Cardiff or Swansea to Llanelli or Wrexham. With the exception of industrial Carmarthenshire, mentioned earlier, the proportional ability to speak Welsh is under 40 per cent, although numerically the language is far stronger than in the Anglicised Lowlands. Demographic trends are variable, tending to be overshadowed still by the economic and social trauma of the 1930s, when in the chronic unemployment and mass emigration of the Depression years Wales lost over 5 per cent of its people. Thus Merthyr Tudful was down by 6·7 per cent and Rhondda by 12 per cent in the decade 1961-71, but Swansea and Newport were up by some 3 per cent in each case.

These industrial situations will be analysed in their own right in later chapters, so all that is necessary here is to mention two environmental issues of major consequence. One is the growing concentration of people and employment in south-eastern Industrial Wales, symbolised by Cwmbran new town, the Severn Bridge and Llanwern steelworks, accompanied by the stagnation and decline of some of the uppermost Valleys. The other theme is the proper handling of the inherited artefacts and residue of two centuries of coal mining, smelting and manufacturing, so that the quality of life is not injured by a senseless, disordered mess of dereliction. Aberfan in 1966 showed the special hazards that may occur, while the Lower Swansea Valley Project since 1961 has been attempting to reclaim one of the most bizarre industrial wastelands in Britain, a mausoleum of seven generations of labour in the metal trades. George Borrow saw it in 1854 as a subject worthy of that 'powerful

9

but insane painter', Hieronymous Bosch: 'immense stacks of chimneys surrounded by grimy diabolical-looking buildings, in the neighbourhood of which were huge heaps of cinders and black rubbish. So strange a scene I had never beheld in nature'.

THE WELSH COUNTRYSIDE SINCE 1800 : LANDSCAPES BY DESIGN

Of the more revolutionary processes at work in Wales since 1800 whose effects may be traced in the national landscape, the most powerful has been the emergence of an industrialised society. Its undoubted expression is imprinted completely in both coalfield regions within Wales, but industrialisation should not be allowed to obscure or overshadow another process that has manifested itself during the nineteenth and twentieth centuries, namely the creation of rural landscapes by design. These stand apart from the earlier phases of landscape-making in Wales because the human touch is more deliberate, clear-cut and measurable in them. They reflect the first attempts at what we know only too well as co-ordinated planning, motivated by a specific purpose, following a definite pattern of implementation, reflecting ideas and fashions as well as social or economic needs. They also reveal the handiwork of an increasingly powerful technology, whether wielded by individuals or institutions, and we can compare some of their more tangible expressions in the Welsh countryside as we now know it.

LANDSCAPE GARDENING

Wales enjoys no special reputation, as does England, for the number and excellence of her landscaped parks and gardens, although there was no shortage of deer parks in medieval Wales. Most of the old lordships had stretches of rough, wooded ground where the beasts of the chase were hunted, but by the sixteenth century they were disparked and thrown open. When Saxton tried to mark them on his maps of the Welsh counties, published between 1574 and 1579, the surviving parks were few and far between. Not a single one was shown in five of the most mountainous counties, but they were comparatively plentiful in border counties like Denbighshire and Monmouthshire, with seven and eight respectively. Only twenty-seven deer parks appeared in the whole of Wales, fewer than Saxton could include in his maps of single English counties like Staffordshire or Hampshire. This generally low number and uneven distribution, moreover, was to set the scale of later and more ambitious varieties of parkland, because the Elizabethan deer parks generally came to serve as the nuclei of expanses of ornamental parkland in the seventeenth and eighteenth centuries. England has plenty of great houses ensconced in landscaped settings of a formal geometrical type of layout, as at Badminton, and of the more subtle version of landscape design found at Blenheim or Harewood in the eighteenth century, when Nature was copied and 'improved' on a grand scale with belts and clumps of planted trees, serpentine lakes, lawns, walks and cascades.

10

Wales played a minor part in both movements, and two reasons may be suggested for its slowness to participate. There were too few landowners of great wealth living in Wales, where the landed estates tended to be numerous, small and scattered. They could not generate the right kind of social and economic climate under which ambitious schemes of landscaping might emerge. In Glamorgan alone, for example, at the close of the eighteenth century, it was calculated there were as many as ninety landed gentry, many of the wealthiest being absentees such as the Duke of Beaufort or the Earl of Plymouth. If this was a practical reason, there was also an intellectual barrier in the minds of the landscape architects themselves, who were wise enough to see they could rarely compete with or improve Nature when the natural scenery was so splendid. Humphrey Repton was working at Rhûg on the upper Dee in the 1780s, and there he realised that with open vistas in abundance it was pointless to plan a large park which would then be dwarfed by its scenic surroundings. Instead he designed a lawn of just 50 acres, arranging within it as much as possible to embellish 'the variety of its surface and the diversity of objects it contains'. Such was the reaction of the landscaping masters when they undertook the occasional assignment in Wales, concentrating their efforts in a relatively small compass, as 'Capability' Brown did in his transformation of the house and park at Wynnstay in Denbighshire in 1777.

A similar course of modest design was followed by a fair number of enthusiastic landowners who did what they could to beautify their surroundings, implementing their own ideas without calling in the services of a professional master. A good instance is Thomas Mansel Talbot. In the early 1770s he was designing the landscaped parkland around his new house at Penrice Castle in Gower, as well as continuing to plant trees at Margam: as he put it in a letter to his gardener, written from Nice, "The alterations I propose making at Penrice I wish to plan myself'. Talbot planted extensively the new woodlands, the trees including elm and beech, oak, pineaster, larch, stone pine, and various firs; among these 'firs' were probably the native Scots pine and the common or Norway spruce, which was first introduced to Britain early in the seventeenth century. Innovators like Talbot were to make a great contribution to the landscape as private planters of trees, a contribution that has not had the recognition it deserves. No doubt it does not compare with the planting of massive woodlands by the Duke of Atholl in Perthshire (14 million trees between 1764 and 1826), but it was still on the grand scale in Wales. In particular, Thomas Johnes planted 4 million trees at Hafod in Cardiganshire between 1796 and 1813, a yearly average that compares well with Atholl's operations. Like most of his fellow enthusiasts Johnes favoured the European larch above all other species, believing that the mountain sheep found it unpalatable and so left the young trees alone. But where the motive for planting was mainly ornamental, the trees were more varied, including the hardwoods to a greater degree, and the giant conifers from California that began to appear after 1853. The trend continued in the gardens of flowering shrubs, especially rhododendrons, planted at Bodnant by Lord Aberconway earlier in this present century.

PARLIAMENTARY ENCLOSURE

The hill pastures of Wales are often carved into great blocks of rough grazing, separated one from the other by stone walls or fences that snake their way over the shoulders of the hills. This pattern was brought into being in large part by the parliamentary enclosures of open pasture during the nineteenth century. To understand how it worked we must remember two of the most important of the geographical facts of life in Wales, largely cause and effect. One-quarter of the whole country is higher than 1,000 feet above the sea and suffers severe restrictions on the use of its land under the climate as it is at present; and 38 per cent of Welsh farmland is still classified as rough grazing on commons and farms. The Acts of Parliament were aimed at the margin between enclosed farmland and open grazings, or between pastures that were used intensively and less intensively, so we would find it useful to know just how much waste and common land there was at different times when the acts were formulated. The statistics are difficult to standardise, but for 1843 we find a figure of 38 per cent for open common land, whereas by 1874 it was estimated that 26 per cent was either waste used by farmers in common or waste attached to individual farms.

The difference between these percentages must reflect in part the progress of parliamentary enclosure and the linked improvement of what had been open upland grazing. About half a million acres were affected by all the acts passed between 1733 and 1885, with 213,000 acres taken in by the acts that came thick and fast in the 'war period' of 1793 to 1815. Enclosing was at its maximum where the uplands offered most scope for it, with its highest incidence in Montgomery, Cardigan, Radnor, Denbigh and Breconshire. Large blocks and parcels of rough pasture were demarcated in and beyond the *ffridd*, allotted to farms already in existence rather than giving rise to entirely new farms, and sometimes lying at a distance from the old farms to which they were allotted. This was because the intakes had to be wherever the moorland margin happened to run, and although it lay at about 1,000 feet in much of mid-Wales its course on the ground was very irregular. It was nothing more, after all, than a temporary balance struck between a series of powerful forces. Some were physical, the margin running high where the slopes were sheltered and gentle, lower where they were exposed and steep. Others were economic and reflected the encroachments on common land by squatters and big landowners alike. Such enclosures were the immediate settings of some of Caradoc Evans's *Stories of the peasantry of West Wales*, as a little quotation will show: 'The land attached to Penrhos was changed from sterile moorland into a fertile garden by Simon and Beca. Great toil went to the taming of these ten acres of heather into the most fruitful soil in the

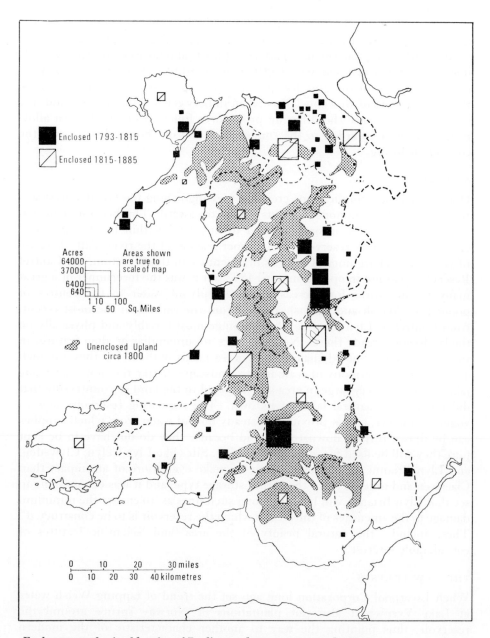

Enclosures authorized by Act of Parliament between 1793 and 1885

Areas enclosed 1793-1815 and the limits of unenclosed upland *circa* 1800 are from Figs. 8 and 12 respectively in D. Thomas, *Agriculture in Wales during the Napoleonic Wars*, University of Wales Press, Cardiff, 1963; enclosures 1815-85 are from Ivor Bowen, *The Great Enclosures of Common Land in Wales*, The Chiswick Press, London, 1914, pp. 47-56.

13

district', and again, 'by the sweat of his limbs he kept profitable the twenty acres of gorse land attached to Ty Hen; he tilled and digged and drained'.

After enclosure, too, the new patterns of fields and farms could vary according to the status of those who had benefited from it. Nowhere is this more perceptible than in the grandest piece of parliamentary enclosure in Wales: the Great Forest of Brecknock was taken in between 1815 and 1818, and it is still possible to trace the differing procedures followed on the Crown allotments, on those awarded to the commoners, and on those sold to cover the costs of enclosing.

NEW LAKES

One of the legal complications created by extinguishing the Great Forest was the basis of the commoners' rights under the award. This became critical in 1884 when Cardiff Corporation tried to buy land within the Commoners' Allotment for a new reservoir in the upper reaches of the river Taff. Because of years of legal argument Cardiff's first venture in this direction, the Cantref Reservoir, was not in operation until 1892 but it was the forerunner of a great many public works for increasing the supply of water to the centres of population, Welsh and English alike. From the earliest to the most recent, from Cantref to Llyn Brianne, they impinge most forcibly and physically on the landscape already there. Not that lakes are unfamiliar or alien features in the Welsh scene: Snowdonia can show at least sixty of them, but they are small and raise no disharmony of scale in the landscape, unlike the new man-made lakes which are very large in area and are sited in the kind of countryside that did not possess natural lakes of its own. The regulating reservoirs now in vogue, moreover, aim at providing a steady flow of water from which supplies can be drawn further downstream, and because they do not have to be kept pure they will be used for sailing and fishing. Sites like Llyn Celyn, Clywedog, and Llyn Brianne are therefore likely to make even more of an impact than Claerwen and other lakes of the earlier storage type, and it was encouraging to see that Llyn Brianne will be built along such lines as 'to ensure the minimum damage to the amenities of the area in which the reservoir is to be constructed'. These include 'the natural beauty of the area' and 'scientific features of considerable interest'.

THE NEW FORESTS

When Liverpool Corporation long ago set the trend of tapping Welsh water at Lake Vyrnwy it also put plantations of Norway spruce around the reservoir, thus pointing the way to another characteristic of the modern landscape. The tree planting on private estates in Georgian and Victorian Wales has become totally overshadowed by the massive planting of new forests during the last forty years, which has revolutionized the appearance of ample stretches of countryside. Given the steady increase in these coniferous forests and in the man-made lakes as well we may see in the future the face of

Upland Wales transformed into a replica of Finland, perhaps accompanied by a second Sibelius to express our reactions to it. The new forests are the handiwork above all of the Forestry Commission. Wales has 496,000 acres of woodland, which is slightly more than the acreage of temporary grassland on all its farms. The Forestry Commission's holding accounts for 300,000 acres of this, and is almost equal to the acreage of all crops and fallow land on Welsh farms. For sheer magnitude of its estate, the Foresty Commission has more power to make or mar the appearance of the countryside than any single agency in the history of Wales.

From Coed Morgannwg in the south to Gwydyr Forest in the north, the seventy-four forests are located principally on the bleakest uplands, some of them transcending the natural treeline to heights of 1,400 feet on westward-facing slopes and 1,700 feet on those facing east. Their absolute upper limit is 2,000 feet above sea level. As the Commission was created to increase home production of pitwood, pulpwood and building timber, it is not surprising that its energies have been directed at quick-growing, hardy coniferous trees. Thus we find in the forest year 1965 that of 18 million trees of all species planted by the Commission in Wales the Sitka spruce accounted for 9 million, the Norway spruce and Lodgepole pine for $2\frac{1}{2}$ million each, and Japanese larch for one million plants. The concentration on conifers has generated one of the main criticisms of what the Commission is doing, namely that the State Forests have distorted the landscape by imposing their geometrical blocks of regimented trees which cannot reflect the seasons' change like the native species. So far, indeed, the dark ranks of the spruce and pine forests have not inspired a second Dafydd ap Gwilym, who loved his religion of the birch and oakwoods,

'When May comes in its green livery,
with ordination for the fresh leaves.'

But in fairness we now find the Commissioners saying that their forests should play a part 'in improving the landscape and in providing opportunities for open-air recreation'. Principles have been worked out for designing the plantations in such an individual way that the earlier blemishes of the 'mass effect' can be avoided, as by planting tongues of broadleaved hardwoods to soften the edges of dark evergreen plantations, to integrate them with agricultural land, to bring out the natural modelling of the hills instead of smothering it. It should be rewarding to see how a more imaginative and aesthetic approach to planting will work out in practice, for such considerations bring us face to face after all with the modern complexities of conservation, amenity, recreation and economic use of land at a time of growing population and new social attitudes. These various demands or pressures (represented, for instance, by three National Parks, by many Areas of Outstanding Natural Beauty and National Trust Properties, or by king-sized caravan camps, military training areas, prospecting by Rio Tinto Zinc), can sometimes be harmonized, but at other times they fall out. Probably no part of Britain poses these issues so acutely or in such close conjunction as Wales, and the lives of its people will be increasingly influenced by them.

Note. On pages 8 and 9 the population statistics for the period 1961-71 are based on the *Preliminary Report* of the Census of Population, H.M.S.O., 1971.

SELECT BIBLIOGRAPHY

Margaret Davies, *Wales in Maps* (Cardiff, 1951).

E. G. Bowen (ed.), *Wales: a physical, historical and regional geography* (Cardiff, 1957, 2nd ed., 1967).

E. G. Bowen, 'Le Payes de Galles', *Transactions of the Institute of British Geographers*, 1959, p. 1.

E. H. Brown, *The relief and drainage of Wales* (Cardiff, 1960).

T. M. Thomas, *The mineral wealth of Wales and its exploitation* (Oliver and Boyd, 1961).

E. Jones and I. L. Griffiths, 'A linguistic map of Wales, 1961', *Geographical Journal*, 129, 1963, p. 192.

J. Oliver, 'A study of upland temperatures and humidities in South Wales', *Transactions of the Institute of British Geographers*, 35, 1964, p. 37.

H. Carter, *The Towns of Wales* (Cardiff, 1965).

E. G. Bowen, H. Carter and J. A. Taylor (eds.), *Geography at Aberystwyth* (Cardiff, 1968).

F. V. Emery, *The World's Landscapes: Wales* (London, 1969).

THE CLOUDS OF WITNESSES

THE WELSH HISTORICAL TRADITION

PRYS T. J. MORGAN

II

ONE evening, some years ago, I was listening to the Welsh news on the wireless, and one item told of two goats being sent by rail from Ystradgynlais in the south to Bryncir in the north. It was still possible to do the journey by rail in those days. The two goats were stranded for a long time on the platform at Aberystwyth station, because they had eaten the labels around their necks which stated whence they had come and whither they were going. The news item has always stuck in my mind as a parable of the relationship of the Welsh people with their history. Although foreigners imagine that the Celts are all afflicted with melancholy, and that one aspect of that melancholy is a regret over 'old unhappy far-off things and battles long ago', the Welsh in fact know only a fragment of their own past, and this contributes not a little to their sense of frustration.

The Welsh, of course, have a history, and historical writing. When one considers the anatomy of a country what part does history play? The total past experience is too much: the vast impersonal forces of meteorology, geology and geography, are of fundamental importance for the development of a country, just as human biology is for a person. The historian, however, is concerned with the mind in that body, and above all, the faculty of memory. With a country, this means the fitful growth of self-awareness, or national identity. Fitful growth, because in comparison with the English, the Welsh historical tradition is more confused, deprived as it is of the back-bone of the unbroken development of a political state over a millenium or more. But while other lands find their historical continuity in dynasties or diplomacy, a mixture of elements has given the Welsh theirs, fundamentally 'the intermingling of a territory with a particular language', as the philosopher J. R. Jones has put it.

Yet history is not made up of territory or language but people. The Welsh people through the ages have had different images or pictures of themselves, and it is these images I wish to survey in this chapter.

For the majority of Welshmen their history begins with the fall of Rome, the coming of Christianity, and the attacks of the Anglo-Saxons. This was the basis of the picture of Welsh history up to the eighteenth century. In a sense it is quite true. The 'Welsh' (meaning probably, Romanised foreigners, to the Saxons) are referred to before the battle of Deorham in 577 cut off the Britons of the south-west from those in the Welsh peninsula, and the word 'Cymry' (meaning fellow-countrymen in Welsh) was used by some, at least, of the Britons before the battle of Chester in 613 or 616 cut off the Britons of the Welsh peninsula from those in Scotland and what is now the north of England. The Saxon attacks did begin at the fall of Rome, and are intimately connected with the collapse of Roman rule. The coming of Christianity is more complex, but here again, although there were Christians in the small Roman settlements in Wales, Christianity appears to have been spread in Wales more effectively in the sixth century by saints such as St. David, who owed little directly to Rome.

In the older versions of the traditional picture, if an origin for the Welsh more ancient than A.D. 500 was needed, then it might be found in fables such as that of Britain being founded by Brutus himself after the fall of Troy. The pattern was Virgil's *Aeneid*. But since the early eighteenth century the Welsh have been aware of their most ancient origins, and it is this awareness which makes us turn to the Celts.

Our knowledge of the Celts comes from the often hostile reports of ancient Greek and Roman writers, and from the evidence of archaeology. The Celts were ancient people who conquered large areas of Europe before 500 B.C. and, among other things, they invaded Britain and imposed their language and culture on the aboriginal peoples here. The Welsh are probably descended mainly from these aborigines, not from the Celts, but history being the past which is relevant and thus memorised, Welsh consciousness goes back to these small Celtic warbands, with their love of beer, horses, gold ornaments and bardic poetry. Welsh is descended from the language of these warbands, and since about 1700 the Welsh have been dimly aware of it. This Celtic linguistic heritage connects the Welsh to the Scots, the Irish, the Cornish and the Bretons. Even in the middle ages there was some awareness of this, in the writings of Giraldus Cambrensis, and in the Welsh legends. The traditional legends, written down in their present form, the so-called *Mabinogion*, in the twelfth and thirteenth centuries, paint a picture of a Britain before Saxon invasions, peopled with what we now know to be Celtic gods and goddesses.

One further aspect of the ancient Celts is very important for Welsh historical awareness, that is the religion of the Celts and the cult of Druids. We have only fragmentary knowledge of the cult, which was powerful in Britain and Gaul in the century before Christ; but these ancient priests, doctors, professors, sooth-sayers and bards, leading national resistance to Roman conquest, have exercised a potent charm over the imaginations of scholars and antiquaries in and outside Wales since the sixteenth century. It was wrongly believed that the druids had built the megalithic monuments such as Stonehenge (which are much earlier remains, in fact). They proved most attractive to the romantic-historical imagination in the late eighteenth century, caused a large literature to be produced on them (during the nineteenth century) and gave rise to the best-known public ceremony in modern Wales, that of the 'Gorsedd of Bards' at the annual Royal National Eisteddfod. Much of the druidic history of ancient Wales was pure balderdash, much of it concocted by a Glamorgan stonemason of genius, Iolo Morganwg, and we can see that Iolo jumbled together three separate cultures in his fevered imagination: the most ancient megalith-builders (long before Christ), the genuine druids around the time of Christ (every schoolboy knows of them from the *Gallic Wars*), and the long line of medieval Welsh bards from the sixth to the sixteenth centuries. Balderdash maybe, but every society needs heroes, and the myths helped to give colour, continuity and interest to Welsh history, and the Celts helped to extend backwards by a thousand years the Welsh historical tradition, giving it an origin which was independent of Christianity and independent of the Anglo-Saxons.

Before the eighteenth century, however, the Welsh historical tradition was very vague about Roman times. Some memories of the Roman conquest had percolated into the middle ages, for instance the ancient pre-Roman kings Llŷr and Cynfelyn must have been remembered in legend long enough for them to reappear at the end of the middle ages as Shakespeare's *King Lear* and *Cymbeline*. The resistance of Buddug (Boudicca or Boadicea) queen of the Iceni in eastern Britain was not so much remembered in the Welsh tradition as the efforts of the other lowland British prince Caradog (Caratacus or Caractacus) to whip up resistance to Rome in wild western Britain, and who was taken captive to Rome before A.D. 51-52 and whose nobility deeply impressed the Romans. The other fragments remaining in the tradition come from the gradual downfall of Roman rule, one most interesting medieval legend being devoted to Magnus Maximus, pretender to the imperial throne in A.D. 383. He was remembered through the middle ages as *Macsen Wledig*, and connected in a vague and cloudy way to Helena, mother of Constantine. The Roman roads in Wales were known as *Sarn Elen*, 'Helena's Causeways', in the middle ages, because of this tradition. Stories, legends, traditions thicken with the total collapse of Rome rule in Britain around A.D. 400-425 under the pressure of attacks by the Picts, the Irish and the Anglo-Saxons. It is interesting that in the middle ages the English were nicknamed *Plant Alys* 'the children of Alys or Ronwen' (Rowena is a romantic form of the name), the daughter of the British king Vortigern, who betrayed the island of Britain to Saxon warbands under Hengist and Horsa.

In the traditional picture of Welsh history the coming of the Saxons and their conquest of England in two stages of conquest, one in the later fifth century, and the second in the later sixth and early seventh centuries, was seen as a battle between kings. History was seen through the genealogies of leaders, English or Welsh; just as Buddug and Caradog personified resistance to Roman conquest, so the native kings who appeared from the shadows of the fallen empire, Urien of Rheged, Mynyddog Mwynfawr of the Gododdin (both in what is now southern Scotland), personify the Britons' resistance to the Anglo-Saxons. The bards and the monkish chroniclers of a later period, such as Nennius, kept alive the memory of the native kings who first met the Saxons in battle because they were the forefathers of later Welsh dynasties. The eighth-century monk Nennius, for example, refers to Cunedda and his sons coming from south Scotland to north west Wales to rid the land of Irishmen, and staying to found various Welsh princely houses. Edeirnion in east Merioneth apparently takes it name from Eternus (Edern) one of Cunedda's sons, and his grandson Marianus (Meirion) was apparently the founder of Meirionnydd (Merioneth). The tradition fits in with what we know about the way the late Empire shifted useful native troops from threatened frontier to threatened frontier as required. Cunedda's period seems to have been early in the fifth century. Strange to relate, the Cunedda tradition, maybe because of its genealogical connexion with later dynasties, is a good deal stronger than that of Arthur. Arthur later became world-famous in lore and story, because he inspired many twelfth-century European romances. He is identified by modern historians with a Romanised leader of the Britons whose victory against the Saxons at 'Mons Badonicus' around A.D. 500 (the exact date and place are unknown) gave the Britons a respite for some generations.

The historical tradition was largely that of princely genealogies, or associated fables of good and bad kings. But we cannot ignore one further picture which is ancient and in many ways just as important. Countless names, placenames, and names of other topographical features such as wells, keep green in every corner the memory of the early saints, missionaries and hermits, who evangelised Wales and all the lands bordering the Irish Sea in the sixth and seventh centuries. The unity of the Christian church was pretty questionable at this time. In any case, the ascetic evangelists owed more to the vigour of Ireland than to Rome. The Irish had been converted by Britons such as Patrick, and then Ireland became the power-house of religious energy. The pagan Saxons cut off the 'Celtic peoples' from the east. The pagan invaders were largely converted to Christianity by missions from Rome. In various stages during later centuries the church in the far west was reconciled to Rome, and absorbed into the Roman church by the time of the Norman conquests of Wales and Ireland. Wales never became an independent archbishopric with its own primate. After the Norman conquest around 1100 Canterbury marched in at the tail of the Norman cavalry, as it were. Many Welsh churchmen—the most famous was the semi-Norman Gerald de Barri, 'Giraldus Cambrensis'— tried to fight a rearguard action, in vain, to make St. Davids an independent archbishopric.

Unsuccessful, and yet the memory of the so-called 'British' church of the Welsh, overwhelmed by the Roman Catholic influence the Normans brought in, always remained. It is possible that the survival of St. David's memory as patron saint is due in part to Welsh suspicion of Norman churchmen. In any case Protestants in England and Wales in the Reformation period were intrigued by this ancient church, independent of Rome, and they tried to show that the British church was the same as that founded at Glastonbury by Joseph of Arimathea himself.

It would be fair to say that there were some other forces preserving the memory of the medieval kings of Wales besides the bards who kept the long genealogies. The lawyers, in the twelfth century at least, kept the memory of Howell the Good (Hywel Dda), king of most of Wales in the early tenth century. The impressive corpus of Welsh medieval legal texts preserved the

21

tradition that the first great codification of native law was made by Hywel at Whitland. King of *most* of Wales, for the native princes, of whom Cunedda's sons were only some, rarely succeeded in uniting Wales. England even before 1066 had one of the most exceptionally unified monarchies in western Europe. English chroniclers present us with a terrible picture of Welsh princes, poverty-stricken squabblers stabbing each other in the back. But recent historians have told us that this is somewhat exaggerated. In the ninth century peaceful marriage alliances, rather like those of diminutive Habsburgs, managed to unify nearly the whole of what is now Wales, under princes like Rhodri Mawr and Hywel Dda. The trouble was that the Welsh kingdoms, Gwynedd, Powys, Deheubarth, Morgannwg and Gwent, all co-existed in an English sphere of influence. They were not unlike the jostling states of the Balkans in the nineteenth century, or Indo-China in the twentieth.

The kings were assailed in almost every generation between the reign of Cadwaladr the blessed, the last Welsh king to claim suzerainty over all of Britain (around A.D. 600), and the Norman conquest. But the English only succeeded in conquering small pieces of territory inside the Welsh peninsula. Offa the Great, king of Mercia, in the mid-eighth century, made a frontier dyke all along the borders of Mercia and Wales, and its memory remained remarkably vivid through the centuries. The dyke, although it touches the present Welsh border in places, runs through the middle of Flintshire to Prestatyn. With the decline of Mercia (and the rise of Wessex) the Welsh drifted eastwards again. The challenge of the Normans after 1066 was akin to that of the first waves of Saxons. William I conquered England in a *blitzkrieg*, but the Norman conquest of Wales was a slow infiltration, in a sense, not complete till 1282. In some ways the Norman attempts resembled the Roman imperial strategy of pinning down the Welsh mountain tribesmen from the fortress towns of Chester, Wroxeter, and Gloucester. The Normans attacked from Chester, Shrewsbury, Hereford and Gloucester, and by the 1090s had considerable success, for the northern and southern lords and princes were killed or exiled, or forced into submission. Rhys ab Tewdwr, who died in 1093, remains in Welsh tradition the last king of South Wales. But even before 1100 there were signs that the Norman hold was shaky, and the grandson of Rhys ab Tewdwr, Rhys ab Gruffydd (the Lord Rhys) later became effective ruler of the south (though with English and Norman agreement). In the north, there was a more real and more striking revival of Welsh independence, under prince Gruffydd ap Cynan (died 1137) and his successor Owain Gwynedd (died 1170). The northern dynasty—descendants of Cunedda and of Rhodri Mawr—regained its hold with Irish help. Indeed Gruffydd ap Cynan was partly Irish-Viking, and his reign saw considerable Irish influence on things Welsh. The fact that this 'Welsh resurgence' was led by the north-western kingdom of Gwynedd, between about 1100 and 1282, lies at the heart of the tradition (well-known to foreigners) that the area around Snowdon is somehow the most 'Welsh' part of Wales. In Welsh tradition the house of

Gwynedd appeared to be the torchbearers of Welsh independence, because the princes of Powys in the east and of Deheubarth in the south, were often puppet-rulers in the control of Norman lords or English kings.

For the historians before modern times, the 'Welsh resurgence' was a dynastic matter, a rise in the fame of the princes of Gwynedd. But modern historians have discerned many more elements of revival and resourcefulness in the Welsh people in the period 1100-1282. In literature, one finds a flowering of court poetry, a codification of the rules of poetry and music, and the earliest recorded example of an Eisteddfod held by the Prince Rhys ab Gruffydd at Cardigan in 1176. One finds vigorous attempts to make St. Davids an archiepiscopal see separate from Canterbury. The Welsh laws were codified in Latin and Welsh at this period, although the lawyers claimed, with the typical conservatism of lawyers, that they were merely recording the work done in the tenth century. The collections of ancient Welsh legends, called by their nineteenth century editors, the *Mabinogion*, were first compiled in this period. One of the most celebrated books to come out of Wales, the *Historia Regum Britanniae*, was written by Geoffrey of Monmouth (Bishop of St. Asaph) in 1136. A few contemporaries, such as Giraldus Cambrensis, saw through the fables about the foundation of Britain, the wonderful hero Arthur, with his knights of the Round Table, Excalibur and the Isle of Avalon, but it had a profound influence on Welsh tradition, for its picture of a hero who had gone away to return in some future hour of crisis, fitted into the picture of history given by the prophetic semi-political poetry of the Welsh bards. Although Geoffrey was attacked by Tudor historians such as Polydore Vergil, much of Geoffrey's writing was accepted as history up to the nineteenth century, and it even now profoundly moves the imagination.

The greatest princes of the 'Welsh resurgence' were, ironically enough, the last ones, Llywelyn ab Iorwerth, Llywelyn the Great or Llywelyn I (died 1240), and his grandson, Llywelyn ab Gruffudd, Llywelyn the Last or Llywelyn II, who was killed at Cilmeri in 1282. They had learned much from their Norman enemies, and sought to absorb other Welsh territories to form a feudal state policed with stone castles. Before this the Welsh had no tradition of feudal obligations or stone building. At this time the remaining princes of south Wales declined or disappeared, and the north-eastern princes, the dynasty of Powys (which on some occasions had taken the lead in Welsh affairs, as around 1100) turned more and more to English help in self-defence against the growing aggression from Gwynedd. Llywelyn I had to contend with a moderately weak English king, Henry III, and he did this subtly and carefully. Llywelyn II, however, had as his enemy the most powerful of English medieval kings, Edward I. When England was divided by barons' wars in the 1240s and 50s, Llywelyn II rose to great heights, and came, by the Treaty of Montgomery in 1267, to control nearly all of Wales. But a policy of war subsequently led to reverses and near downfall by the Treaty of Aberconway 1277. Edward needed only bide his time before making Llywelyn quarrel at a bad moment. That opportunity came in 1282. During the Welsh war Llywelyn was killed in a chance foray near Builth. Despite considerable resistance under Llywelyn's brother Prince David, a man who had had a most stormy and chequered relationship with Llywelyn, Welsh defences soon collapsed, and the English armies occupied the whole of western Wales. Even at the time, the Welsh felt this was the end. One or two fine poems were written on Llywelyn's death, the most famous being the long elegy by Gruffudd ab yr Ynad Coch, which is full of a remarkable sense of historical destiny, the ancient lineage of the house of Gwynedd, its recent pretensions to greatness, and historical tragedy, the awesome character of its collapse.

The Welsh chronicle *Brenhinedd y Saeson* says under the year 1282 that 'Wales was cast to the ground'. Yet for those for whom history was princely titles and genealogies, the history of Wales was continued after 1282 by the fact that Edward I, having conquered western Wales, created in 1301 the English principality of Wales, henceforth to be a private possession of the eldest sons of the English kings. It was believed that the history of English princes like the Black Prince, with his Welsh troops at Creçy in 1346 wearing leeks in their bonnets, formed part of Welsh history. The principality, as a fiscal unit in royal finances, continued to exist up to the late eighteenth century, and by that time, the titular 'Principality' was almost the only official recognition of the very existence of a 'Wales' at all. The colourful investiture ceremonies of the Princes of Wales held in 1911 and 1969 helped to revive this somewhat unreal picture of Welsh medieval history, but we must note that it forms a very important element in Welsh historical writing (especially writing in English).

The military conquest of 1282 was regulated by an edict of the king at Rhuddlan in 1284, and the conquest became a reality with the building of those enormous castles such as Caernarvon, and with the increasing hold of Canterbury over the Church in Wales, introducing something like a regular pattern of ecclesiastical parishes. The bards ceased to sing for princes, and turned their talents to the praise of the gentry. They sang to the English conquerors sometimes, and sometimes they sang strange prophetic poetry to incite the Welsh to rebellion. The native upper class sometimes took part in unsuccessful plots, such as that of Llywelyn Bren in Glamorgan, but generally they compromised with the new regime. The most famous poet of the fourteenth century, perhaps the greatest Welsh poet, was Dafydd ap Gwilym: he came from a family high in English government service in west Wales. Most ambiguous are the vagaries of the family of Ednyfed Fychan, the seneschal of Prince Llywelyn, whose descendants survived as gentry, who were implicated deeply in the rebellion of Owain Glyndŵr 1400-1410, and then reappeared as the forefathers of the Tudor dynasty. Perhaps the chief feature in Welsh history after 1282 is the way a class of gentry landowners emerged out of a semi-tribal world, and came into their own in Tudor times.

It is perhaps a fiction to speak of one Wales in the later middle ages. Wales

24

was not united to England in 1284. The king merely became the largest, most powerful marcher lord in Wales. The lords marcher (or marcher lords) are an important element in the tradition. Originally they were Norman warriors given licence to carve out little kingdoms as best they could for themselves, or to step into the shoes of the princelings of Wales. So great Norman families came to have their own small private kingdoms beyond the reach of the king of England. Because the hold of the native princes was maintained to some degree over western Wales between 1100 and 1282, the marcher lordships of these families were mainly in the east, Gower and Glamorgan being two examples. The marcher lords interfered in English politics at any point of royal weakness, and because of their implication in the 'Wars of the Roses', they were the bugbears of Tudor historians or apologists.

Many aspects of the final English or Anglo-Norman domination of Wales must have been unpleasant, and by the mid-fourteenth century plagues, rapid agrarian changes and social discontents (as in England) added to the misery of the Welsh. As we have said the bards wrote political prophesies and aided and abetted plots by descendants of native princes or chieftains against English rule. The raids of one of the descendants of Llywelyn I, Owain ab Tomos ab Rhodri, called also Owain Lawgoch (Owen Red Hand), were quite unsuccessful but they entered into historical tradition and legend. Far more important than he is the slightly later Owen Glendower, or Owain Glyndŵr, who led a long-lasting rising against Henry IV from 1400 to 1410, when he disappeared. Glyndŵr's rebellion was so successful that it gave rise to great English hatred for the Welsh and much anti-Welsh legislation. His rebellion was accompanied by lawlessness and destruction. Welsh historians from the ranks of the Tudor gentry and other Tudor apologists (not least William Shakespeare) believed Glyndŵr was a rebel and traitor, whose rebellion was only put down by Henry of Monmouth (Henry V), whom Fluellen claimed as a 'Welshman', at least for the sake of an argument.

Glyndŵr's revolt began as a private quarrel between the chieftain of a small Welsh lordship and a great marcher lord, Grey de Ruthin. Glyndŵr was an exceptional man, and able to take advantage of English civil wars after the coup-d'état of the Lancastrians and the deposition of Richard II in 1399. Glyndŵr used old dynastic claims which he had to the crown of Powys and (tenuously) to the crown of Deheubarth in the south, to bolster his rebellion. He also drew on terrible agrarian and social discontents of the period, frustration which needed some vent, however desperate. Glyndŵr goes beyond the purely social or dynastic: he was crowned Prince of Wales, he called Welsh parliaments, tried to set up the structure of a monarchy with a civil service drawn from a proposed Welsh university and an independent Welsh church.

No writer had a good word, however, for this noble and tragic failure of a prince, whose rebellion collapsed in 1410, until the romantic period. Thomas Pennant in the late eighteenth century is said to have begun his rehabilitation,

25

which went on apace in the nineteenth century, not merely in frothy romantic patriotic odes and stage-plays, but because his proposals for a Welsh church and university were of deep interest to the Victorians who were attempting to disestablish the Anglican church and set up a Welsh university too. Modern historians have been able to show how Glyndŵr's revolt fits into a general pattern of discontent and revolt in Europe around 1400, and have debunked him as a patriotic hero pure and simple.

If one looks at them coldly, these princes such as Glyndŵr are unsuitable heroes, their images of romantic failure are not very relevant to twentieth-century Wales, with its markedly democratic penchant. But if we realise that Welsh patriotism or nationhood in the middle ages could be expressed only through a dynasty or monarchy, then their struggles can be seen in a different light. Rhodri Mawr and Hywel Dda in the ninth century, the Llywelyns in the thirteenth, and Glyndŵr in the early fifteenth, came nearest to founding a unified Welsh state by the standards of their times, and these attempts have haunted Welshmen ever since. Without these experiments, Welsh history would be quite non-political, merely social and cultural history.

The Tudor historians such as George Owen of Henllys and Sir John Wynn of Gwydir drew a black picture of the fifteenth century, but if one looks at the reams of Welsh poetry written during that century the picture is quite different: a lively society of gentry, vigorous and resourceful in getting round the anti-Welsh penal legislation, and learning to run their communities while the English were immersed in their civil wars. Even the robbers and raiders living in the forest are painted in brilliant Robin-Hood-like hues. The native-born rose to positions of great prominence in Wales, and by the mid-century Welshmen like William Herbert, Earl of Pembroke, rose to positions of unheard-of prominence in England. Although Glyndŵr had disappeared in 1410 (and was probably dead by 1415) the bards often wrote anti-English prophetic poetry, creating a public opinion in Wales which might expect some deliverer, a second Arthur as it were. It was thought to be William Herbert until he was killed (with a great train of Welsh gentry) at Banbury in 1469; then it was seen to be Henry Tudor. The bards transmuted his return from Brittany in 1485 and his victory at Bosworth into a peculiarly Welsh triumph. The Tudors were willing for the Welsh to cultivate the myth, because it suited them to have a popular base of support in so large a region. For those to whom history was family history writ large, Henry appeared as the descendant of native Welsh princes and even as the ultimate descendant of Cadwaladr, last Welsh king of all Britain. Henry used what was supposed to be Cadwaladr's Red Dragon standard at Bosworth, and this, superimposed on the Tudor green and white livery, eventually came to be the national emblem of Wales.

The Tudor period is one of the most disputed parts of the Welsh historical tradition. The appearance of printed books, interest among the English in things Welsh because of the Welsh origins of the royal house, and the large numbers of Welshmen coming to London, gave rise to considerable writing on

Wales in the sixteenth century. The Tudors were praised for having extended so many favours to Welshmen (the Herberts and the Cecils were merely the most successful of a vast array), for having reformed the government of Wales, and for having brought the Reformation to the benighted Welsh. It is quite true that nearly all the Tudors gave marked favours to Welshmen, though few of them attained really high office. Henry VII began to remove the legal disabilities of Welshmen bit by bit from 1505 to 1507. The early Tudors also humbled the marcher lords such as the Duke of Buckingham, lord of Brecknock, and reduced the congeries of Welsh lordships and principalities to unity and order by the Welsh ordinances of 1536. The lordships were turned into thirteen counties on the English pattern, which survive more or less intact to the present day. The ordinances, called later the 'Act of Union', delivered the *coup de grace* to the surviving native laws of Hywel Dda, and ended what official status the Welsh language had had in administration. A second set of ordinances in 1542, also called the 'Act of Union', cleared up many anomalies in the act of 1536, and gave Wales and its borders a special regional administration set up by statute. An irregular and informal council had met at Ludlow since 1471, but this was in 1542 turned into a permanent administration, which lasted till 1689. Wales was given a system of courts of law separate from Westminster, and these lasted till 1830. The newly formed county of Monmouth was excluded from this arrangement, and attached to Westminster courts on the grounds that it was nearest to London. This began the anomalous position of Monmouthshire in the eyes of lawyers, for Monmouthshire did have an English legal system right up to 1830.

The so-called 'Act of Union' did not as an act figure very large in the older histories of Wales. It must have appeared unquestionably beneficial to those who wrote Welsh history, for it gave opportunities for unchallenged power in all parts of Wales (and England) for any able Welsh gentleman. But the Tudors, after being praised for so long by Welsh and English writers, were accused in the nineteenth century of tyrannical behaviour, and Welsh writers began to see the Act of Union as an act destroying the existence of Wales, and cruelly proscribing the Welsh language and laws. The gentry had risen fast in the sixteenth century, and they had within two or three generations forgotten their Welsh; hence the act appeared to be not only the beginning of the woes of the language, but also one cause for the separation of gentry from the folk or *Gwerin*, a social separation which had become complete by the late eighteenth century, and which was one of the obsessions of Liberal or Radical writers in the nineteenth. What did it matter to the *Gwerin* that the Tudors had quashed marcher lords such as Sir William Stanley, if they replaced them by selfseeking gentry like Sir John Wynn of Gwydir?

Since 1900 the Tudors, who have never ceased to have their defenders, have also been attacked from a patriotic point of view. Law and order and opportunity for progress certainly were brought by the Tudors, but there is more uncertainty about the long-term effects, effects which the Tudors

27

themselves perhaps did not foresee. Historians of literature—who after all, are historians—added fuel to the fire by showing how soon after 1536-42 the old cultural growth of the bards, their guilds and schools, meetings and practices, began to wither, only to be replaced by a London grown culture disseminated over Wales by schools like Shrewsbury School or Queen Elizabeth Grammar school, Carmarthen, and how the native culture fell into atrophy soon after 1600.

Much more acrimonious, perhaps, has been the debate over the Reformation. Every schoolboy knows how much ink has been spilt over Henry VIII's divorce and Bloody Mary's martyrs in England. The debate has been rather different in Wales. The reform of the Anglican church came fast on the heels of the 'Act of Union', and the Welsh acquiesced in the changes more peacefully than many parts of England. From the mid-sixteenth century onwards the Anglican church was controlled in part by the Welsh gentry, and hence the changes were shown favourably by those who wrote on Welsh history. It was realised by the 1550s that the new changes were being hampered because the Welsh people were not receiving propaganda in their own language. As a result of the strenuous efforts of a most remarkable group of Welsh clerics such as Richard Davies, Bishop of St. Davids, and scholars such as William Salesbury, the Elizabethan government of 1563 began to use Welsh as one of the two languages of the Anglican church in Wales, and an edition of the Common Prayer appeared, together with a New Testament, in Welsh in 1567. The whole Bible was completed by William Morgan, later Bishop of Llandaff and St. Asaph, in 1588. A revised version came in 1620 (this is the Welsh 'King James Version'), and popular pocket editions in 1630. It might be said that although the use of Welsh was proscribed in secular matters of state in 1536, the act of 1563 did give a seal of official approval to Welsh in religious matters. This is the origin of the dichotomy which surprises visitors to Wales, to find the Welsh language so often used within the bounds of the churchyard and so seldom outside.

The greater part of Welsh historical writing in modern times has been about religion, and most of it has been written either by nonconformists dissenting from the Anglican church, or by those working in a nonconformist atmosphere, and hence the unfavourable light cast so often by Welsh writers on the Anglican church. Suspicion or dislike for its present role was cast back at its apparent origins in the Tudor period, and the Anglican church therefore appeared as an alien church, imposed by law against the will of the Welsh people, living in a kind of limbo, which lasted until the religious revivals of the eighteenth century. The 'Act of Union', according to this Dissenter image of Tudor history, appears as a 'softening-up process', preparing the Welsh upper classes to accept the Reformation and put it into practice in the remote provinces. This old image was added to in the late nineteenth century by Radical and Liberal Welsh writers, because the chief upholders of the Anglican church, by then the church of a minority in most parts of Wales, were the Welsh country gentry, who were for purely secular reasons the bugbears of these writers.

Professor A. H. Dodd, writing in 1953, complained that the whole of the seventeenth century had a needlessly feeble image in Welsh historical thought. This is probably because nothing striking happened to Wales: on the surface it was merely a sleepy, down-at-heel province of the Stuart monarchy, slow-moving, conservative, and fitting perfectly into the neo-Marxist English view of the mid-century upheaval between King and Parliament whereby Wales in common with 'backwoods' areas in the north and west of England supported the King, while the progressive south and east supported Parliament. What striking changes did occur, for example, the abolition of the Council of Wales in 1641, and its wraith-like existence once again from 1660 to 1689, were negative or unattractive. For historians such as the Radicals of the nineteenth century, or the historians of nonconformist 'causes', the seventeenth century was a period of darkness, the alien church finding no roots in the people, the gentry growing more and more alienated from their tenantry, while the peasants turned to the degraded pleasures of the flesh and the alehouse. For those who wrote on literature the period was one of sad decay, because of the atrophy of the bards who had more than anybody else given a solemn continuity to Welsh tradition, and the decay of the bards was hardly compensated by the growth of Protestant literature, religious history and apologetics, because so much of what appeared in Welsh was derivative, if not downright translation. Nonconformists, of course, found something to praise in works of devotion, and in the fact that the origins of many later nonconformist causes could be found in the 'gathered churches' of the Commonwealth period. There were one or two congregations of Puritans in Wales before 1640, but the Welsh had clearly ignored the appeals of John Penry of Cefn-brith, implicated in the Elizabethan Martin Marprelate tract controversy, and executed. It was only in the late nineteenth century that he was rediscovered by Welsh nonconformity as its morning-star. Later non-conformity looked back at the Commonwealth period as its heroic age, for the musketry of Cromwell's forces had protected the early Welsh Puritan causes against popular dislike, and indeed, from 1650 to 1653 the act for the propagation of the Gospel in Wales gave Wales special treatment (to be sure because Wales appeared to be so benighted to English eyes). The small congregations founded about 1650 struck roots quite soon, and endured through Caroline persecutions, and became the 'mother churches' of many congregations. For those who wrote on the progress of Welsh education, the seventeenth century, as with nonconformity, was a period of glimmering twilight before the true dawn; one thinks of the schools of the Welch Trust founded by Thomas Gouge, of the work of educationists like Stephen Hughes and Charles Edwards (also a distinguished religious historian in Welsh), and the hundred or so schools founded by the S.P.C.K. in Wales between 1700 and 1740. Similarly the work of the Welsh scholars in the seventeenth century, although it now seems a valuable work of rescue at the eleventh hour, seems to have the air of preparation for great things to come rather than an achievement in itself.

The image of the seventeenth century in Wales has suffered because the eighteenth century has so much more positive an image; to most modern writers the latter century has seemed the true dawn or bright morning of modern Welsh history. We have mentioned the industrious scholars of the Stuart period preparing the way for the Welsh literary revival which many would choose to start with the publication in 1707 of Edward Lhuyd's examination of the Celtic tongues in *Archaeologia Britannica*. We have also mentioned the Welch Trust and the S.P.C.K. schools in the late Stuart period, but these were feeble and shortlived compared with the incredible success with 'instant literacy' for thousands, of the movement of Circulating Schools run by Griffith Jones, vicar of Llanddowror, from 1730 to 1761. For religious writers the dissenting causes of the seventeenth century were like violins tuning up before the full orchestra played the music of the Methodist Revival of the period after 1735. The greatest formative influence of all, the changes called the Industrial Revolution, was only clearly visible in Wales during the latter half of the eighteenth century. All these changes, cultural, educational, religious and industrial, have their full effects in the nineteenth century: the dissenters were still a minority in 1800, and areas which had become fully industrialised such as Bersham in the north and Merthyr in the south, were exceptional before 1800. It is equally true to observe that many of the profoundest changes had occurred in the late seventeenth century: the appearance of a sizable Welsh literate middle class for the first time; or the appearance in England of those economic forces which would change Wales in the wake of England. Nevertheless, in the Welsh historical tradition, it is the eighteenth century which claims a positive reputation as one of the great turning-points in Welsh history.

There is probably an element of exaggeration in all memorable historical images. Recent historians have told us not to take for granted the picture of Welsh culture painted by the rather self-important literary revivalists of the mid-eighteenth century, the publicists Richard, Lewis and William Morris, and their protégé the poet Goronwy Owen. The Glamorgan stonemason Iolo Morganwg disliked the Morrises and, for all his fantasies, rightly emphasised that in many parts of Wales there never had ceased to exist small coteries of bards meeting quietly in alehouses to judge each other's stanzas over beer and cheese. Welsh scholarship, with its considerable volume of publication of Welsh literary and historical texts, owed much to Edward Lhuyd, but he in turn owed much to those circles of literary parsons and squireens in, among other places, the Vale of Teifi, the Vale of Clwyd and eastern Denbighshire. The tide may have been ebbing and turning around 1690-1700, but by 1751, when the Morris brothers and their convivial London friends founded the first 'Welsh society' the Cymmrodorion, the tide was flowing fast. The strenuous efforts of individuals in the first half of the century led to something like a web of organisation in the latter half, printers and publishers appear for the first time in Wales, and we have a scene of humming activity, from collections of poetry to dictionaries to raise the status and improve the public knowledge of the language. The cultural revival was mostly literary, or linguistic, but it also had its musical side: the ancient custom, now rapidly falling into desuetude, of declaiming odes as a false-burden or descant over well-known harp tunes (known as *penillion* singing) linked poetry to music; the cultural revivalists devoted considerable energies to collecting and publishing Welsh music, and reviving the dying art of *penillion* singing, thus beginning the modern image of the Welsh as a 'musical nation'. The culture revived was that of the princely past of ancient Wales: but it was revived for a literate middle class of yeomen and merchants, and even civil servants and manufacturers in London. It was a later century that was to develop this culture for a popular democratic audience. For instance, the alehouse competitions of the bardic coteries were reorganised, and publicised in newspapers and thrown open to the public for the first time in 1789. Truly popular *eisteddfodau* came a good deal later after the new roads and railways made it possible for crowds to come together, that is after 1850.

Something parallel happened with the religious revival in the eighteenth century. The Methodist revival, which began in the diocese of St. Davids in the 1730s, and spread rapidly through south and mid-Wales, together with later revivals of evangelical fervour in the small dissenting sects, have long given the eighteenth century a most positive image, though patriots most deeply concerned for folklore and country dances have always accused the Methodists of killing what was carefree and jolly in the natural culture of the peasantry. The picture of Wales in 1700 given us by Methodist historians and others is of a 'Wales lying in a dark and deathly sleep', as William Williams of Pantycelyn, the great hymnwriter put it. Further evidence of the appalling state of religion in the Anglican church in Wales is presented by Erasmus Saunders in his view of the Diocese of St. Davids in 1721. But modern historians remind us that things were already stirring in the diocese long before the great Methodist preachers got to work: there were societies concerned to improve the morals of the lower orders, and efforts to found schools. Griffith Jones, who successfully ran the educational revolution of the Circulating schools, was a clergyman of the diocese, and brother-in-law of Sir John Philipps, the great patron of the schools of the S.P.C.K. During the eighteenth century the hellfire Methodist preachers made a considerable popular impact, but the permanence of their organisation owed much to the growth in Wales of a sizable literate middle class. If it can be said that some elements of the sixteenth century European Renaissance seem to reach Wales by the mid-eighteenth century, it might be added that Wales does not experience the sixteenth century Reformation fully until the same period.

Although the evangelical revivals of the century, the Methodist revival within the Anglican church, the attendant revivals in sects like the Baptists or Congregationalists (Independents, as they are called in Wales), had English and other foreign origins, the enormous success of the movement and the myriads of Welsh converts, made the movements autonomous, and making great use of the Welsh language, cultivated the language for all public purposes, so that they produced a very large Welsh literature, not the least part of which was a whole corpus of religious history. The anti-Methodists also tried their best to spread their propaganda in Welsh: a redoubtable enemy of the evangelicals was Theophilus Evans, rector of Llangammarch in Breconshire, who wrote the most widely read history book in Welsh in the eighteenth and nineteenth centuries, *Drych y Prif Oesoedd* (1716, and second edition 1740), which gave a wonderfully vigorous picture of Welsh history, showing how the good old Anglican church was the true successor of the 'Celtic' church first founded in Britain about the time of Christ. It had the merit of giving to the Welsh public in a digestible form the work of Edward Lhuyd and others on the ancient Celtic conquerors.

The industrial revolution was no less important in Wales than in England, but in Wales its impact was rather different. From being one of the poorest areas in western Europe Wales suddenly became one of the richest. The revolution had fewer antecedents in Wales than in England. Welsh agriculture had been notoriously backward and poor, but in the latter half of the eighteenth century Wales had some of the most progressive agricultural societies, that of Breconshire, for example, one of whose founders, by the way, was the great Methodist evangelist Howell Harris of Trevecka (died 1773). During the century, industrial activity, financed sometimes by English capitalists like Bacon and Crawshay at Dowlais, or John Wilkinson at Bersham, or sometimes by native squires like Thomas Pryce of Neath in west Glamorgan, spread sporadically throughout Wales—there were new slate quarries in Caernarvonshire, great copper mines in Anglesey, iron works in east Denbighshire and in the hills of the Brecon-Glamorgan borderland, woollen mills rose up in the green countryside, as at Newtown in Montgomeryshire. Newtown was the birthplace (in 1771) of the prophet of the new world order, Robert Owen. It was only after 1800 that the industrial centres of north and mid-Wales began to decline in comparison with the miraculous development of the industries based on coal, along the southern belt from the hinterland of Llanelli in the west to that of Newport in the east.

This industrial development, though enormous, has given rise to conflicting historical images in Wales as it has in England. Every coin has two sides. But the picture until recent years given of the coming of industry has been unduly hostile; Welsh historical writing has not come from people reared in industrial areas. Dark Satanic mills glowered over the green and pleasant land of Wales, too. Many factors have gone to make up a picture of dirt, darkness, of Welsh workmen being exploited by alien capitalist masters, and many writers in Wales have emphasised the disruption of the social life of Wales by the way industry attracted English and Irish workmen in hungry droves. From another direction, a good deal of local or county history has been written in Wales since the late eighteenth century, and that usually by learned antiquaries, to whom industry appeared as the great destroyer of beautiful old monuments and picturesque customs, to the gentry writers industry appeared to bring vulgar standards of moneyed wealth, to the clergymen who wrote, industry appeared to destroy the old parochial pattern and give fresh opportunities for the evangelical efforts of nonconformists.

But for other writers, industry in Wales has had a beneficent image. These remind us that migrant workers came chiefly not from England or Ireland but from rural Wales into industrial Wales; that, furthermore, the Welsh economy expanded so consistently well throughout the nineteenth century that migration out of Wales to America and elsewhere was small, small compared with the proportion of emigrants from England, and infinitesimal compared with those from Ireland abroad. Circles of amateur poets appeared in coal mining or slate-quarrying villages just as they had done in rural villages. The choirs which made Welsh music so famous did not come into existence before the 1820s and then made their first appearance in the large industrial settlements. Industry brought new wealth, and with wealth money to build chapels, buy musical instruments, build printing presses, pay for books, newspapers and sheet-music. The large provincial and national *Eisteddfodau* could not exist without modern methods of transport, cheap excursion tickets on the railways, for instance. As for the fate of the Welsh language, this is a moot point, but suffice it here to say that Welsh was the language of most industrial areas up to 1900, even 1914, and Welsh survived better there than in many rural areas, for example, eastern Monmouthshire, the Vale of Glamorgan, and rural Breconshire or Radnorshire.

It is impossible to separate the historical image of the eighteenth from that of the nineteenth century, what we believe about the former will affect what we believe about the latter. In passing it should be said that during this period, the end of the eighteenth and beginning of the nineteenth centuries, there was a great increase in the books written about Wales and things Welsh. This is partly because of the efforts of Welshmen themselves, the travel books of Thomas Pennant or the paintings of Richard Wilson; partly the result of the romantic movement which sent many foreign travellers into Wales in search of rugged landscape and ancient abbeys and castles. Stories of noble failures such as Caradog (Caractacus), Llywelyn II and Edward I's slaughter of Welsh bards were given fresh currency.

The nineteenth century was a century of great advance in historical studies in Europe; it was also the century of nationalism. The new feeling that the nation should contain the whole of the people, and that the national history was that of the whole people, was bound to have an effect sooner or later on Wales. It appeared at the time of the French Revolution in 1789. Though the Revolution had some faint echoes in Wales—a number of prominent Welshmen such as Richard Price supported the Revolution in its initial stage, and there was considerable sympathy amongst Glamorgan craftsmen and literati, such as Edward Williams, 'Iolo Morganwg'—sympathy in Wales was killed by the fear of revolution in Ireland and by the vain French invasion of Pembrokeshire in 1797. The combined elements of romantic patriotism and democratic nationalism were only later to have a profound effect on the Welsh historical tradition: the rehabilitation of Owain Glyndŵr as a suitable romantic-nationalist hero is one aspect of it. Another aspect of the change is seen in the way the number of excellent county histories of Wales (such as that of Breconshire by Theophilus Jones) pay considerable attention to the manners and customs of the people, and efforts were made to collect historical materials—the Welsh Manuscript Society was not founded till 1836-7, and the Cambrian Archaeological Society not till 1846. A good example of the broader interest of historians is the work of the nationalist circle of Augusta Hall, Lady Llanover in Monmouthshire during the first half of the nineteenth century. Lady Llanover contributed much to the Welsh myth with her work on what she imagined was 'Welsh national costume' with the tall black hat and *pais* and *betgwn*. Her friend Thomas Price 'Carnhuanawc' published a fine modern history of the Welsh people in 1842.

But the Welsh could carry their romantic-nationalism too far. One of the most powerful influences on historical tradition in this period was the erratic genius Edward Williams, 'Iolo Morganwg', who amongst other things bedevilled much of Welsh history for many years by his fantasies and forgeries. One reason why he could 'get away with it', was that Welsh historical and literary materials were scattered all over the place, and often locked out of sight in gentry libraries. After 1830 the Welsh courts, the Courts of Great Sessions, were closed, and their records were carted away to London. Further, with no Welsh colleges, there was no school of academic criticism. Iolo's greatest invention was his ceremonial freemasonry of the Gorsedd of Bards of the Isle of Britain, whose ritual was first held in 1791, and united to the provincial (and later national) *Eisteddfod* in 1819. He wrote a great deal to support his historical and literary fantasies, and spurred others to do the same. However warped his imagination may have been, he certainly succeeded in giving wide publicity to Welsh history, and gave its most ancient elements an attractive and interesting public image.

The mid-nineteenth century was the Golden Age of Welsh-language publishing, with dozens of magazines pouring from the presses, for a populace hungry for literacy and knowledge, learning to read and write in the network of Sunday schools (for adults as well as children) which were the true successors in the nineteenth century of the Circulating Schools of the previous age, and learning to sing anthems in 'Singing-schools' after chapel service, or in the vast numbers of classes learning Curwen's Tonic Sol-fa. It is only since 1900 that, on looking back, Welsh writers have found fault with the optimists of the previous age.

The larger part of this mass of popular writing was concerned with religion, in some way or other, and much of it was religious history. The number of chapel histories and biographies, nay, hagiographies, of religious leaders great and small, run into hundreds. The Welsh Victorian nonconformists had little to tell but a success story; they created their own heroes and myths: they recovered the long-forgotten John Penry, they reprinted Puritan classics of the seventeenth century, and painted a black and white picture of a gloomy *ancien régime* of Anglicanism, before the Revival. The Anglicans of course played an important part in Victorian Wales—Lady Llanover's nationalist circle was Anglican, for example—but they did not create its 'image' in modern Welsh history. The dissenters were a minority in Wales in 1800, even in 1815. But they soon became a majority concerned not just for religion, but for Welsh secular culture, education, and politics. They came to see themselves as the guardians of everything Welsh, and they put their stamp on all things Welsh during the period 1840-1914.

Nonconformity owed a great deal to industrialism (though it spread in country areas very quickly) because it was the rising standard of living which made it possible for men to devote money to building hundreds upon hundreds of chapels all over Wales. For a small congregation to afford a church organ would have been unthinkable in the eighteenth century. The population of Wales probably rose about 40 per cent in the eighteenth century, slowly at first and rapidly later in the century; in the first half of the nineteenth century the population increased by over 70 per cent. Even as early as 1851 over 60 per cent of Welsh people worked in non-agrarian occupations, which means that Wales can be counted one of the most profoundly industrialised countries in the world. The early nineteenth century age of iron gave way to that of coal and steel, which lasted from about 1870 to 1918. The Welsh countryside declined relatively in population till 1851, and then began an absolute decline which has tragically continued ever since. The image of industry as we have said is not untarnished. The time of war against Napoleon had been one of great prosperity, but peacetime brought great problems, great poverty after 1815, and with poverty, unrest, and even rebellion.

Unrest and rebellion in Wales between 1815 and 1850 are very important because they bring the Welsh people to political maturity, and thus they add an important new dimension, a political dimension, to the Welsh historical tradition. The raw new industrial areas, Brynmawr, Blaenavon, Merthyr, and others, were torn by para-military strikes and riots. The most serious was the Merthyr rebellion of 1831, which was put down by troops, and after which Dic Penderyn was hanged in Cardiff jail. Dic became the first hero of the Welsh working classes, and just as the nonconformists had to find heroes and myths in the persecution of seventeenth century Puritans, so the Radicals and Liberals found their heroes and myths in the riots of 1815-50, especially in 1831, and in the Chartist riots in Newport in 1839 led by John Frost. Those riots were industrial, but some parts of the countryside were torn by social unrest and riots, the most celebrated being the Rebecca Riots in west Wales from 1839-1842. The verse in Genesis mentioning the daughters of Rebecca possessing the gates of her enemies, was a good advertisement for the outward symbol of oppression attacked was the tollgate of the turnpike system. The causes and motives of all these uprisings and protests were varied, but they provide useful myth for Left-wing writers, and nationalists at the same time have been able to find in them a suitable picture of a downtrodden people rising against alien masters, alien capitalists, alien police and troops, alien stewards, and tollgate keepers.

The 'hungry forties' were as hungry in Wales as in England; it is during this decade that one discerns first a familiar pattern of events in Welsh political life. The present hunger and the upheavals of the 1830s gave rise to a demand for government action in Wales. Action would have to be preceded by inquiry. In 1846 the commissioners of the government carried out an exhaustive inquiry into education in Wales, but it turned into an inquiry into religion and all aspects of social life. When published as Blue Books in 1847 it caused a storm of protest throughout Wales, a storm which showed how well-knit 'public opinion' had become, how self-consciously Welsh the people felt. A leading nonconformist journalist Evan Jones, 'Ieuan Gwynedd' castigated the reports as the 'Treason of the Blue Books', an historical echo of the 'Treason of the Long Knives' whereby Vortigern around A.D. 400 had supposedly betrayed the island of Britain to the Anglo-Saxons. The Welshness of the reaction came out, one must admit, because the commissioners attacked things Welsh at the same time as they attacked all things nonconformist. Whatever the rights and wrongs of the Blue Books, the scandal jerked the Welsh into action, to give Wales a decent modern system of education, and resulted in campaigns between 1847 and 1870, to set up training colleges, schools and university colleges; secondly, it jerked the nonconformists, even the rather quiescent and noncommittal Methodists, into involving themselves in politics.

The truth about the Welsh political awakening in the nineteenth century is complex, many-sided, but it has a clear image in the modern historical tradition. Wales had little chance to throw off the hold of the Tory squirearchy in the early nineteenth century, for the 1832 Reform Act made little real difference in Wales in the short run. The 1867 Reform Act of Disraeli was more significant, because it offered a much wider popular franchise, and because the Welsh had come to take an interest in politics between 1832 and 1867. The election of 1868 was long considered to be the turning point, the first election where the views of the ordinary people of Wales—the *Gwerin*—had affected the vote, an election (although many Tories continued to represent Wales, and although most of the Liberals returned were Anglicans) which seemed to usher in the 'Golden Age of Welsh Radicalism'. Radicalism became more orthodox Liberalism, and Liberalism went into a decline after 1922, but the predominantly radical or left-wing world of Welsh politics since 1922 still chooses to look back at 1868 as an *annus mirabilis*.

Welsh Radicalism, according to its own publicists, aimed to rid Wales of oppression, to destroy the tyranny of the squires over the peasantry, the injustice of the Anglican state church in Wales, of which only a tiny fraction of the Welsh were communicants, and to improve the status of the Welsh people by better cultural and educational institutions, which would give the Welsh the same advantages as the English. One advantage the English had was the English language, and so this would have to be taught as quickly as possible to all Welshmen. The radicals also claimed to be Welsh nationalists, though political nationalism only came to the fore for a short time, when Radicalism was influenced in the *fin-de-siècle* by the 'Young Wales' or 'Cymru Fydd' movement. It would be truer to say that the radicals were more non-conformist than nationalist, and that the impetus for some of their causes—sabbatarianism, teetotalism, disestablishment of the church—came from England. In 1862 the Liberation society, aiming to disestablish and disendow the state church everywhere, started to work with considerable success in Wales. Radicals made these things, however, appear like Welsh national causes. In 1872 a University college was opened in Aberystwyth, and by 1893 this had spawned other colleges, to form a federal University of Wales. In the 1880s the radicals obtained various measures of legislation for Wales, the Sunday closing of public houses, the founding in 1889 of a network of grammar schools—called 'County Schools'—for Wales, and a long campaign by the radicals eventually obtained a bill to disestablish the Anglican church in 1914. It is difficult to avoid the conclusion that there was an element of nationalism in radicalism, however. One or two lonely figures, such as the Reverend Michael D. Jones, and the Reverend Ambrose Jones ('Emrys ap Iwan'), were nationalist patriots pure and simple. Mazzini, Kossuth, and other European nationalists had a number of Welsh admirers, and many Victorian ballads and songs were full of yeasty nationalist romanticism. Michael D. Jones and others were infuriated by the way the Tory Anglican landowners oppressed the Welsh-speaking, radical dissenting peasantry and believed the solution lay in founding a Welsh-speaking dissenter 'colony' abroad; the attempts to found one in North America failed, but in 1865 a Welsh 'colony' was founded in the uninhabited uttermost tracts of Argentina. The venture, though in its way a success, did not solve what the Radicals saw as the Welsh land problem, and their agitation led to a number of inquiries into landowner-ship in Wales. The Reports of the Royal Commission on Welsh Land published in 1896 are amongst the fullest documents ever compiled on Welsh society. A combination of social pressures and economic circumstances eventually persuaded great Welsh landowners to sell their land to small peasant proprietors, but this was after the First World War.

One consequence of the Welsh political awakening since the 1840s was that Radical writers—W. Llywelyn Williams and Owen M. Edwards, were also Liberal politicians, among other things—changed the historical tradition from the age old concern for princes and kings, which had been given a new lease of life by the Romantic tradition, to one in which the ordinary folk (the *Gwerin*) of Wales were the real heroes. A *cliché* of their thought is the picture of the thatched cottage in the shadow of the gaunt Norman castle, the castle's ruins symbolising the fate of conquerors, the cottage expressing the eventual triumph of the sons of the soil. This view of history is expressed on many levels—the Welsh poetry of W. Crwys Williams among others made it memorable for ordinary men. This picture was more suitable for the history of the last two centuries. I think that what occurred around 1900 was a split or dichotomy in Welsh history: the academic standards of other countries came to Welsh history through the history departments of the new University of Wales, but most of the academic historians concerned themselves with medieval history, the period when Wales had princes, politics, and foreign policy. J. E. Lloyd (later Sir John Lloyd) was the doyen of these men. Recent Welsh history was written in more popular, even journalistic books. There was a great demand for books about Wales in English at this time, because of the fame of Welsh politicians at Westminster from the 1890s onwards, and a number of the politicians, Tom Ellis of Merioneth, Herbert Lewis of Flintshire, and most famous of all, David Lloyd George, appeared to typify the myth of the *Gwerin* school of writers, rising to fame from the peasantry.

Poets, historians, and not least, politicians on platforms, hammered home their new popular version of Welsh history: but they did not merely dwell upon the injustices of the alien Bishops, or alien Tory squires, or alien capitalists, they also—as befitted good Victorians—emphasised the present excellence of the *Gwerin* of Wales. In contrast with drunken Papist murderous Ireland, Wales was 'Land of White Gloves', where the assize justices had no crime to deal with. The Welsh peasant was the best educated, the most temperate, the most pious, and the most upstanding, politically, in Europe. Or at least, this was the picture. The Welsh peasantry might be lacking in painting and architecture, but who could compare with them for music—were the mammoth choirs of the Welsh not world-famous after 1870, at Crystal Palace Music Festivals, International Fairs and Exhibitions, even at Victoria's Windsor Castle? The political representatives of the *Gwerin*, with the help of men like Mr. Gladstone (who was considered more-or-less-a-Welshman since he lived at Hawarden in Flintshire), seemed to be about to achieve great things for Wales: various Welsh legislative measures were passed between the 1880s and 1914, which created a precedent for later administrative devolution in Wales, and up to 1922 a number of small measures of domestic home-rule were discussed briefly at Westminster.

The First World War caused an abrupt change. No doubt the image of the *Gwerin* was like the Victorian and Edwardian English one writ-democratic. But the changes which struck Wales after 1918 were more sudden and more harsh. Despite the apparent Liberal triumph before 1914, factors for change had already appeared; by 1891 already Wales had a higher proportion of Trade Union members than did England, and after 1900 when Keir Hardie was elected Labour M.P. for Merthyr, Socialism began to spread rapidly, though it did not oust Liberalism till the period between the First and Second World Wars. The Labour tradition in Wales created its new myths, traditions and heroes, just as other movements did before—it looked back to Dic Penderyn in 1831, but found fresher, more relevant heroes in Keir Hardie, in the long lock-out and strike in the Penrhyn quarries around 1900, in the violent strikes (as in Tonypandy) in 1910-12, and above all, in the coalminers' strikes and the General Strike of 1926.

The First War was a deep disappointment to those optimists who had held that the Welsh were particularly pacifist people, symbolised by the great radical politician Henry Richard, secretary of the Peace Society. For those concerned for Welsh culture, it was alarming that, although the absolute total of Welsh-speakers had risen with every census to 1911, the numbers fell noticeably after 1921. The membership of Welsh churches had reached an all-time peak in 1911, probably as a result of the Welsh evangelical revival of 1904-5 led by Evan Roberts of Loughor, but the membership declined noticeably after 1918. Interest in Home rule and devolution also declined in the period. Wales's very own international hero, Lloyd George, was in the political wilderness after 1922. The feature which created the gloomy, even cataclysmic image of the Wales of the twenties, was however the slump. The history of the great depression is well known. It hit the heavy industries dominating the Welsh economy particularly hard. From 1921 to 1939 some 450,000 Welshmen emigrated, and yet in July 1935 there were still over 203,000 unemployed left in Wales. The 'Green Revolution' in the countryside, when the great estates gave way to little farms, was followed by agrarian depression in the thirties.

But if the period around 1920 saw the end of discussion of measures of Home Rule at Westminster, it also saw the beginnings of modern political nationalism in Wales. Out of the moral crisis of the World War, the Irish civil wars, and the difficulties of Liberalism, the Welsh National Party (*Plaid Cymru*) was born in 1926, with the aim of securing a self-governing Welsh state. Political nationalism has had a considerable effect upon the historical tradition, especially in the Welsh language, because many of its founding members concerned themselves with revaluing the past: one thinks of the critic Saunders Lewis, the scholar G. J. Williams, and on a more popular level, the historical writer Ambrose Bebb. Like the larger and more successful Labour movement in Wales, the nationalists castigated the moral failures of Victorian Welsh Liberalism and Radicalism. Like the Liberal and Labour parties, the nationalists have discovered their own traditions, myths and heroes in the past —the noble failures like Llywelyn II and Owain Glyndŵr make a reappearance. More important perhaps was the burning by three prominent nationalists of the Bombing school in Caernarvonshire in 1936 and the subsequent imprisonment of the three. Since 1936 the nationalist and non-nationalist interpretations of Welsh history have, obviously, played no small part in

39

literature. The twenties, further, have a rather paradoxical image in Welsh history, because despite the cataclysmic effects of the slump, the twenties saw an advance in opening and developing the national institutions envisaged late in Victoria's reign, the Federal University (expanded during the twenties and thirties), the National Museum, the National Library, all of which contributed to the greatest advance in our knowledge of Welsh history and Welsh literature. In Welsh letters the twenties saw men like Caradoc Evans, Saunders Lewis, W. J. Gruffydd, and R. T. Jenkins attacking, debunking, criticising the complacencies of the last two centuries with vivacity and vigour.

In so many ways the present patterns or tendencies of Welsh life were laid down in the period immediately after the First World War: the fragility of the Welsh economy, rural as well as industrial, in the early seventies, reinforces this impression—the same pattern of devolution of administration inherited from the Lloyd George era, the same debates between the nationalist and non-nationalist, the same decline of religion and the native language. Yet, because the problems have gone unsolved so long, there is an almost frantic search for identity, for a basis of self-awareness. Some have claimed that a knowledge of Welsh history could give all Welshmen this firm unity: but most Welsh people are taught British and English history more than Welsh history, and Welsh historians have written little save for their own fellow-academics. There is no great apron stage, near the audience, as it were; little or no interpretation of history in strip-cartoons, television historical costume dramas, and popular historical novels, for Welsh history.

What can we say, in conclusion, of our anatomy of the Welsh historical tradition? We can see how each generation or each movement has looked for its fresh heroes and myths in the past. But the Welsh mind or memory is patchy and imperfect. One reason for this is that so much of our history is locked in the Welsh language, the key to which has been lost by the majority in the twentieth century. Another reason is that much of Welsh history is a long tale of woe. Workaday existence cannot go on without some reference to past standards, even a past as recent as the early twentieth century. The modern Welsh poet Waldo Williams has a line which might be roughly translated as 'What is love of country? Keeping house in a cloud of witnesses'. Statesmen used to say that history should be taught to the young to instil patriotism: but, on the surface, Welsh tradition seems eminently unsuitable for this purpose, with its lamentable decline from those marvellous centuries before Christ, when the ancestral Celts had a hegemony over ancient Europe. Young people in Wales sing with fervour about princes like Llywelyn II and Glyndŵr. Such great men should appear in the 'clouds of witnesses'. But are they the ones who really make 'housekeeping' worthwhile? It may be, that for all their uncritical enthusiasms, the Liberal, Radical and Left-wing writers have been nearer the mark with their picture of a stubbornly heroic self-reliant Welsh folk, determined to improve themselves, their land and their culture, against all odds, and, even when cast down in the terrible years of the slump between the two World Wars, determined to rise again. But for one reason and another, the Welsh people are still searching for their identity, for a basis for their self-awareness. This is why they still seem to me to be like those two goats, who have nibbled their own direction-labels, stranded on Aberystwyth station.

SELECT BIBLIOGRAPHY

A. GENERAL

The biographies of those mentioned in the article should be seen in detail in the *Dictionary of Welsh Biography* (London 1959).

Details of books may be seen in the second edition of the *Bibliography of the History of Wales* (Cardiff 1962) to which supplements are published periodically in the *Bulletin of the Board of Celtic Studies*.

The most valuable work on Welsh history is to be found in articles in historical journals, such as *The Welsh History Review*, and the *Bulletin of the Board of Celtic Studies* (both published by the University of Wales Press, Cardiff); *Archaeologia Cambrensis* (published by the Cambrian Archaeological Association); and the *Transactions of the Honourable Society of Cymmrodorion* (published in London by the Society).

An excellent guide to books is A. H. Dodd, 'Welsh History and Historians in the Twentieth Century', in *Celtic Studies in Wales—A Survey* (ed. E. Davies) (Cardiff 1963), pp. 49-70.

See also *Wales through the Ages* (ed. A. J. Roderick) (2 vols. Llandybie 1959, 1960); E. Inglis Jones, *The Story of Wales* (London 1955); R. Coupland, *Welsh and Scottish Nationalism—a survey* (London 1954); *The Historical basis of Welsh nationalism* (ed. A. O. H. Jarman) (Cardiff 1950); chapters on Wales by G. Evans and I. Rhys in *Celtic Nationalism* (ed. O. D. Edwards) (London 1968).

Two recent short studies of Welsh historiography by G. Williams are: 'Local and national history in Wales', *Welsh History Review*, V (1), 45-66; and 'Language, literacy and nationality in Wales', *History*, LVI, 1-16.

B. MEDIEVAL

E. G. Bowen, *Settlements of the Celtic Saints in Wales* (Cardiff 1954).
N. K. Chadwick, *Celtic Britain* (London 1963).
M. Dillon and N. K. Chadwick, *The Celtic Realms* (London 1967).
G. Edwards, *The principality of Wales 1267-1967* (Caernarvonshire Historical Society 1969).
H. T. Evans, *Wales and the wars of the roses* (Cambridge 1915).
C. Fox, *Offa's Dyke* (London 1955).
W. F. Grimes, *Prehistory of Wales* (Cardiff 1951).
K. H. Jackson, *Language and History in Early Britain* (Edinburgh 1953).
J. E. Lloyd, *History of Wales from the earliest times to the Edwardian Conquest* (London 2 vols. 1911, many editions since).
J. E. Lloyd, *Owen Glendower—Owain Glyndŵr* (Oxford 1931).
V. E. Nash-Williams, *Early Christian Monuments of Wales* (Cardiff 1950).
V. E. Nash-Williams, *The Roman Frontier in Wales* (new edit. ed. Jarrett, Cardiff 1970).

W. Rees, *South Wales and the March 1284-1415* (Oxford 1924).
W. Rees, *An historical atlas of Wales from early to modern times* (London 1959).
R. E. M. Wheeler, *Prehistoric and Roman Wales* (Oxford 1925).
A. H. Williams, *An Introduction to the History of Wales* (2 vols. Cardiff 1941, 1948).
G. Williams, *The Welsh Church from conquest to reformation* (Cardiff 1962).
G. Williams, *Owen Glendower* (Oxford 1966).

C. MODERN

P. M. H. Bell, *Disestablishment in Ireland and Wales* (London 1969).
E. T. Davies, *Religion in the industrial revolution in South Wales* (Cardiff 1965).
A. H. Dodd, *The Industrial revolution in North Wales* (Cardiff 1951, 2nd ed.).
A. H. Dodd, *Studies in Stuart Wales* (Cardiff 1953, 2nd ed. 1971).
T. Evans, *The Background to modern Welsh politics* (Cardiff 1936).
H.M.S.O., *Education in Wales, 1847-1947* (London 1948, reprinted since).
A. H. John, *The Industrial Development of South Wales* (Cardiff 1950).
H. A. Lloyd, *The Gentry of South West Wales* 1540-1640 (Cardiff 1968).
D. Mathew, *The Celtic peoples and Renaissance Europe* (London 1933).
K. O. Morgan, *Wales in British Politics 1868-1922* (Cardiff 1963, 2nd ed. 1971).
K. O. Morgan, *Freedom or Sacrilege? The History of the Campaign for Welsh Disestablishment* (Penarth 1966).
G. D. Owen, *Elizabethan Wales—the social scene* (Cardiff 1962).
J. F. Rees, *Tudor policy in Wales* (Cardiff 1936).
W. Rees, *The union of England and Wales* (Cardiff 1948).
J. Thirsk (ed.), *The Agrarian History of England and Wales*, vol. iv 1500-1640, pp. 357-396, 767-814.
D. Williams, *John Frost* (Cardiff 1939).
D. Williams, *A History of Modern Wales* (London 1950).
D. Williams, *The Rebecca Riots—a study in agrarian discontent* (Cardiff 1955).
G. Williams, *Welsh Reformation Essays* (Cardiff 1968).
P. Williams, *The Council in the Marches of Wales under Elizabeth I* (Cardiff 1958).
W. O. Williams, *Tudor Gwynedd* (Caernarvon 1956).

SOCIETY IN WALES

IORWERTH C. PEATE

III

TO understand the structure of Welsh society throughout the ages, one has to begin with the Laws of Hywel Dda which, while they were codified in the tenth century, must represent custom practised in earlier centuries. In these laws, the main classes recognized were (a) the royal class—the king or lord and his entourage; (b) the *bonheddig* or the freeborn *uchelwr*, the free 'man of lineage'; (c) the *aillt* or *taeog* who had considerable rights and freedom but these were not as complete as those of the *uchelwr*; (d) the *alltud* or men of foreign blood resident in the country; and (e) the bond-servant, the *caeth*.

T. P. Ellis has stressed that there are distinct differences between this Welsh classification and other legal systems. For instance, 'in no system is the position of the "foreigner" class so clearly indicated as it is in the Welsh Law'. Indeed, it may be that this is one reason, beyond that of language, why it has always taken such a long time for the 'foreigner' to be accepted in many close-knit Welsh communities. Nor was 'nobility' recognized. There were 'lords' in Welsh society but they had no superiority of blood and no privilege not possessed by the ordinary freeman. The stress was upon unity not class division, the unity of the whole of Wales within the larger unity of the Isle of Britain. It was a unity however of at least three geographical parts, Gwynedd, Powys and Deheubarth, with their capitals at Aberffraw, Mathrafal and Dinefwr. Each of these territories had its own 'king' or 'lord', theoretically with an acknowledged supremacy resident in Gwynedd. It was a conception of unity by federation, an ideal always dear to the Welsh heart. In actual fact, the three provinces were themselves federations, if such a modern term can be admitted. Deheubarth was merely a geographical expression which included Gwent, Morgannwg, Dyfed, etc. Powys became divided into Powys Fadog and Powys Wenwynwyn. Through the traditional rule of succession by which each son was given an equal share in his father's estate, divisions into smaller units became inevitable. Indeed, the *cwmwd*, the commote, as a small territorial unit, was one of the striking features of early Welsh social organisation, and remained so throughout the years. Each commote had its lord, and its sense of community was strong for reasons which were simple. Communal help and co-operation among free and unfree are notable features of the early Laws. The statement by Giraldus Cambrensis that the Welsh lived not in villages but scattered about the countryside is well-known and one comes to the obvious conclusion that the occupiers of separate holdings would not keep plough-oxen to plough each holding separately. Co-tillage was practised and the practice of communal aid, *cymhortha*, must have been considerable.

The second main element in the Laws which is of importance to a study of the Welsh social structure is that of kinship, *cenedl* (the modern term for 'nation'). Every man had relatives, related to him within nine degrees. Within such an orbit, every person was kin to a man who therefore, in law, had rights and duties to all such persons. T. P. Ellis has summed up the situation adequately:—

"The ties of computable relationship between persons descended from a common stock, agnatically or cognatically, were real and important factors in Welsh law and society; but there was no necessary uniform grouping of men so related into any organism . . . Such relationship might but did not necessarily coincide with the tribe or clan."

I hope that it can be shown that these main principles underlying the early laws have unconsciously dominated society in Wales throughout the centuries.

Naturally the intrusion of Norman and English influences throughout later centuries blurred the influence of the older laws on Welsh society: indeed, with the Act of Union in the sixteenth century the Welsh laws were officially discarded and English law fully introduced. This is one of the essential differences between the union of Wales with England and that of Scotland. Scotland retained its legal system but Wales did not, and the effect was considerable. But the organization of society and the basic features of social life in Wales throughout medieval and modern times still owed much to the main bases of Hywel's laws.

To the thirteenth century, the Welsh social system remained but eroded gradually by the alien feudal system. Edward I's policy was 'to make Welshmen Englishmen as soon as possible' and his aim has been aped by many politicians and others ever since. The tragedy of his policy was this attempt deliberately to exterminate a nation and to abolish the law by which the Welsh people had been organized. Part of his purpose was achieved by the Statute of Rhuddlan in 1284. But the commonly accepted system continued to be that of Hywel Dda, and the Welsh language—then as now the nation's only bastion against extermination—continued in general use.

The pasturing of flocks and herds remained partly the economic basis of society with much monastic activity helping the development of mixed farming. Giraldus had averred that in his day most of the land served for grazing and that little of it was used for tillage, but well before the fifteenth century Giraldus's statement was shown to be false. Indeed, the detailed attention given to the ox and the ploughman in Hywel's laws serves to emphasize the importance of tillage in Wales even in pre-Norman times. Mr. Ffransis Payne has given ample evidence of Welsh tillage and its social implications from the tenth to the fifteenth century. Sheep were, of course as the monks knew to their advantage, of inestimable value and formed a solid part of the basis of Welsh social life.

The tide of the Middle Ages ebbed in the second half of the fifteenth century and in the first half of the following century. The year 1453 saw the fall of

Constantinople; the year 1485 saw the victory on Bosworth Field of Henry Tudor, a Welsh-speaking Welshman; the year 1492 marked Columbus's discovery of America; in 1517 Martin Luther began his dialogue with Papal authority; the year 1536 saw not only the Union of Wales with England but the publication of John Calvin's *Institutes of the Christian Religion*. In Huizinga's phrase, the 'diapason of life' was changing; the Renascence, the Protestant Reformation, world colonization, the emergence of national states—all these were to affect society profoundly.

In 1587 Thomas Churchyard could compare Wales with England and declare 'that Wales, methinks, is now the soundest state' adding that its market was:—

> "good, and victuals nothing deare,
> Each place is filde with plentie all the yeare,
> The ground manurde, the graine doth so increase
> That thousands live in wealth and blessed peace . . .
> They have begun of late to lime their land
> And plowe the ground where sturdie okes did stand,
> Converte the meares and marrish everywhere
> Whose barraine earth begins good fruite to beare.
> They teare up trees and take the rootes away,
> Make stonie fieldes smooth fertile fallowe ground,
> Bring pastures bare to beare good grasse for hay
> By which at length in wealth they will abound.
> Wales is this day (behold throughout the sheares)
> In better state than was these hundred yeeres . . .
> I meane where weedes and thistles long hath growne
> (Wild drosse and docks and stinking nettles vile)
> There Barley sweete and goodly wheate is sowne
> Which makes man rich that liv'd in lacke long while."

This is a view of rural life in Wales in the sixteenth century which contrasts markedly with the observations of some of the English travellers whom Churchyard castigates as 'spiteful tongues'. An 'account of the social condition of the people of Anglesey' written about twenty-five years later (1613) gives aspects of country life not mentioned by Churchyard. It complains against the 'secular and lay ministers and officers of justice' for not carrying out their duties, thus allowing 'beggars, rogues, vagabonds and idlers' to force householders 'to bestow more food in a month than would serve their own family in a fortnight'. But this account too mentions 'houses and grainyards stored with corn and grain and fields with cattle'. *Cymhortha* also is discussed but interpreted here as the 'gathering of alms' only. There is also a significant reference to the importance of kinship in the social scene of that period. During her period of *cymhortha* 'the good young wife must take an old impudent drab with her that can allege either kindred, alliance, nursery or some affinity or other with all men'. Here, many centuries after the codification of the Welsh laws, appears still an insistence upon the individual's duty towards one of his own kin. In such *cymhortha* in seventeenth-century Anglesey, 'cheeses, wool, hemp, flax and such commodities' were obtained. The women concerned even earned the name of *gwragedd cawsa* (women cheese-gatherers).

If one may consider briefly another feature of social life, buying and selling, this Anglesey account throws light on contemporary weights and measures. At 'the two usual markets of Bewmares and Caernarvon' two sorts of corn measures were found—the 'true' Winchester measure and the Welsh measure, 'the one bigger to buy and the other lesser to sell'. There were also the Welsh and English yards: 'the English yard is certain and known; the other is uncertain and unlawful, $3\frac{1}{2}$ or $3\frac{5}{8}$ inches longer than the English yard. The one is used by all merchants, mercers, pedlars, masons, carpenters, land meeters and others: the other by all tailors, weavers, fullers, housewives and such like.' There were also the Welsh and English gallons. The Welsh gallon was used to measure butter, tallow, honey and the like and 'is thought to be seven quarts and a half or, as some hold, eight quarts English'. *Pwys y garreg wlân*, the wool pound, was used to weigh butter, cheese, yarn, wool, etc., and by it all housewives delivered their yarn to the weavers.

A Welsh social commentary during this transitional period in Welsh society was given by Siôn Tudur who died in 1602 and was buried at St. Asaph. Taxes, he complained, were high for the common people, bishops lived well but had no thought for preaching. They were concerned only with amassing wealth. No-one received holy orders unless he paid bribes, but if one spoke English '*fe gai urddau ar redeg*' (he would receive orders at once). The same was true of the justices:—

> "Ac yn ôl yr aur melyn
> Y byddai y farn yn canlyn
> [judgement followed the yellow gold]."

Siôn's list of 'craftsmen' is of interest. It includes barkers, leather-workers, shoemakers, glovers, felters, cobblers, smiths, saddlers, gardeners, tinkers, miners, goldsmiths, bellringers, clerks, carpenters, stonemasons, slaters, and bards.

The change in Welsh society after the Act of Union was to prove profound. The Welsh language was outlawed, the Marcher lordships were abolished and Wales was finally fully divided into counties. The *uchelwyr* were now to abandon the Welsh tradition and to adorn the English court—the Cecils (*Seisyllt*) were notable examples—to become part in due course of the English upper class and totally alienated from the Welsh tradition. The old bardic system gradually disappeared although an occasional house maintained a family bard down to the eighteenth century. For a period the traditional society was leaderless.

Nor must the fact be overlooked that Wales was now officially a Protestant country. It was a religious 'reformation' without revelation and resulted for a considerable time, as observers like John Penry stated, in a widespread deterioration into 'paganism'. One result was the Elizabethan act of 1563 to translate the Bible and the Book of Common Prayer into Welsh (but note the reason why) so that 'such as do not understand the [English] language may be conferring both Tongues together the sooner to attain to the knowledge of the English Tongue'. And this too was the consummation which stimulated the translators, excellent Welshmen though they were.

The Act achieved the reverse purpose. Into the spiritual vacuum created by the cataclysmic changes, the Welsh Bible, the Welsh Book of Common Prayer and the metrical Psalms of Edmwnd Prys saved the language from deteriorating into a mean patois. It resulted in new standards and with the development in the seventeenth century of the older Nonconformist sects, the language gained a new dignity which produced the magnificent prose of Morgan Llwyd o Wynedd (1619-59) and gave the Welsh people new leaders—the minister and the preacher took the place of the now-anglicized *uchelwr*.

Here we return to that other notable event of the early sixteenth century, the publication of John Calvin's *Institutes of the Christian Religion*: it was to have a fundamental influence on Welsh society. John Penry, the Welsh Independent martyr who was executed in 1593 was himself a convinced Calvinist believing in predestination and that man's fate was finally determined at death. Indeed all the Nonconformist leaders—Independent, Presbyterian, Baptist and the later Calvinistic Methodists—based their philosophies, in the main, on Calvinism. Welsh society as a whole throughout the preceding centuries had been imbued with the same philosophy for St. Augustine had fixed a large part of Calvin's theology and the Catholic church had imprinted it on the minds of generations of Welsh folk. The new version of the old theology filled the gap left by the Tudor rejection of the old Catholic church. I have noted elsewhere the continuity of the old Catholic tradition into some of the newer sects, the 'new presbyter' was indeed the 'old priest writ large'. But whatever the theology of their members, the early Nonconformist churches' great contribution to Welsh life was—to use G. P. Gooch's words—'to familiarize the mind with the operation of democratic principles [and to] teach the individual to consider himself in a special sense the instrument of some great purpose of God'. This was to result later in the development of radical, and indeed socialist, thought.

The decline of the old bardic schools has been mentioned. Indeed, Elizabeth I commissioned an eisteddfod at Caerwys to license bards and so to diminish what had become, in English eyes, 'vagabondage'. At the same time, anglicized Welshmen established grammar schools in centres such as Abergavenny, Bangor, Carmarthen, Cowbridge, Presteign and Rhuthun, while the monastic school at Abergwili was removed to Brecon (because of the Welshness of the people of Carmarthenshire!) where it became Christ's College. All this was to enable Welsh boys 'to attain the same success in England' that had fallen to the lot of the founders. In the same way, in 1571, a Welsh college, Jesus College, was founded in the University of Oxford. The educated youth of Wales were to be uprooted from the old tradition to turn their eyes to England. The seed was sown of an idea which was to flower in all its absurdity in more recent times when many Welshmen have believed that culture is synonymous with the knowledge of the English language and that an M.A. (Oxbridge) represents the ideal in education and culture.

The early Nonconformists established many academies and schools as did the Anglican Society for the Promotion of Christian Knowledge and, also, in the eighteenth century, Griffith Jones, the rector of Llanddowror, Carmarthenshire. Much of this activity too was based on the need for teaching English and particularly for the saving of Welsh souls. But its ultimate effect was to revivify and strengthen the Welsh language and to inculcate in Welsh men and women a fervid enthusiasm for education. The Circulating Schools were the precursors of the Methodist Movement which, founded on the Welsh language and an acceptable theology, became a vehicle of expression for the whole life of the nation. Its appeal was not to the intellect as was the older Nonconformist movement, in great part, but it was a cry to men's hearts. As Mr. A. H. Williams has well remarked:—

"Daeth yr hogi meddwl yn y man—gyda'r Ysgol Sul a'r dadleuon diwinyddol: ond gwreiddyn y drwg yng ngolwg y gwir Fethodist oedd calon lygredig dyn."

[The sharpening of men's minds came later—with the Sunday School and the theological disputations: but in the true Methodist's view the root of all evil was man's corrupt heart.]

The influence of the Movement on Welsh society was immeasurable: it was harmful as well as beneficial. Harmful in the sense that it placed an exaggerated importance on the individual's concern for saving his own soul, on the 'world to come' and on man's degradation and sin. The great poet of the Movement, William Williams of Pantycelyn could declare with conviction:—

"Llwch wyf i, o'r llwch y deuthum,
Pryf yw 'mrawd, y ddae'r yw 'mam,
Eto 'rwyf i'n mofyn teyrnas
Ddisigledig, bur, ddi-nam.
Pryf y ddaear,
A ddaw hwnnw mewn i'r nef?"

[Dust am I, from dust I came, my brother is the worm, the earth my mother. Yet I seek a kingdom immutable, pure, faultless. The earth's worm, shall it too enter into heaven?]

But countless generations have sung his hymn without his conviction or vision.

The eighteenth and nineteenth century reformers had a simple vision of the Heavenly City but their Jacob's-ladder was too often not:—

"Pitched betwixt Heaven and Charing Cross."

Their city was 'invisible', 'intangible', 'unknowable' and 'inapprehensible' and the pain, grime and cruelty of the rapidly-developing industrial valleys and the long hard day's grind of the rural labourer were not their concern. To them, religion was a separate entity. They eschewed politics and social welfare; religion was concerned only with the saving of the individual soul and not with man's occupation and daily life. They were openly inimical to much of men's activities—music, dance, drama and the visual arts were too often 'sinful' occupations. For example a 'ballad' by a devout young woman in the nineteenth century denounced even the new tonic sol-fa notation as a 'sin'. It was the Methodist Fathers, unlike the earlier reformers, who insisted on the sanctity of the 'Welsh Sabbath' and tried hard to ban the harp, the 'interlude' and the country dance from the Welsh scene. The Kingdom of Heaven belonged to the 'world to come' and to enter it one did not whistle on Sundays or read novels or practise the morris dance. These activities persisted well into the twentieth century, and when, in the 1920s, a Calvinistic Methodist minister, one of the true saints of our time, chose to question and disregard some of the outmoded tenets of his denomination's 'Confession of Faith', he was excommunicated.

The Movement permeated the well-established earlier Nonconformist sects which became 'methodistized' in different degrees. Those comparatively uninfluenced were the Unitarians, the heirs of the early Presbyterianism (whose churches were designated 'black spots' despite their enlightened belief in toleration) and the Quakers whose number had been severely diminished by persecution.

But the beneficial effect of the Movement was substantial. It created a literate Welsh nation and gave it a serious purpose. Here now was a national community which could read, write and discuss not only theology but politics, literature and all things of human concern; in this activity the contribution of the earlier sects was outstanding. By the beginning of the nineteenth century, considerable areas of Wales were becoming industrialized and the process continued throughout the century. But they were not anglicized. In the third quarter of the century, Thomas Gee could produce a new edition of the *Myvyrian Archaiology* (1250 pages) at a profit, as well as *Y Gwyddoniadur*, a ten-volume encyclopedia which went into a second edition within ten years. In 1870, two publishers, at Aberdare and Liverpool, could produce and sell dictionaries of Welsh biography (1300 and 1100 pages), while publishing firms in London, Glasgow, and Edinburgh, such as William Mackenzie, Blackie and Son, Fullerton and Co., and Virtue and Co., all of whom paid their editors and writers, found it profitable to produce in Welsh substantial volumes such as the works of William Williams of Pantycelyn (816 quarto pages) and works on Welsh and world history, all in the Welsh language. The inhabitants of the industrial valleys bought a substantial proportion of these works, the remainder going to the more sparsely populated areas of rural Wales. Why did a Welsh industrial society bother itself with copies of the *Myvyrian Archaiology of Wales*? The answer is simple: it was still a society concerned with its own roots, the inheritor of the tradition of the Welsh schools of the eighteenth century, of the Independent academies, and of the bardic schools. Wales in 1870 was ripe for a system of Welsh-medium schools.

What it received in that year was the notorious Education Act which led to the English-orientated system of intermediate schools, to the first university college, Aberystwyth, opened in 1872, followed later by other colleges at Cardiff and Bangor and the creation of the University of Wales. In all these schools and colleges, the medium of learning was English and the effect on the national character of the Welsh society was disastrous; even in the rural primary schools where most of the pupils were monoglot Welsh speakers, the speaking of Welsh was cruelly punished.

However, the Sunday Schools continued to flourish, and in them the Welsh language was the only medium of instruction. Even in my own youth in the early years of the present century, an occasional farmer, bred in the pre-1870 tradition and self taught, was known to produce in his Sunday-school class a copy of the Greek New Testament and quote from it to prove a point. Such men were the products of rural communities which produced philosophers such as Sir Henry Jones of Glasgow University, a Denbighshire shoemaker's son, and many of those Welsh leaders, such as Sir Owen Edwards, who were to counteract the effects of the anglicization of Welsh education.

*   *   *

We have travelled far from the society of the Welsh Laws. Through all the centuries of change, of social upheaval and religious and educational ferment, did any of the ancient elements of Welsh society persist? In my view, the continuity of Welsh social tradition, and with it the survival of the Welsh language, is the most remarkable phenomenon in our history. Ellis's statement that in our ancient laws a 'noble' class was not recognized has remained true. Throughout the centuries class distinction in the 'blue blood' sense was never important. When the Tudor *uchelwyr* (noblemen) abandoned their language and culture for the fleshpots of the English court, the only element which could have become a Welsh 'upper class' disappeared. Thenceforward, the only national leaders were those who proved themselves by force of personality, ability, and culture, preachers, poets, teachers and business men alike, all members of *y werin* (the folk). The *gwerin* was not a lower class; if the term must be used, it was the *only* class. During the heyday of Welsh Nonconformity, all men were 'equal before God', and the farm labourer and his

51

master could share in the diaconate. But when the churches ceased to be communities of true believers, independent of the 'world', especially in the post-1870 period when the Samuel Smiles brand of English education became fashionable in Wales, the churches ceased to function as the 'salt of the earth' and espoused 'the world'. Worldly success now became the criterion of leadership, and a Welsh 'middle class' whose hallmark was respectability not integrity tended to emerge. As the late W. J. Gruffydd once said, 'the stockbroker entered the big pew'—not because of his saintly qualifications! The consequences can be seen in the pathetic unimportance of the churches in our own day.

The importance of kinship and the commote has remained significant to this day as a part of twentieth-century society. Throughout the centuries, Welsh loyalties have been local. The concept of *bro*—no English word adequately conveys its meaning, district, region, vale, moorland are all inadequate—has always been more important than that of nation. This accounts for much of the internecine strife of medieval times; one recalls too the variety of small towns which competed for the honour of being capital of Wales in recent times. Bro Hiraethog, bro Uwchaled, bro Ddyfi, bro Morgannwg, bro Gŵyr, gwlad Llŷn, Arfon, Môn, and Ceredigion, to name only a few, still attract more loyalties than the national concept of Wales itself or even the concept of individual shires except where their boundaries coincide with those defined in the early laws. Here, it seems to me, emerges the stupidity of those modern political administrators who in planning the reconstruction of local government consider county boundaries sacrosanct but ignore the older administrative units. For instance, to Arwystli and Cyfeiliog, Mawddwy is meaningful but Elfael and Brycheiniog are not. Yet such affinities are ignored.

And kinship. In my youth, every district had its *teulu ni* ('our family'). Our love of genealogical studies is well-known. Family pride has shown itself constantly in a delight in tracing relationships even to the ninth degree. In my native *bro*, the local genealogist was the Methodist historian, Richard Bennett, and there were few families in the area which did not elicit his help to trace relationships to a bewildering degree. Pride in and responsibility for family relationships have always been features of Welsh society: in this con-nexion, one should note the old Welsh system of nomenclature. For example, the fifteenth-century poet from bro Ddyfi was not merely Dafydd Llwyd: he was indeed Dafydd Llwyd ap Llywelyn ap Gruffudd, bearing in his name the name of father and grandfather also.

In such small close-knit communities, folk memory has always proved to be strong and ancient custom slow to disappear. Practices such as *cymhortha* therefore tended to persist and have done so to the present day, strengthened and sublimated by the Christian emphasis on duty to one's neighbour. Helping one's neighbour at ploughing, reaping and shearing has been normal practice in rural communities, while assistance in gifts of money or goods at weddings

52

or to surviving relatives at death has always been a feature of the Welsh society. Indeed, the *gwylnos* ('wake') remained a social occasion, an exemplar of *cymhortha*, in my childhood days and may still be so in many districts. At least, partaking, generally in the chapel vestry, in a funeral 'tea' with contributions from neighbours has always been a popular (in the literal sense) event, redolent as one well remembers of the smell of caraway-seed cake!

I have discussed elsewhere how the Welsh community has always emphasized the dignity of craftsmanship and how also the tenets of the Calvinist Methodist Movement corresponded in many ways with those of the medieval church, even to the belief in the *index* and excommunication. But traces of a still older order have also remained, reverting occasionally to pre-Christian practice such as in the case of many faithful church-goers who in time of trouble have always consulted a local 'conjurer'.

The twentieth century however has brought cataclysmic changes to the social order in Wales as elsewhere; the ruthless disintegration of country life and the acceleration of the spread of an urban conception of society may have far-reaching effects. On the other hand, other recent developments have helped to fuse local loyalties, without destroying their identity, into a new national unity which augurs well for the future. But the present belief of large sections of the Welsh society in bilingualism as the panacea for all its ills only sows the seed of that society's destruction. Wales will survive only if it is Welsh.

SELECT BIBLIOGRAPHY

T. P. Ellis, *Welsh Tribal Law and Custom in the Middle Ages* (Clarendon Press, Oxford 1926).

R. T. Jenkins, *Gruffydd Jones Llanddowror* (University of Wales Press 1930).

Ffransis G. Payne, 'Cwysau o foliant cyson' in *Y Llenor* (Hughes a'i Fab Caerdydd 1947), 3-24.

Iorwerth C. Peate, *Tradition and Folk Life: a Welsh view* (Faber and Faber Ltd. London, 1972).

A. H. Williams, *The Background of Welsh History* (Cardiff 1930).

Griffith J. Williams, *Y Wasg Gymraeg Ddoe a Heddiw* (Llyfrau'r Faner, Y Bala 1970).

53

THE WELSH ECONOMY

GRAHAM L. REES

IV

ONE of the main features of Welsh history over the past two centuries or so has been the massive increase in population, enjoying a standard of living well beyond the reach of its forebears' imagination. During the century or so before 1914 the expansion of the population was phenomenally rapid: when the nineteenth century opened the population of Wales was only just over half a million, but in little more than a hundred years, as the accompanying table indicates, it was more than four times as great.

The Population of Wales

				thousands
1801	..	..	..	587
1851	..	..	..	1,163
1901	..	..	..	2,019
1911	..	..	..	2,421
1921	..	..	..	2,656
1931	..	..	..	2,593
1939	..	..	..	2,567
1951	..	..	..	2,597
1961	..	..	..	2,644
1971	..	..	..	2,724

Despite the disruptions of war, numbers continued to grow through the second decade of the twentieth century. During the 1920s, however, gains were replaced by losses as the great exodus began, and in the early 1930s, as economic difficulties intensified, so the drain continued. In fact, so great was the emigration between 1921 and 1939 that Wales not only lost the equivalent of its natural increase of 259,000, but a further 191,000 as well, to make a net loss by migration of not far short of half a million people; a staggering rate of loss for such a small country.

After the second world war numbers rose after demobilization, but even so the population of the Principality had increased by a mere 6,000 at the 1951 Census by comparison with the last previous complete Census taken twenty years earlier. There was a more substantial gain, of some 45,000, over the next ten years to 1961, but it continues to surprise many that the population at this date was nevertheless still somewhat lower—in fact 12,000 less—than the level attained in 1921. The preliminary results of the 1971 Census indicate that the population is now not very far short of two and three quarter millions, a gain of almost 80,000 people since 1961. The story of the growth in our

56

numbers is thus a remarkable one and, as already intimated, closely bound up with the economic changes which have occurred over the period. Therefore, though considerations of space make it impossible to present a detailed analysis of the transformation in the Welsh economy which has occurred over the period of the Industrial Revolution, even a brief outline of the evolution of the economy will, it is hoped, provide insights into its present strengths and weaknesses.

*   *   *

The rudimentary metallurgical processes of the earlier phases of industrialization required such large quantities of coal in relation to ore as to localize industry firmly upon the coalfields. Moreover, there were particular factors, notably the geological configuration of the coal measures and the carboniferous limestone strata in which iron ores are found, which determined that the early Welsh ironworks would be located on the bleak northern rim of the South Wales coalfield. The area, as Professor Glanmor Williams has pointed out, has in fact a strong claim to the distinction of being the cradle of the world's industrial civilization. With such innovations as that of Crane and David Thomas at Ystalyfera (which enabled the western end of the South Wales coalfield, consisting of anthracite coal, to be exploited) the region grew in strength as a leading sector in British economic growth. During the first half of the nineteenth century the iron rails poured from these works in an ever-mounting stream so that, whereas in 1788 iron production in South Wales amounted to some 10,000 tons, by 1823 it had grown twenty-fold to 200,000 tons. Subsequently, for almost all of the following 40 years or so the area was Britain's most important producer of iron. By 1860 there were 165 furnaces in blast in Wales, producing almost a million tons of pig-iron out of a U.K. total of 3·6 million tons.

At the southern end of the South Wales coalfield, copper smelting, which had had early beginnings in the area, was very highly localized and shortly after the middle of the nineteenth century, of the 18 copper works in Britain, 17 were located in the hinterland of Swansea. There were good reasons for this, in the shape of the coal, the water, and the port facilities available there, for this smelting industry's ore supplies came by sea; in fact by mid-century the bulk of the supply came not from Cornwall and Anglesey but from as far afield as Chile, Australia and South Africa.

By 1850 the four major canals called into being by the inadequacy of the old turnpike roads (i.e. the Glamorgan canal to Cardiff, the Neath canal to Giant's Grave, the Monmouthshire canal to Newport and the Swansea canal along Cwmtawe) were themselves half a century old and in the process of being superseded by the new railways. The first of these followed hard upon the opening of Cardiff docks, in 1841. It was Brunel who built this railway from

Merthyr to the second Marquis of Bute's docks, with branches down the Aberdare Valley and across to the mouth of the Rhondda Fawr to the coal pits at Dinas and Cymer. Brunel, too, was responsible for the trunk line from South Wales to London, though it was preceded in time by George and Robert Stephenson's railway from North Wales to the capital, which owed its early start to the importance of the Irish mail service to Holyhead. However, despite this advantage of an early trunk route to the metropolis, industrial development in North Wales failed to flourish. This has been attributed not only to the difficult nature of the terrain and the exhaustion of its mineral wealth, but also to its inability to attract capital investment. At all events, by 1850, as Professor David Williams has pointed out, 'the region had returned to agriculture'.

Naturally, therefore, when we examine the distribution of the increase of a population which had nearly doubled during the first half of the nineteenth century, we find that the growth was greatest in Glamorgan and Monmouth-shire. The rising centres of industry developed urban populations to serve them, drawn, for the most part, from rural Wales, though workers were also attracted from nearby English counties. Merthyr Tydfil, a mere hamlet in 1750, already had a population of 7,705 in 1801 compared with Swansea's 6,831. At that time both Cardiff and Newport were small townships of less than 2,000 people. By 1851 Merthyr's population had rocketed to no less than 35,000 to make it, by a considerable margin, the largest township in the Principality. In the meantime, Cardiff had also registered a considerable advance in numbers to more than 20,000.

Despite this great growth in the population centred on the South Wales coalfield, the population of Wales' predominantly rural areas also grew by about two-thirds during the first half of the nineteenth century. Improvements in farming techniques were widely introduced in the Principality during this period and large areas of land were brought into regular cultivation for the first time. It was a process of internal colonization, as Ashby and Evans have pointed out, based on the family farm employing, on the average, two or more labourers in addition to the farmer and his relatives. Typically, the economic organization in these rural communities was one of subsistence farming, over and above which rents and tithes were paid from the sale of store cattle, sheep, wool, butter and cheese. The expanding metal industries of South Wales and their associated mining activities attracted farm labour—and it was the labourers rather than the farmers who left the land—but the family farm remained much as it had been. The indications were that many Welsh farms benefited appreciably from the improved methods introduced during the period. In fact the 1850s and sixties proved to be the high tide of arable farming in Wales; thenceafter tillage declined while the importance of grassland grew; the number of livestock increased and subsistence farming gave way to an increased specialization and dependence upon the outside world.

*   *   *

From about the middle of the nineteenth century to the first world war the Welsh economy grew even more rapidly than during the first half of the century. Above all else it was a period when the economy was dominated by the export of coal which now became much more important than iron had been at an earlier date. Wales became more specialized and highly dependent upon world markets for its prosperity. In fact, so prosperous was it during periods of high activity that, as Professor Brinley Thomas has pointed out, the emigration peaks of England, Scotland, Ireland and Sweden in the 1880s failed to find a reflection in the Welsh figures. During the first decade of the twentieth century this contrast was even more marked, for while neighbouring countries were experiencing large losses due to emigration, in Wales the net flow was inwards at a rate of some 45 per 10,000. It is a remarkable fact that during this period Wales was absorbing population at a rate not much below that of the U.S.A.

The dynamic was provided by the enormous growth of what used to be called 'sale coal'. The iron and copper smelters frequently owned their own mines in order to ensure their coal supplies, and when their smelting activities ceased some of these enterprises remained in being to mine and sell their coal. However, the great impetus which subsequently linked South Wales indissolubly with coal was the exploitation of the smokeless steam coal which began when these rich seams were tapped at Abercanaid and elsewhere, especially in the Aberdare and the Rhondda valleys. It was an age in which coal had no rival as a fuel, and the aggregation of the demand for it from domestic consumers, the railways, industry, and eventually from the Royal Navy and the merchant marine, converted the valleys of South Wales into a vast black Klondyke.

It is now becoming fashionable to question the accepted belief that Welsh businessmen played a leading role in the development of the South Wales coal industry. In fact, however, their names frequently bespeak their origin, and even when this is not so—as for example was true of Walter Coffin—we find that they were previously resident in Wales. Many of the most famous made large fortunes. Thomas Powell became the world's largest coal exporter and the Powell Duffryn Steam Coal Company, formed after his death, subsequently owned most of the Aberdare valley. In the Rhondda valleys, as Dr. E. D. Lewis recounts, David Davies, the 'topsawyer' and builder of railways in Mid-Wales, proved the most audacious of them all. The shafts which he and his partners needed to sink had often to be driven to impressive depths before they came to the 'six feet seam' which helped to make their fortunes. Before his death 'Davies yr Ocean' (i.e. The Ocean Coal Company Ltd.) had broken the virtual monopoly held by the Marquis of Bute and his powerful agent W. T. Lewis (the Lord Merthyr of later years) in the shipment of coal from Cardiff. This he did by leading a successful campaign to build new docks at Barry with a direct link from the Rhondda valleys—and what is more, followed this up by actually building the dock. Cardiff docks had, in any case, become inadequate by this time, especially following John Cory's enterprise in establishing bunkering stations, some 80 in all, the world over. Barry Dock was completed in 1889 and subsequently extended. In 1913, total shipments from this dock complex alone amounted to more than 11 million tons of coal, compared with 10·6 million from Cardiff. Within a generation, therefore, Barry had, by a small margin, wrested from Cardiff the title of the world's largest coal exporting port. It was all a far cry from 1782, when the official customs report for Cardiff declared that 'We have no coal exported from this port, nor ever shall, as it would be too expensive to bring it down here from the internal part of the country'.

The second half of the century was the great era of dock building; following the Marquis of Bute's first great venture in 1839, Bute East Dock was completed in 1859, Roath Dock in 1887 and the Queen Alexandra Dock in 1907. A few miles away, Ely Harbour was completed in 1859, Penarth Docks in 1865, and at Newport the Alexandra and South Docks were added in 1875 and 1892 respectively. In Swansea the North and South Docks were built in 1852 and 1859; the Prince of Wales Dock followed in 1881 and King's Dock in 1909. Improved docks were completed at Briton Ferry in 1860, at Port Talbot in 1898 and at Llanelli in 1903. Port developments were accompanied by railway extensions and 1886 saw the opening of the Severn Tunnel. This cut the rail journey to London by one hour and proved a considerable advantage to the coal trade. However, as D. A. Thomas pointed out, many years ago, even after the opening of the Tunnel it still cost less to ship coal to Port Said (to one of Cory's bunkering depots) than it did to convey it from the Rhondda to London. The world's voracious demand for Welsh coal gave rise to a gross imbalance between the Principality's exports and its imports: the total trade of the South Wales ports in 1913 was 89 per cent exports, amounting to some 42 million tons, of which coal comprised 37 million tons. Imports totalled just over 5 million tons, of which 1·7 million tons were iron ore, the single most important item.

By 1913 imported ore had long been important in Welsh iron and steel production. The ironmasters were faced with a major difficulty in the conversion of indigenous ores to steel, which was by the third quarter of the nineteenth century supplanting iron in a variety of uses, but most importantly for the world's railways. The difficulty lay in the phosphoric content of the native ore, resolved, as is now widely known, by the Gilchrist-Thomas discovery that this phosphorus could be separated out by lining the Bessemer converters with a basic material such as limestone. However, Welsh ore supplies were, in any case, rapidly becoming depleted, a situation which put the established ironworks in the uplands away from the seaports at a grave disadvantage. Ultimately, it resulted in a major shift in the location of the industry to the coast. During the early years of the twentieth century the number of steel works in Wales numbered some 35 and their production amounted to rather more than a million tons of steel ingots a year.

With the shift in emphasis to steel, iron production in South Wales more or less stabilized, and the area of growth became that of tinplate manufacture. This was centred at the western end of the coalfield and associated with the higher quality Open Hearth steel and the port of Swansea, for the tin had always come in by sea. By the time of the passage of the U.S. McKinley tariff in 1890, U.K. tinplate exports—almost exclusively Welsh—were of the order of half a million tons. The American action threw some 10,000 out of employment and some works closed permanently. As Professor Minchinton has emphasized, the industry was partly saved by a subsequent major shift to galvanizing. Investment was in fact very heavy in the years leading to the first world war, with the production of galvanized sheets attaining a peak of 848,000 tons in 1912.

The golden age of South Wales copper smelting lay in the thirty years or so ending about 1890, before the Americans unearthed their massive ore deposits, and before the smelting of domestic ores was started in Chile and Australia. Those were the days when the renowned Cape Horners were a familiar sight in Swansea docks, and when that town's Metal Exchange was the acknowledged world centre of the trade. The industry was almost exclusively confined to smelting and, as Mr. R. O. Roberts has made clear, its virtual loss before 1914 had more than a little to do with the monopolistic behaviour of the smelters. Because they were at one time the sole buyers the smelters found that they could, by acting in close collusion, keep down the price at which they bought the ores and maintain the price at which they sold refined copper.

According to the 1851 Census of Population, the numbers then engaged in non-ferrous metal smelting in South Wales was 2,253. In 1911 the figure was 3,769, the decline in copper production from the 1880s having been offset by the growth in zinc smelting. The latter industry drew upon the metallurgical experience of the area, and relied for its supplies upon imported ores from New South Wales. It was this same experience which also attracted the more important Mond Nickel works. This was established at Clydach, the country of origin of the ores in this case being Canada.

Outside the South Wales industrial belt the industry which flourished for longest was slate-quarrying in North Wales. This reached its zenith at the turn of the century with an output of about half a million tons. Its decline, however, was a rapid one, for production had already, by 1914, fallen to about a half of its peak figure. By today, its employees are numbered only in hundreds.

The period from the 1850s to the first world war was thus one of remarkable industrial growth in the history of Wales. During these decades it became very much an export economy, responding to fluctuations in overseas demand for coal, steel and tinplate, especially from the Western Hemisphere. Its dynamic growth during the period, moreover, served to ensure, in conjunction with improvements in agricultural techniques, that a high proportion of its surplus rural population was absorbed internally by the growth of Welsh industry. This was especially true from the 1880s, as Professor Brinley Thomas has pointed out, thus providing a startling contrast with Ireland, the population of which was almost halved between 1841 and 1911 (i.e. from more than eight million to less than four and a half million). Thus Jack Jones' famous novel title *Off to Philadelphia in the Morning*—borrowed from a popular song at the turn of the century—did not actually apply in general nearly as much to the Welsh population as to that of any of the other three countries comprising the United Kingdom. (The annual rate of migration to the U.S.A. per 10,000 mean population between 1831 and 1930 measured decennially never exceeded 8 for Wales, which was for 1881-90. Over the same ten-year period the English figure was 25, the Scottish was 39 and the Irish was as much as 133.)

*   *   *

When the tide of economic prosperity turned for Wales after the first world war, the depression was as deep and cruel as the era of prosperity had been remarkable. The Principality's industrial economy was specialized and depended for prosperity to a very considerable degree upon basic industrial production—the extraction of coal, the manufacture of iron, steel and tinplate and the hewing of slate—rather than upon the manufacture of finished goods for final consumption. In this sense Wales was a specialized 'peripheral' economic area; a supplier of raw materials and intermediate goods to manufacturing industries which were centred elsewhere. Following the collapse of war-time demand for coal and steel, and the end of the postwar boom in 1922, the history of the interwar period for the world economy was one of shrinking export markets with the growth of economic nationalism and the imposition of restrictions upon international trade. For the U.K. the position was additionally complicated by the Government's determination to return to the gold standard in 1925 at the pre-war exchange rate parity despite the fact that the price level had risen appreciably in the meantime. Our exports were thus made much less competitive in foreign markets. For Wales these economic difficulties were further intensified by the specialized nature of the economy. In no sector was this more marked than in coal. During the 1920s the Americans dominated the Canadian market and those of Central and South America, while the French and Italian markets almost vanished under the weight of German coal reparations. As though this were not enough, the British and other navies, followed shortly by much of the world's merchant marine, began to convert from coal to oil and thus added enormously to the straitened circumstances of the Welsh coal industry.

The world, moreover, was learning how to make its own steel and tinplate, or else buying an increasing proportion of its supplies from the U.S.A. and Belgium. The Cyfarthfa works finally closed in 1921 and in 1930 the closure of the Dowlais steel works followed, the latter alone throwing more than 3,000 men out of work. The general bitterness was increased by the actions of firms such as that of Richard Thomas and Co. which, having joined a quota rationing system in the tinplate industry, proceeded to buy up and close small going concerns for the sake of their quotas, which were then produced elsewhere.

The price of agricultural produce continued to rise after 1918, and a number of the gentry took advantage of this rural prosperity to sell their land, thus bringing about the virtual eclipse of the large landowner in Wales. However, as Professor David Williams so rightly remarks, though the farmers were thus relieved of any petty tyranny they may have suffered, they bought their land at highly inflated prices and from this time forward the real landlords of Wales were the banks. Guaranteed high prices for cereals disappeared with the repeal of the Corn Production Act in 1921, and brought about a considerable decline in arable cultivation in Wales. Milk production increased, assisted by the ability of motorized transport to get it to market from all but the remotest farms. Milk production was economical in its use of labour, and this, together with ever-increasing mechanization, contributed to the acute unemployment problem in Wales for almost all the inter-war period. The proportion of the work force which failed to find employment varied from place to place throughout the period and at one time in 1932 unemployment amounted to about one-fifth of the entire population of Wales and Monmouth-shire. In terms of the total work force it reached 38·2 per cent in June 1932, while individual areas such as Merthyr Tydfil and the Rhondda valleys endured the desolating experience of an unemployment rate which amounted to over one half of the insured male working population.

The unemployment led in turn to a movement of population. As we have already emphasized, some 430,000 people migrated from Wales in the inter-war period. In the Rhondda valleys alone numbers fell by 13 per cent from 162,000 in 1921 to 141,000 in 1931; twenty years later its population was down to 111,000. In all cases it was the younger element which left, especially the males, a fact which was reflected most markedly in the female to male ratios for the country. Though the great mass of this sad migration was from the industrialized valleys of South Wales, there was also, as we have already remarked, a flow of agricultural workers from the rural areas. The regions least affected were those of the non-industrial towns of North Wales, some of which actually gained population during this period. This was true of Bangor, Caernarvon, Colwyn Bay, Llandudno, Rhyl, Conway, Prestatyn and Abergele. Flintshire as a whole actually registered an increase in numbers over the inter-war period with the establishment of new industries there.

*　　　　　*　　　　　*

The evolution of the Welsh economy in the period since the second world war has in many respects provided a remarkable contrast with both the pre-first world war era and the stagnant inter-war period. To start with, the period has been characterized by the continued run-down of the once supremely important coal industry. Output in South Wales, which had been 57 million tons in 1913, was 35 million in 1939, and by 1945 was down to 20 million tons. As for numbers employed, from having reached 270,000 in 1920, these were barely 100,000 in 1945. As Mr. Leslie Jones has remarked 'The amount of coal exported from South Wales was down to where it was in 1860; in the lifespan of one man it had gone full circle from 1·7 million tons to a peak of 35 million and then down again to 1·6 million'. By today, the numbers employed for Wales as a whole have fallen to some 41,000 (1970) while Welsh coal output is of the order of 13 million tons. It will already be evident from these figures that the N.C.B's closure policy has exercised a major impact upon the Welsh economy in recent years. Without the assistance of immigrant manufacturing concerns which have to some extent closed the gap left by the run-down of the coal and certain other traditional industries, therefore, the Welsh economy could have been left in a very parlous state indeed. As it transpired the economy has become very much more diversified since World War II, a process to which the inducements afforded by successive governments have contributed. In brief, over the past generation or so the Welsh economy has become, broadly speaking, very much more like the British economy generally. In other words, when we examine the 'economic profile' of the Welsh economy in terms of the proportionate disposition of its work force in basic, manufacturing, and service industries, we find that it has evolved to greater conformity with that of the 'economic profile' of Britain as a whole. In considering the growth and prosperity of the Welsh economy in the future, therefore, the concern must be, if the basic industries continue to decline in importance, that their place will be taken by manufacturing and service industries on a sufficient scale to prevent 'job opportunities' from declining in relation to the numbers seeking work. It is from this standpoint that anyone concerned with the future of the Welsh economy must view Development Area policy and government attitudes towards the infra-structure of the country; that is, its roads, railways, ports and other major items of capital investment. In these respects the economic indicators and certain events over the past few years cannot but give rise to some concern.

Wales' share of the population of the U.K. continues to fall. It was 5·6 per cent in 1931, but by 1971 it was only 4·9 per cent. Moreover, though there appears on balance to have been a small net gain of people into the Principality since 1961 this conceals the fact that what has really happened is that the economy has had an influx of retired—and therefore non-productive—people, and an efflux of the economically active. This has been especially true of the North Coast area of the planning sub-division known as North-West Wales where the total net migration increase between 1951 and 1969 was more

Changes in employment in Wales and Great Britain in Index form, 1948 = 100

Industrial Order 1958 S.I.C.	*1969* Wales	G.B.
Agriculture, Forestry and Fishing	37·6	42·4
Mining and Quarrying	42·8	52·6
TOTAL EXTRACTIVE	41·7	47·3
Food, Drink and Tobacco	97·1	115·3
Chemicals and Allied Industries	126·9	117·0
Metal Manufacture	117·1	112·3
Engineering and Electrical	216·8	151·9
Shipbuilding and Marine Engineering	28·4	56·3
Vehicles	79·7	90·9
Metal Goods	140·9	91·1
Textiles	155·3	71·0
Leather, Leather Goods and Furs	112·5	71·5
Clothing and Footwear	147·4	79·7
Bricks, Pottery, Glass and Cement.....	100·0	113·0
Timber, Furniture, etc.	146·0	114·0
Paper, Printing and Publishing	210·8	137·6
Other Manufacturing Industries	318·2	147·7
TOTAL MANUFACTURING	131·6	108·6
Construction	115·3	111·5
Gas, Electricity and Water	167·2	125·6
Transport and Communications	71·6	86·7
Distributive Trades	115·6	132·6
Insurance, Banking and Finance	160·0	162·1
Professional and Scientific	216·3	209·0
Miscellaneous Services	106·5	114·8
Public Administration and Defence	94·0	94·6
TOTAL SERVICES	117·4	124·2
GRAND TOTAL	105·6	110·9

Source: Department of Employment.

Percentage distribution of employees in Wales and Great Britain in June 1969

Industrial Order 1968 S.I.C.	*Wales*	*G.B.*
Agriculture, Forestry and Fishing	1·5	1·7
Mining and Quarrying	6·4	2·0
TOTAL EXTRACTIVE	7·9	3·7
Food, Drink and Tobacco	2·1	3·7
Coal and Petroleum Products	0·7	0·3
Chemicals and Allied Industries	1·6	2·1
Metal Manufacture	9·7	2·6
Mechanical Engineering	3·2	3·2
Instrument Engineering	0·4	0·7
Electrical Engineering	3·0	4·0
Shipbuilding and Marine Engineering	0·3	0·9
Vehicles	2·4	3·6
Metal Goods not elsewhere specified	2·5	2·8
Textiles	2·0	3·1
Leather, Leather Goods and Fur	0·2	0·3
Clothing and Footwear	1·7	2·2
Bricks, Pottery, Glass and Cement	1·1	1·5
Timber and Furniture	1·0	1·4
Paper, Printing and Publishing	1·4	2·8
Other Manufacturing Industries	1·9	1·5
TOTAL MANUFACTURING	38·2	38·5
Construction	7·8	6·6
Gas, Electricity and Water	2·3	1·7
Transport and Communication	6·6	6·9
Distributive Trades	10·4	11·9
Insurance, Banking, Finance and Business Services	2·0	3·9
Professional and Scientific Services	12·9	12·1
Miscellaneous Services	7·7	8·4
Public Administration and Defence	6·8	6·1
TOTAL SERVICES (incl. Construction)	56·5	57·6
Persons not classified by Industry	0·4	0·2
GRAND TOTAL	100·0	100·0

Source: Department of Employment.

than 24 per cent of its 1951 population. In fact, for a number of years past there has been a tendency for an increasing share of the Principality's population to concentrate near the north and south coasts. In South Wales the drift has been from both West South Wales and from the Central and Eastern valleys, but most markedly from the latter. This has occurred partly because of pit closures and the concentration of steel production at the Abbey Works Port Talbot, and the Spencer Works at Newport, leaving only the Ebbw Vale works on the northern rim of the South Wales coalfield. Tinplate production is now centred upon the coast at Trostre (Llanelli), and Velindre (Swansea), virtually all the old hand mills, which extended well into the Swansea hinterland, having closed down with the technological revolution to electrolytic tinning.

The contrasting experience of the various planning sub-divisions of Wales is also reflected in the relative change in numbers in the four South Wales county boroughs over this period. In the coastal belt the population of Cardiff increased by more than 20 per cent in the forty years from 1931 to 1971, and is now 278,000. The number of inhabitants in Newport increased by some 14 per cent to 112,000 over the same period. A few miles away the township of Cwmbran, which has come into being only since 1945, is now 32,000 strong. By contrast, the population of Swansea in the West South Wales planning sub-divisions has increased by less than 5 per cent since 1931, and now stands at 172,500. Over the same period the population of Merthyr Tydfil has fallen by more than 20 per cent and is now only 55,000. Its day as the largest town in Wales is long since over and its status as a county borough is being increasingly called into question.

In 1971 no less than 76 per cent of the Welsh population lived in Flintshire, Denbighshire, Glamorgan and Monmouthshire, though, as we have already intimated there have also been strong population movements of recent years within the county boundaries, towards the north and south coasts. Meanwhile, the drift of population away from Mid-Wales continues to be a matter of concern to many, not least to the local authorities who find it increasingly difficult to maintain community services from inadequate rate incomes. The withdrawal of some rural bus services provides the latest major example of the economic difficulties to which a very sparse population gives rise, to say nothing of the earlier closure of the Aberystwyth—Carmarthen, and other railway lines. Between 1956 and 1969 the civilian population of the Mid-Wales area fell from 179,483 to 174,620, i.e. a decline of 2·7 per cent. As the figures show, the total number of its inhabitants is now only marginally greater than that of the county borough of Swansea though its area, as Professor Beacham has pointed out, is one hundred times as great. The preliminary Report of the 1971 Census shows quite clearly that the populations of the Mid-Wales counties resumed their negative intercensal change after 1951, having registered increases between 1939 and 1951. The data are summarized in the accompanying table. It is interesting to note by contrast that Glamorgan, which has 5·9 persons to the hectare (a hectare

	Intercensal Change in Population						Persons per Hectare 1971
	1939–1951		1951–1961		1961–1971		
	No.	% per year	No.	% per year	No.	% per year	
Radnorshire	473	0·20	—1,522	—0·79	— 209	—0·11	0·1
Montgomeryshire	1,160	0·22	—1,825	—0·40	—1,404	—0·32	0·2
Carmarthenshire	54	0·00	—4,026	—0·24	—5,695	—0·34	0·7
Breconshire	3,968	0·62	—1,323	—0·24	—1,951	—0·36	0·3
Merionethshire	1,605	0·34	—3,155	—0·79	—3,033	—0·82	0·2

is equivalent to 2·471 acres) is one of the most densely populated counties not only in Wales, but in the whole of the United Kingdom. However, its population density is still comfortably below Warwickshire's exceptionally high figure of 8·2 persons to the hectare. The sharp contrast between this density figure and those of the relatively empty Mid-Wales counties—with which Warwickshire lies in quite close juxtaposition—will doubtless be increasingly borne in upon planners in the future when looking for possible overspill sites for Midlands industry, and ultimately for establishing residential conurbations.

The population of Wales has other interesting facets, the simplest explanation for which derives from economic conditions. At the beginning of the century, for example, Wales, as has already been stated, had a relatively low female to male ratio of 99 to 100—a characteristic feature of expanding 'peripheral' economies dependant upon extractive and other basic industries—certainly the ratio showed that there were relatively far fewer females than for the U.K. as a whole, which had a ratio of more than 105 to 100. However, the figures for subsequent Census years have revealed an increase in the female to male ratio for Wales by contrast with that of the U.K., which has remained fairly constant. In 1968 the ratios were approximately the same for both entities, at between 105 and 106 females to 100 males. The explanation usually offered for the rising ratio in Wales is the migration of male workers from Wales due to industrial depression, and the fact that the main part of the rise is apparent when comparing the 1931 and 1951 figures lends credence to this view. As compared with the U.K., Wales has greater proportions of both sexes over the age of 39, and a markedly greater proportion of females to males over the age of 59 than is true of the U.K. Finally, the break-down of population by socio-economic structure indicates that Wales has a smaller proportion of males in both professional and skilled occupations than is true of Britain as a whole. (Note that where comparisons are made, they have sometimes to be made with Britain, and at other times with the U.K., according to the availability of statistics).

At 0·2 per cent, the rate of growth of the working population of Wales since 1948 has been even less than that for Britain (which was 0·7 per cent). In fact there has been a sharp decline in the figures since 1955 for both Wales and Britain. When the emqloyment figures are examined, we find that since 1948 male employment in the Principality has actually fallen by some 40,000 people. The rise in the number of females employed has been an equally notable feature of the times.

The proportion of males employed in manufacturing is now approximately 40 per cent both in Wales and in Britain as a whole, but in terms of the proportion of the male labour force employed, the extractive industries— especially mining and quarrying—are still twice as important in Wales, where they employ 11·3 per cent of the male work force, compared with 5·3 per cent for Britain. On the other hand the service industries (excluding construction) are relatively more important in Britain, where they employ rather more than 52 per cent of the male labour force compared with somewhat less than 50 per cent in Wales. However, as we would expect, Wales employs a significantly greater proportion of its male labour force in metal manufacture (13·5 per cent compared with 3·6 per cent) than Britain generally; it also employs a rather greater proportion on construction (11·3 per cent compared with 10·0 per cent). By contrast, Britain employs a higher proportion of male workers in food, drink and tobacco (3·5 per cent compared with 1·8 per cent), mechanical engineering (6·9 per cent compared with 4·0 per cent), electrical engineering (3·9 per cent compared with 2·4 per cent) and vehicles (5·0 per cent compared with 2·8 per cent).

Females, who now account for as much as one-third of the labour force in Wales, are employed primarily in the service industries and to a somewhat lesser extent in manufacturing.

The numbers engaged in mining and quarrying—which as we have already remarked were far below end World War I levels at the end of World War II— decreased by the quite startling figure of 84,000 between 1948 and 1969. Over the same period the numbers employed in agriculture also suffered a drastic reduction, of some 24,000 (i.e. about 57 per cent). The work force in transport and communications suffered an even greater reduction, some 26,000, representing a curtailment of more than 60 per cent of the industry's labour force. Shipbuilding and marine engineering shed some 7,000 workers over the period, while the vehicle manufacturing industry had some 6,000 fewer workers in 1969 than in 1948, though there has been an increase of rather more than 40 per cent in the numbers employed in this sector since 1959.

The Welsh Office considered, in 1967, in *Wales: The Way Ahead* that between 1966 and 1970, the steel industry would divest itself of between 6,000 and 10,000 workers. Though this has not yet taken place, overmanning in the industry is still being discussed and in the increasingly competitive atmosphere, it would be wrong to dismiss the Welsh Office forecast as being completely in error. In the coal industry a new militarism has emerged as the miners have

69

become increasingly conscious that their position on the 'league-table' of wages is not what it was. Should they succeed to any marked degree with their demands for betterment it must necessarily mean a further substantial run-down in the industry.[1]

Some of these displaced workers were absorbed by the engineering and clerical industries which took on some 35,000 additional workers over the same period. The paper, printing and publishing industries expanded by more than 7,000, textiles registered an increase of almost 7,000, and a category consisting of manufacturing industries not individually named employed in total an additional 12,000 workers.

However, though the number of employees in manufacturing industries has grown comparatively more rapidly in Wales than in Britain as a whole, Wales has grown more slowly overall than Britain. This, in broad summary, has been due to the slower growth rate in the service industries and to the higher rate of decline in the extractive industries. The upshot of this situation has been a proportion of the insured population out of work in Wales, of some 3·1 per cent on average between 1954 and 1970; that is, almost twice the comparable figure for Britain as a whole. At no time during this period has unemployment in Wales been below the percentage figure for Britain; the range of variations was in fact between 2·6 and 4·1 per cent for Wales during this time and indicates a situation where even the former figure is above the British average of 1·8 per cent. from the end of World War II to the end of the 1960s. We must, however, be careful to maintain a balanced perspective in considering this situation; it might help to remember, for example, that in 1937, a comparatively prosperous pre-war year, unemployment in the London region was as high as 6·3 per cent (the basis of the figures is not exactly the same, but this does not affect the comparison greatly). The peaks and troughs in the demand for labour in Wales follow those for Britain quite closely, the effects of government 'stop-go' policies having produced simultaneous upturns and downturns in the numbers of people registered as unemployed. However, it is less true than formerly that 'when Britain sneezes, Wales contracts pneumonia'. Despite this, there is little cause for complacency, especially in view of the fact that if we examine the figures of employees in employment, we discover that for males these declined by no less than 64,000 between 1964 and 1970. The loss of 'job opportunities' reflected in this figure highlights the nature of the problem as far as Wales is concerned. In other words, when unemployment encourages workers to migrate, or else discourages them from registering as looking for further work, the official unemployment figures no

---

[1] Since the above was written, the Coal Board has settled with the miners (March 1972) for a very substantial rise. Indeed, Lord Robens, in a widely quoted comment, forecast that the settlement might mean the loss of some 50,000 to 55,000 jobs. Should this turn out to be the case—and this depends to a considerable extent upon whether the government intervenes to assist the industry—then the loss of jobs in the Welsh sector could be as high as 10,000.

longer takes cognizance of them. However, their disappearance as statistics does not imply the elimination of the problem, and perusal of the fall in the numbers of those in employment helps us to remember this.

We have already referred, albeit briefly, to the direction of population flow within Wales, so it will be no surprise to discover that there is a close correspondence between the regions which are experiencing population losses and the areas of greatest unemployment. These lie in such sub-divisions as, West Wales, and the Central and Eastern Valleys of South Wales. It is also true that workers have tended to remain unemployed for longer periods in Wales than in Britain as a whole and, not surprisingly, that over half the male unemployed are men aged 40 and above. Moreover, more than one-third of these turn out to have been unemployed for periods of one year or more. Of recent years, examination of unemployment figures, and their comparisons with unfilled vacancies, has been supplemented by other indicators of the economic well-being of a community, prominent among which have been the development of activity rates. These constitute a broader measure than employment percentages, of the extent to which human resources are being utilized in the particular areas to which they refer. (Thus the employee activity rate expresses the estimated number of employees in an area as a percentage of the corresponding estimated number of persons in the population of the area.) An examination of activity rates reveals that, when properly calculated, the total activity rate for males does not deviate very much from the overall U.K. proportion, in fact, as far as men are concerned, the labour 'reserve' in Wales consists very largely and straightforwardly of the registered insured unemployed. However, there is one category of 'reserve' productive power in Wales which is not revealed by either measure; this is, those males engaged in relatively unproductive work. We hear a great deal about 'concealed' unemployment in less developed countries, but in Wales (and in some other parts of the U.K.) their nearest equivalent is to be found among self-employed farmers. Self-employed persons comprise a higher proportion of the population in Wales than in any other part of the United Kingdom except Northern Ireland and South-West England. (The proportion is about four per cent for Wales.) Many of them are small farmers and for the last Census year the income of self-employed persons in agriculture in Wales was as low as 63 per cent of the U.K. average.

By contrast with male activity rates, those for females have been rising rapidly for some time in the Principality, but are still relatively low by comparison with those for Britain as a whole. This indicates the presence of a 'reserve' labour force in Wales and thus comprises a hidden asset for the country which could be utilized should the demand materialize. The rise in female activity rates for more than a decade has been due very largely to the growth of industries employing a relatively high proportion of females compared with industries already established. In fact, this change is a further facet of the evolution of the Welsh economy to closer similarity with that of

Britain as a whole. (In 1969, the female employee activity rate for Wales was 30 per cent compared with some 40 per cent for Britain as a whole).

Manufacturing employment in Wales increased by more than 14 per cent during the 1960s, or, to put it in another perspective, Wales, with some 5 per cent of Britain's population and 7½ per cent of Britain's unemployed, received more than 9 per cent of the total extra jobs claimed for new industrial development over this period. Much of this new industry, moreover, appears to have originated outside Wales. By 1965, establishments set up since 1945 by outside enterprises provided rather more than 30 per cent of manufacturing employment accounting for two-thirds of the increase recorded between 1960 and 1965. Closer study serves to throw up further interesting facts about this post-war invasion; for example, leaving out of the account the very new establishments because of their newness (i.e. those opened since 1960) we find that the remaining post-war immigrant firms increased their employment of labour at a rate no less than twice that of firms already in Wales. This has happened despite the less fortunate experience of the firms which established in the Principality during the abnormal early post-war years, for nearly one half of these subsequently closed down. More recently, the immigrant firms appear to have established more firmly in rapidly expanding sectors of industry and there is some evidence to support the view that employment in Welsh branch factories is often more buoyant than in their parent works.

A sample enquiry initiated at Aberystwyth in 1970 indicated that a sample of Wales' new manufacturing concerns were very much involved with the

Wales and Great Britain - Unemployment Rates, 1954-1970
(monthly average percentages)

world outside the Principality. They traded predominantly with firms outside Wales, and managerial staff were recruited mainly outside Wales, though this proportion appeared typically to decline over time in favour of more Welsh recruitment. It was interesting, too, to discover that these firms' contacts with government departments were largely with the Welsh branches of the main departments, although some still found it necessary to maintain their contacts with the headquarters of government ministries. These firms stated that, on the whole, they experienced little or no difficulty in obtaining government assistance in establishing their factories.

For all that, the failure of the Principality to achieve as good an employment percentage as prevails for Britain generally, together with the relatively low activity rates, especially of the female population, rightly continues to be a matter of considerable concern. Attempts to alleviate this relatively poor performance of the economy in the use of its resources mostly hinges upon government concessions to the Development Areas, and almost the whole of Wales comes into this category. A discussion of the details of Development Area policy falls outside the scope of this essay, but there are other related issues which call for comment. This is most certainly true of the argument that what Wales needs above all else is an improvement of its 'infra-structure', particularly transport and communications. How inadequate are they?

*   *   *

The most convenient comparison for the examination of transport statistics is not between Wales and the U.K., or with Britain, but with England and Wales. As far as roads are concerned, Wales has 11·7 per cent of the public road system of England and Wales, and judgment of its adequacy hinges upon whether this proportion is measured against the ratio of land areas, which is 13·7 per cent, or of the population, which is only 5·7 per cent. The population of England and Wales is to some extent mobile, of course, which leads to a difficulty in determining whether there are proportionally more English cars on Welsh roads than vice versa! During parts of the summer season this is probably so, when some of the Welsh roads become very congested. In fact the roads along the north and south coasts are by far the busiest and carry a volume of traffic of the order of some six times the north-south traffic within Wales. About 80 per cent of the freight tonnage originated inside Wales goes by road rather than by rail, and about three-quarters of it is for delivery inside Wales. (The comparable proportion of rail freight is not known.) Reliance upon personal transport is high in Wales, and this is especially true of the rural areas, where it is increasing appreciably. There are further increases in prospect with more rail closures threatened, not to mention the withdrawal of bus subsidies by local authorities. There is an obvious need for a rationally planned transport service which comprehends road and rail in the more sparsely peopled areas of the Principality. Meanwhile, its road network is growing appreciably more slowly than that of England; between 1963 and 1969 the the rate of growth of trunk roads was 4·2 per cent in Wales and 6·3 per cent in England; that is, half as much again. The growth in the ordinary road network shows a similar ratio, of 2·8 per cent and 4·1 per cent respectively.[1] As far as rural Wales is concerned the inadequacy of the system shows itself more in terms of lack of uniform standards (and the need for sufficiently long straight stretches where fast moving traffic may overtake the slow) than in failure to cope with the density of traffic. The inadequacies of the system from this latter point of view are, however, becoming daily more apparent in parts of Glamorgan, Monmouthshire and North East Wales.

Of the 624 miles of passenger rail-routes left in Wales, all except about 60 miles have some grant-aided services. The surviving railway routes are clearly orientated to flows between Wales and England. The Principality's routes have been subjected to a good deal of unfavourable scrutiny during and since the Beeching era, but the remedies have been partial and piecemeal. Incredible though it may appear, some places such as Ebbw Vale, Abertillery, Brynmawr, Dowlais and Aberdare where rail services were duplicated, and even triplicated, lost *all* their passenger rail services because when they were all open not one could show a profit, and the irrationality of total closure to passengers was then perpetrated in the name of rationalization. In the South Wales valleys, car ownership tends to be relatively low, and in a situation where nationalized industry is contracting rapidly, proposals to withdraw even fairly costly passenger trains should be looked at very carefully in the national interest. The question which requires to be asked is whether it is entirely expedient for a nationalized enterprise to abandon its services in a particular area at the very time when other nationalized enterprises have, through local closures, made many redundant who henceforward have to travel to any work obtainable. The same sort of argument, which really reduces to a plea to the government to look at the overall picture, applies generally in Wales, since almost the whole of it is a Development Area and therefore in receipt of government concessions. It is hardly rational to divert considerable grant payments of one sort and another to an area and take no cognizance of these efforts to sustain economic activity when other government agencies seek to withdraw services in order to save money. A pioneering cost-benefit study of the threatened Cambrian Coast railway (from Machynlleth to Pwllheli) by the Ministry of Transport recently served to demonstrate how rudimentary and partial such a technique can be in this respect. There are some genuine problems of intangible elements, such as measuring the sense of remoteness experienced without a rail service, and of quantifying problems of time (e.g. whether to value long periods of travel pro rata to short ones). More importantly, we have to ask ourselves whether we

---

[1] There was, however, a subsequent large increase in total road expenditure for Wales. It rose from £34 million in 1969-70, to some £41 million the following year. Special expenditures to combat unemployment are excluded from this figure.

have any criteria which would help us to determine how worthwhile it is to arrest rural depopulation. Then we must ask ourselves whether, and to what extent, railways and bus services play a part in helping to stem the process. The answers to questions such as these could well differ according to their origin; there could, in particular, be interesting discrepencies between answers supplied in London on the one hand, and Cardiff on the other.

Finally, there is little doubt that a close scrutiny, not only of the rationality of grant payments to rail as opposed to road transport, but to other closely-competing claims for public money, might pay handsomely. For example, the total road expenditure programme increased by a remarkable jump of more than 20 per cent in 1970-71 over the previous financial year, i.e. from £34 million to £41 million. As G. N. Rubra has pointed out, this increase of £7 million would be more than enough (without counting in the further Development Areas expenditure upon roads implemented for employment reasons) to cover the total subvention needed to keep all public transport in being in Wales at its 1969 level, for which a sum of some £5 million a year would be needed. (This works out roughly at £4 million for rail services and £1 million for road services.) Further food for thought is provided by the same economist's calculation that the remission to bus operators in Wales of the remaining fuel tax would, at some £0·7 million for 1969, have just about covered the operating deficit on all buses. The abolition of the fuel tax could thus serve as a more convenient means of retaining bus services than the payment of grants?

With the exception of Milford Haven, the traffic of which is almost exclusively in oil, each of the South Wales ports serves the same hinterland. They have played a major role in attracting many industries to the area, and continue to play an essential role in this respect. In North Wales, Holyhead is the only port of any size and serves as the main British passenger terminal for Irish traffic. In traffic bound for Eire, Fishguard remains of some importance despite the development of modern facilities at Swansea.

Of recent years cargo vessels have increased so appreciably in size as to preclude the use of many Welsh ports, the notable exception being again, Milford's superb natural harbour. It will surprise many to learn that this port is now the second largest in Britain by tonnage handled. Swansea is Wales' second largest port, handling some 7½ million tons of traffic in 1969, but this makes it eleventh only in the British list in order of size. The day of the massive coal tonnages, as we have already remarked, has passed long ago and the other Welsh ports now occupy an even more modest place on the list of British ports. The degree to which the Welsh ports rely upon bulk cargoes is nevertheless considerable. This is shown by the fact that though 17½ per cent of total British cargo passes through Welsh ports, the same comparison broken down by category of trade reveals a proportion of 8·3 per cent for manufactured goods and only 3·2 per cent for foodstuffs, while basic materials (e.g. iron ore etc.) come to 14·6 per cent, and fuels as much as 21·2 per cent. Most of the

75

last named consists of oil rather than coal. In brief, basic materials and fuels account for 94 per cent of the total port traffic of the Welsh ports. Because of this, most of the traffic has either originated in Wales, or else has Wales as its destination. The exceptions are Cardiff and Newport which also handle some shipments for the Midlands.

By contrast with the above description a substantial amount of general cargo destined for, or originating in, Wales does not use Welsh ports. Sometimes the reason is that the volume of such traffic is too low to warrant a shipping service, and in other cases it is traceable to superior facilities at some convenient English ports. Of recent years the most serious shortcoming of the Welsh ports is their failure to develop containerization at anything like a rate comparable to that of the English ports generally. This constitutes a threat to their long-term future, even though they appear for the most part to have been financially viable during the 1960s.

One of the basic difficulties faced by the Welsh port authorities is, clearly, that their facilities are of pre-first world war vintage. This is also true of much of the social capital of Wales, which follows from what has already been said about the history of the Principality. Space does not permit us to pursue this theme to any great extent but it is worth noting that just short of half of all the dwellings in Wales date from before 1919, compared with a much lower proportion—37 per cent—for Britain as a whole. Moreover, as we would expect, relatively few new houses were built in Wales between 1919 and 1944, the proportion in this category being 16 per cent compared with 25 per cent for Britain. However, an appreciably higher proportion of the housing stock in Wales is privately owned than in the U.K. as a whole. Amenities in houses in Wales generally, however, tend to be significantly inferior to those obtaining in the U.K. as a whole, though superior to those in Northern Ireland. (In 1966, for example, nearly 17 per cent of the houses in Wales did not have the exclusive use of a hot water tap, 23 per cent had no fixed bath, and 4 per cent had no W.C. Only two-thirds of the households had the exclusive use of hot water, a fixed bath and an inside W.C.) Despite these facts, a comparison of the house-starts per 10,000 of the population for Wales and Britain since 1951 reveals that for almost every year the proportion of starts was lower in Wales. (In the entire period 1951-69 the average number of starts per 10,000 was 54 for Wales and 65 for Britain). Moreover, in 1969 the number of dwellings completed in Wales was the lowest total (17,304) for six years, and nearly 3,000 fewer than in the record year, 1967.

In a written reply to a question in Parliament on 2 March 1971 it was stated that there were in Wales 1,327 Primary Schools and 128 Secondary Schools whose buildings were erected before 1903. Proportionately, some 50 per cent of Welsh primary-school children compared with some 44 per cent in England were so housed, while the respective proportions in pre-1903 secondary schools were some 29 per cent and 17 per cent. Obviously, some are in much poorer condition than others, but it is now hoped to modernise or else to replace these old buildings within some six years, at a cost which cannot be put at less than £30 million for Wales. Finally, in hospital bed provision, though there are wide disparities as between one Management Committee area and another, for Wales as a whole in 1968 the number of beds per 10,000 of the population was approximately 91, compared with a rather better provision for England and Wales as a whole, of some 95.

When we turn from a consideration of social capital to the social accounts of the Welsh economy, there are, fortunately, some reasonably up-to-date figures to quote. Mr. C. R. Tomkins has recently produced comprehensive figures for 1965-68, thus extending a series dating back to 1948, the result of pioneering work by Professor Nevin and his associates.

From these social accounts it appears that in 1968 Wales' gross domestic product (at factor cost) was some £1,538 million, compared with £36,500 million for the U.K. as a whole. When we reduce these figures to a comparable basis of production per head of the population, we find that it was £565 for Wales compared with £661 for the U.K. Expenditures per head on the other hand were much closer, being £637 and £666 respectively. The figures imply an 'import' of resources into Wales of some £194 million, or £72 per head of the Welsh population. Most of this (i.e. some £161 million) was covered by a favourable net balance of government expenditure within Wales. The remainder was covered by two items, that is, by a possible positive net contribution of pension and property income flowing into the Principality on the one hand and a net influx of capital on the other. Unfortunately, it is not possible to break these figures down with any great degree of confidence. However, what should be said in connection with Wales' 'import surplus' is that the presence of such a 'deficit' can add nothing to the debate as to whether Wales would be viable as an independent economy. This debate is quite meaningless. The figures in any set of social accounts are the result of a given set of conditions. By changing these conditions—as for example would be the case were Wales to become independent—the figures would change. In any case, a balance of payments deficit does not, of itself, spell catastrophe for a country: the concomitant influx of resources from other countries could well represent the best means for its advancement.

There remains the fact that gross domestic product per head in Wales is, according to the above figures, only some 85 per cent of the U.K. figures. What can we say about this? Basically, that the population structure of Wales, and its employment level, is different from that of the U.K. By comparison with the United Kingdom generally, Wales has a relatively high proportion of 'economically inactive' people—mostly accounted for by differences in the proportions of school children, students, and pensioners in the population. Furthermore, as we have already seen, the 'economically active' population contains a higher proportion of unemployed persons. However, it is possible to allow for these differences by looking at the figures of employees in employment and the self-employed, dividing their total into the gross domestic product. The result, called the gross domestic product per person occupied, has, over the years 1965-68, remained within a percentage point or so, equal as between Wales and the U.K.—and this despite the continuing appreciable difference between the industrial structure of Wales and the U.K. which we have already examined.

It has already been suggested that most of Wales' 'deficit' is covered by a favourable balance—from the Welsh point of view—of government transactions within the Principality. This, therefore, provides a point of departure for the consideration of the hypothetical 'Welsh Budget' published by the Treasury in 1971, covering central government revenue and expenditure attributable to Wales for the financial year 1968-69. What emerges must evidently depend upon what assumptions are made, particularly concerning the 'imperial contribution'; that is, the proportion of expenditure made on behalf of the U.K. as a whole which is allocated to Wales. The main items are defence, debt interest, external relations, and other U.K. services. On current account alone, Wales had a substantial surplus before taking the 'imperial contribution' into account; in fact, total current receipts for 1968-69 were £622 million compared with 'identifiable' current expenditure of £477 million. However, according to the Treasury's reckoning, of this favourable balance of £145 million, some £137 million was swallowed up by an adverse balance on capital expenditure less capital receipts. With receipts thus virtually exhausted, it follows that, in 1968-69 at least, Wales made an almost negligible contribution to external defence, external relations etc., and interest on the national debt. The Welsh 'net borrowing requirement', i.e. its overall deficit on this hypothetical budget, is greatest when the 'imperial contribution' of allocated expenditure is set 'neutrally' (the Treasury's description) according to the ratio of the Welsh to the U.K. population (i.e. 4·9 per cent). On this basis the overall 'deficit' for the Principality worked out at £182 million for 1968-69. A reduction in allocated expenditure in line with the proportion of Welsh *personal income* to that of the U.K. gives a lower 'imperial contribution' (in fact bringing the figure down from £190 million to £144 million) because this ratio is only 3·7 per cent compared with the population ratio of 4·9 per cent. Upon this assumption the Welsh 'overall deficit', or 'net borrowing requirement' fell from £182 million to £134 million for the year in question. Finally, the Treasury, by adopting what it terms 'extreme assumptions'— mainly by halving attributed military expenditure from £118 million to the £50-£65 million range but at the same time increasing national debt interest allocated to Wales—succeeds in further reducing the hypothetical Welsh deficit for 1968-69. Even so, the resulting figure is still some £114 million, from which, the Treasury concludes, 'on any reasonable set of assumptions', there was a large unfavourable balance between central government expenditure and revenue attributable to Wales in 1968-69. For the same financial year, by contrast, the U.K. as a whole had a sizeable overall surplus of £273 million.

What should we make of all this? Clearly, it would be an easy matter to exaggerate the importance of these accounts, and despite warnings to the contrary, there is likely to be misunderstanding and misinterpretation. It is possible to dispute the relevance of the assumptions and to challenge the reliability of the estimates. We leave these matters as passing beyond our brief. Instead, we wish to stress what we consider to be the fundamental issues which lie, as it were, behind the figures. What needs to be stressed is that hypothetical budgets—as indeed is true of all budgets—are the outcome of a certain set of conditions. Thus, the balance between revenue and expenditure depends crucially upon the level of income, since it is very largely upon this that the revenue from taxation depends. In turn, the level of income depends to a considerable degree upon the ratio of the 'active' to the 'inactive' population, the level of employment, and upon the quality of the jobs available in Wales. These, then, are the more obvious fundamentals which largely determine what the government's revenue from Wales will be. The real issue, therefore, must be not whether the Principality happens to have a deficit when a hypothetical budget is calculated, but whether the U.K. economy has been managed with sufficient insight, judgement and skill to provide employment levels in its various regions which do not show a significant and persistent dispersion from the overall average.

Our final task in this essay, therefore, must be to examine the policy problem posed for the U.K. government by the present condition of, and future outlook for, the Welsh economy. In so doing, we should first try to provide some basic explanation for Wales' problem of relatively low employment levels and slow growth, for in the absence of market imperfections the economic pressures generated by relatively high unemployment should in time result in sufficient changes in price relationships to eliminate the problem. In other words, under free market conditions, relatively high unemployment rates in Wales would depress wage rates in parts of the Principality and so give rise to an outflow of labour. Moreover, those remaining would then find employment more readily at the lower wage rates, and this would be reinforced by a tendency for new capital to be attracted to a region of relatively low wages. This would provide a further secondary boost in the demand for labour, and so the unemployment would be mopped up. Given the fact that Wales has a common exchange rate and common structure of interest rates with the remainder of the U.K., the failure of the adjusting mechanisms described above is to be ascribed chiefly to the fact that price relationships have been prevented from changing because many trade union wage bargains are fixed on a U.K.—wide basis, even though 'plant bargaining' makes for appreciable differences in some industries. In other words, differences in the pressure of demand for labour are not permitted to result in sufficient differences in wage rates to enable differences in employment levels to be ironed out by this means. In essence, therefore, the present problem of the relatively depressed regions has turned out to be more than transitional in nature because of a framework which imposes limitations upon the price adjustment process. The economic setting is thus a very different one from that in which the early iron-masters and coal-mining pioneers earned their fortunes. During those early days of industrialization, when labour was virtually unorganized, wage rates tended to be driven up roughly in line with the strength of demand. To quote but one instance from among many, when coal output in the parish of Ystrad-yfodwg increased from less than half a million tons in 1864, to almost two million tons within ten years, Dr. E. D. Lewis informs us that wage rates rose to an estimated 15 to 25 per cent above those paid in the older mining districts such as Merthyr and Dowlais, where output was not increasing at anything like the same rate. In the present situation of wide employment disparities between regions and within each region, free market conditions would result in a much more dramatic outflow of people from relatively depressed districts than has in fact occurred. To the extent that this has failed to occur, differences in employment levels have persisted.

To uncover the basic rationale of the way economic pressures work in the present connection is not, obviously, to be confused with any advocacy that they ought necessarily to be allowed to operate unchecked and so result in a massive emigration of its people from the Principality. On the contrary, the usefulness of this brief exposition lies (it is hoped) in indicating that the present situation of relatively low employment, slow growth and some emigration of the economically active in Wales—and other similar regions—is one for which the United Kingdom authorities cannot avoid responsibility. In brief, Wales' full integration with its sister countries in the U.K. precludes it from a separate adjustment of interest rates or its exchange rate in relation to these countries, as would be possible for it in principle were it a sovereign state. Therefore, some other means of increasing 'job opportunities' within the Principality must be found, and because, given the present institutional set-up, it is only the central government which can do this on a significant scale, the responsibility for doing so must lie at its door.

What can be done? Action can evidently take the form of special expenditures, especially upon public works of various kinds. Their object is to stimulate local demand and employment. In addition to these regional Keynesian remedies the U.K. authorities can also operate via the price system through differential taxes and subsidies. For example, from 1967 a manufacturer in a Development Area not only had his Selective Employment Tax refunded, but also received an additional payment—a Regional Employment Premium—per person. (Both forms of incentive are, however, being phased out.) The Labour administration also paid substantial investment grants, building grants and training grants to firms in Development Areas. The Conservative government which came to power in 1970, however, soon modified this particular group of incentives, though they still sought to work through the price system by means of accelerated depreciation allowances. Clearly, the authorities can also intervene even more directly by controlling the location of economic activity, and in the United Kingdom some attempt has been made to do this through the issue of Industrial Development Certificates.[1]

Few Welshmen will need to be persuaded of the need for action through the channels described above in order to compensate for the impediments to the adjustment of the economy occasioned by its total integration with that of the United Kingdom. Long-term unemployment is even today too recent an experience in Wales for it to be necessary to labour the theme of its crushing effect upon the human spirit. From a social scientist's viewpoint relatively high unemployment rates also represent a waste of economic resources, while a greater reactivation of relatively depressed areas would add to the rate of growth of the U.K. as a whole and enable it to achieve higher overall levels of employment before wage inflation becomes a major problem.

As it is, Wales has doubtless been greatly assisted by the enormous growth of financial assistance extended to the relatively less prosperous areas during the 1960s. For example, by the end of the decade more such assistance was given to Wales during the one year 1969-70 than was given to the whole of Britain for a comparable period at the beginning of the decade. Notwithstanding this increase in the application of Development Area incentives by the Labour government, it cannot but be a cause for considerable concern that unemployment has continued to grow. Between 1966 and 1970, for example, there was an increase of some 12,000 in the number of unemployed in Wales and a fall of 3,000 in the number of employers and self-employed. Of even greater significance is the decline of no less than 51,000 in the number of employees in employment over the same period, for it is the decline in job opportunities reflected in this figure which must be presumed to have given rise to most of the emigration of the young economically active population. However, of the three separate figures for employees in employment in Wales quoted in this essay, the single most impressive one is the decline—taking males only—of no less than 64,000 between 1964 and 1970.

More than one projection exists which seeks to forecast the extent of the shortfall of jobs which we are likely to witness in the Principality by the

---

[1] Since the above was written, the Chancellor of the Exchequer has presented his 1972 Budget, which included further changes in the package of regional incentives. While the enlargement of the Intermediate Areas and the provision of free depreciation will exercise a 'diluting' effect upon the advantages accruing, the extra investment incentives certainly strengthen the inducements to firms to locate in the Development Areas. Moreover, the government's decision to prescribe a life for them lasting at least until 1978 should be helpful.

As for the Industrial Development Executive brought into being at the same time, though its remit is not limited to the Development Area industries, this body, in conjunction with the associated Regional Development Boards, could be an organization of considerable benefit. Whether this potential is realized must obviously depend upon whether their thinking is directed towards the elimination of, rather than the mere provision of props for, the Development Areas.

mid-seventies. The answers naturally depend upon the assumptions used; Plaid Cymru foresees a shortfall by 1976 of almost 110,000 jobs for males and 67,500 for females, while our own projections at Aberystwyth, using the modest activity-rate aims of the Welsh office, show a shortfall of 49,000 jobs for males and a possible surplus of opportunities for women for the same year. Clearly, all estimates are likely to be falsified by the ceaseless flux of economic life, but it is quite evident that a significant increase in the demand, for male labour especially, is urgently necessary if we are to forestall an acceleration in the emigration from Wales of relatively young people actively seeking work. There is little reason to doubt that the cost to the Exchequer of providing additional jobs for unemployed persons in Wales is still appreciably less than the net return to the state, so there is no justification for any official faltering on that score. These trends in unemployment will be disappointing, if not frustrating, to many Welshmen. After the poignant experience of the fantastically high unemployment rates which led to the massive exodus of the inter-war period we should be at least as keen to prevent its recurrence as, say, the Germans are to guard against a repetition of hyper-inflation, following the monetary misfortunes of that economy earlier this century.

SELECT BIBLIOGRAPHY

A. W. Ashby and I. L. Evans, *The Agriculture of Wales and Monmouthshire* (University of Wales Press 1944).

A. Beacham, *De-population in Mid-Wales* (H.M.S.O. 1964).

D. Law and R. Howes, *Mid-Wales: An assessment of the impact of the Development Commission factory programme* (H.M.S.O., 1972).

E. D. Lewis, *The Rhondda Valleys* (London 1959).

H. Marquand, *Second Industrial Survey of South Wales*, 3 Vols. Thesis submitted for the D.Sc. degree (University of Wales 1937).

W. Minchinton (ed.), *Industrial South Wales 1750-1914* (London 1969).

J. H. Morris and L. J. Williams, *The South Wales Coal Industry 1845-1875* (University of Wales Press 1958).

E. T. Nevin, A. R. Roe and J. I. Round, *The Structure of the Welsh Economy* (University of Wales Press 1966).

Plaid Cymru Research Group, *An Economic Plan for Wales* (Cardiff 1970).

G. L. Rees and Associates, *Survey of the Welsh Economy* (to be published in conjunction with the Report of the Commission on the Constitution).

B. Thomas (ed.), *The Welsh Economy* (University of Wales Press 1962).

R. Thomas, 'The New Investment Incentives', *Bulletin of the Oxford University Institute of Economics and Statistics*, May 1971.

C. R. Tomkins, *Income and Expenditure Accounts for Wales* (forthcoming).

D. Williams, *A History of Modern Wales* (London 1950).

D. Trevor Williams, *The Economic Development of Swansea and of the Swansea District to 1921* (University of Wales Press, 1940).

OFFICIAL PUBLICATIONS

The Welsh Office, *Wales: The Way Ahead*, Cmnd. 3334 (July 1967).

Digest of Welsh Statistics.

Wales: Cymru (presented annually to Parliament by the Secretary of State for Wales).

Census 1971 England and Wales, Preliminary Report.

H.M. Treasury. *A Welsh Budget: Central Government Revenue and Expenditure Attributable to Wales, 1968-69.*

INDUSTRY   IN   WALES

D.   MORGAN   REES

THERE runs through the history of Wales an industrial thread which has been unbroken for 400 years. At times it has been frayed by local, national and political motivations; there have been occasions when it has run slack, and when it has known trials of its tensile strength during periods of transition within itself. It has, despite all, survived to reach a point of great diversification, involving processes as highly developed and as sophisticated as any to be found elsewhere. This diversification which has developed with remarkable rapidity since 1945 was beyond anyone's forecast during the decade preceding the war years.

The second half of the sixteenth century provides the best starting point because it was during this period that industry in Wales began to produce for the market, an expression which embraces the idea of production above local needs and distribution beyond local boundaries. In deciding upon this starting point previous contributions to the technical processes of certain industries and the application of engineering skills are in no way discounted.

For example, the evidence of applied industry during Roman times in Wales, and indeed earlier, has a fascination and provides proof of great technical ability. The workings of the Dolaucothi goldmine the *Ogofau*, near Pumsaint, Carmarthenshire, and the meeting of their demands for water, provide proof of applied engineering of extraordinarily high attainment. Some of the levels, which were driven into hillsides at this goldmine, may still be penetrated to reveal their 'bold and regular workmanship'. The formation of roof and walls is such that it suggests, in some cases, that the level was driven so that loads could be carried hanging from yokes borne on human shoulders. That these levels were driven using hand tools only makes them all the more remarkable.

An exceptional feature associated with this Roman goldmine was the watercourse, which brought water to it from a point on the river Cothi about seven miles away. It followed the steep hillside bounding the eastern side of the river valley running between the 600 and 800 feet contour lines. Along parts of its length continuity was only made possible by cutting channels out of rock or a flat ledge into the hillside. Despite the time which has elapsed, this aqueduct may still be traced along parts of its length enabling it to be recognised as an outstanding feat of water engineering.

IRON

(i) *The sixteenth and seventeenth centuries*
During the second half of the sixteenth century Sussex ironmasters who had,

by royal ordinance, been prevented from using the timbers of the Weald for charcoal-burning came to Glamorgan. Valleys such as those of the rivers Taff, the Cynon and the Aman were well-wooded, sufficiently endowed with iron ore out-crops and able to provide the water power to drive water wheels which operated the bellows which gave ironmaking furnaces the blast of air they needed to create the heat necessary for the smelting operation. Water-wheels were also used to operate the hammers of the forges which shaped the iron after it had first been refined in readiness for this operation.

This migration from Sussex resulted in blast furnaces and forges appearing, between 1564 and 1600, near Tongwynlais, at Pentyrch, Pont-y-gwaith, Pont-y-Rhun, and Blaencannaid in the Taff Valley; they were also established at Cwmaman and Dyffryn in the Cynon Valley. During the same period Sir Robert Sidney developed works at Llanhari, Llantrisant, and Angelton north of Bridgend.

In Monmouthshire the valleys of the Afon Lwyd, the Ebbw Fach and Ebbw Fawr and of the river Usk provided similarly favourable conditions. Ironmaking came to the county some years after it had started in Glamorgan. In 1570 there were works at Cwmffrwdoer, and afterwards at Trosnant, Abercarn and Monkswood, sites fairly near to Pontypool where furnaces and forges were also established. The Tintern wireworks, in the Wye Valley was also emerging during this period, a works associated with Richard Hanbury of Worcestershire, an astute man who realised the importance of acquiring acres of woodland at this time. He also became proprietor of some of the works near Pontypool.

This early iron industry, because of its complete dependence upon natural supplies, has been described as one which was subject to 'the tyranny of wood and water'. Nonetheless it flourished sufficiently to develop an export trade in finished iron from Cardiff and Newport to the midland counties of England, to Bristol, westwards to Carmarthenshire and Ireland, and to the Low Countries. Such consignments are recorded in the Welsh Port Books of the period, but there was also a trade with Spain in pieces of ordnance, one which was not strictly legal as England and Spain were at war with each other at that time.

After 1600 there was a contraction in the exports of finished iron to parts of England in the face of competition from the Midlands and the Forest of Dean. New furnaces and forges were, however, built in Glamorgan, Brecon-shire and Carmarthenshire and production was increased in the Wye Valley by the addition of two more blast furnaces. The scarcity of timber for charcoal fuel within economic reach of established sites inevitably caused closures and the iron industry became more scattered.

The use of coke instead of charcoal as a fuel in ironmaking, first introduced by Abraham Darby at Coalbrookdale in 1709, gradually increased during the course of the eighteenth century. As a result, by about 1775 the charcoal iron industry had practically ceased to exist in Britain. A charcoal furnace, was, however, first worked in Wales twenty years before this date at the village of Furnace, in Cardiganshire. During the first half of the eighteenth century there were sporadic movements towards the establishment of furnaces and forges in the western counties of Wales. In some cases they developed from the need to be closer to timber supplies and in others from this and the availability of local supplies of iron ore. Quaker families—the Darbys, Lloyds and Paytons—were the first promoters of ironmaking and forging in Merioneth at Dolgun, in Montgomeryshire at Dolobran and Mathrafal, and in Cardiganshire at Glanfrêd. A furnace at Bersham, in Denbighshire, was re-built in 1717 by Charles Lloyd of Dolobran—it was reputed to have been casting cannon in 1649—and afterwards was owned and operated until 1808 by the well-known ironmaking family, the Wilkinsons.

During this period finished iron from some of these forges—it came to them in the form of pig iron—was supplied to merchants in Liverpool, Chester and Bristol, to ironmongers in a number of North Wales towns, to a wireworks at Gwersyllt, near Wrexham, and to a tinplate works at Llechryd, Cardiganshire and to other users.

(ii) *The eighteenth and nineteenth centuries*

The year 1775 was decisive in industrial history because it marked the development of the steam engine of James Watt from the experimental to the commercial stage. Its effect on the iron industry marked it as a year which shows 'more clearly than most dates selected as boundary-stones the end of one economic period and the beginning of another'. The final period of the eighteenth century has been identified with the industrial revolution, a concept which may be defined as the time during which the economy of a country changes predominantly from a non-industrial to an industrial economy. This is a concept which can only apply to parts of Wales and it must not be looked upon as being comparable to the movement towards a factory system which followed inventions in the cotton and woollen industries of northern England.

The great change began in South Wales from 1760 with the development and growth of an iron industry in the east of this region, one which was to end in the first concentration of industry within a defined area of the country, the northern rim of the South Wales coalfield. At the heads of the valleys running northwards from the coast of east Glamorgan and Monmouth-shire ' a great chain' of ironworks was developed in barely more than a generation, some of which reached high peaks of production and prosperity. For a long period they were able to work iron ore easily so close was it to the surface; their supplies of limestone were assured—lime was now used as a flux in the ironmaking process; the coal for coking was near at hand in abundance and there were adequate supplies of stone for furnace building.

The blast furnace of the late eighteenth early nineteenth century was essentially a vertical, circular chamber or shaft which widened from the top

88

and bottom towards its middle section. Its inner lining was made of fire-brick, surrounded by subsequent courses of common brick and a rubble of stone as a filling between the brickwork and the stout, outer walls of stone. Externally the furnaces presented square structures, massive in appearance, built to cling to the sides of rising ground to enable easy charging of the prepared materials from platforms which were level with the working areas above and behind the furnaces. The stone-built furnaces were generally replaced during the second half of the nineteenth century by round structures clad in iron plates, and with the introduction of hoists to bring up the raw materials to the charging platforms the furnaces became free-standing although often linked with one another.

In South Wales at the beginning of this period waterwheels were still used to drive the blast-providing bellows, but by the beginning of the nineteenth century steam-driven engines were in general use. It is not always appreciated how much the introduction of steam engines resulted in greater efficiency and in increased tonnages of pig iron and finished iron in different forms.

The size of an ironworks, apart from the demand for iron, depended upon the number of its blast furnaces, because it was their demand for raw materials and their production of pig iron which determined the extent of the preparatory and the finishing processes. There is evidence in paintings of ironworks in production and in photographs of works as they approached their closing stages, usually between 1860 and 1870, of the great areas covered by some of them and the profusion of buildings which made up the overall complexes.

Three water colours by G. Childs, dated 1840, of different parts of the Dowlais Ironworks epitomise the tremendous productive capacity of a large ironworks and possibly suggest that this was the year when this and other works were reaching their peak. One painting shows a general view of the iron-making side in which eighteen blast furnaces are discernible. In attendance on these there were lime kilns, calcining furnaces, coke ovens and engine houses. The second shows a close-up of the tops of a number of furnaces from which flame and smoke pour forth. This also reveals that there were groupings of furnaces—towering structures 45 to 50 feet high—in pairs and threes, arrangements which gave increased production of iron. It shows too, a small group of people, near a charging platform engaged in manual work, one of them being a woman, an indication of the mixed labour element in an ironworks at that time.

In the third painting—the finishing end of the works—is seen the answer to the problem endured by ironmasters in earlier years when they were faced with solving the need to convert pig iron into wrought iron, the problem which brought periodic congestion of production because the production of bar iron could not match that of pig iron. A forest of comparatively short chimneys indicates a proliferation of refining and puddling furnaces. The discovery of a method of decarbonising in large quantities—the puddling process—led to spectacular increases in bar iron. The two inventors, in 1784, were Peter

Onions, a foreman in an iron mill at Merthyr Tydfil, but originally from Coal-brookdale, and Henry Cort a contractor to the Admiralty, well-connected and able to undertake its commercial development, whilst Onions remained unknown.

This discovery was followed by the rolling of iron, and mills were laid down in Dowlais and other ironworks in South Wales. The increase in the production of finished iron was spectacular. In 1803 rather more than 800 tons were carried on the Glamorganshire Canal. Between 1817 and 1830 the total from the four works at Merthyr Tydfil approximated 120,000 tons, the Dowlais Company contributing some 42,000 tons. In 1840, 10,000 people were employed at this works when it was regarded as the largest in the world.

Statistics of output for Monmouthshire during the same period show a similar increase in production. Between 1802 and 1830 the iron transported on the Monmouthshire Canal to Newport was more than 112,000 tons; it was made up of pig iron, puddled bars and blooms, and bars, rods and hoops.

This volume of production cannot, however, be regarded as a criterion of profit. It is true that the large works such as Dowlais and Cyfarthfa made huge profits, but all the smaller works did not escape 'the inevitable ill-consequences of war', which was a notable feature of the late eighteenth and early nineteenth centuries. But the contracts for ordnance obtained during this period have been described as 'Food of the Gods'. In 1762 the Bersham ironworks of the Wilkinsons were re-constituted to cast cannon, shell and grenades on a scale which gave them a European reputation.

Between 1760 and 1850 the iron industry distributed itself throughout the South Wales area, stretching from Pontypool in the east to Stepaside in Pembrokeshire. It touched upon every county. Its greatest concentration was along the northern rim of the South Wales coalfield on the narrow strip of land which traversed the *blaenau*; here too, were to be formed its largest works. It was an industry which became familiar to Central Glamorgan at Maesteg, Tondu and even Cefn Cribwr; to the Swansea Valley at Ystrad-gynlais and Ystalyfera; to Carmarthen and Llanelli, and also to Pembrokeshire. In all there were 45 ironworks.

As the number of ironworks was so large contributions to technical progress in ironmaking would be expected in some of them. Many attempts were made to smelt iron by using anthracite coal as fuel, but none succeeded until George Crane, the proprietor of Ynyscedwyn Ironworks, Ystradgynlais solved 'this difficult problem . . . by making strong and excellent pig iron . . . by means of hot blast with raw anthracite coal'. Crane reported on his discovery in a paper to the British Association in 1838. At another works in the Swansea Valley—the Ystalyfera Ironworks—the proprietor, James Palmer Budd, devised a method for using the heat from the waste gases of a blast furnace by directing them into chambers through which the cold blast passed thus enabling the saving of the cost of fuel and labour employed in heating the blast and raising steam for the blast engine. His achievement was reported to the British Association, at Edinburgh, in 1850.

There can be no doubt that the modern iron industry of South Wales owed its existence to a number of Englishmen of vision and initiative. Among the earliest was John Guest of Broseley, in Shropshire, a county described as 'the matrix of the iron industry in Wales', and Anthony Bacon of Whitehaven and London. They came to Merthyr Tydfil in the 1760s and became identified with Dowlais and Cyfarthfa respectively. In 1782, Samuel, Jeremiah and Thomas Homfray, also of Broseley, began forge operations at Cyfarthfa and afterwards established the Penydarren Ironworks. Richard Hill took over the Plymouth furnace at Merthyr Tydfil and Richard Crawshay established one of the most famous of all ironmaking dynasties at Cyfarthfa. Other names which emerged were the Kendalls of the Beaufort and Clydach ironworks, the Baileys of Nant-y-glo ironworks, the Fothergills of Abernant and Tredegar ironworks and the Harfords of Ebbw Vale.

The decline of the industry was as swift as its rise. Its inland sites, with few exceptions, could not meet new demands and from 1860 plant was dismantled and works' buildings were left to decay and disintegrate.

IRON, STEEL AND TINPLATE: THE FIRST PHASE

There were limitations to the uses of iron. The superiority of steel had been known for hundreds of years, but the technological advance towards its production in bulk did not come until the end of the nineteenth century. The evolution into steelmaking, the use of iron to make steel was inevitable—in a sense it was a natural development.

The first experimenter to succeed was Henry Bessemer, who invented the process of turning molten iron into steel by blowing air into it to remove the impurities thus achieving the conversion. This was in 1856. His converter was not the complete answer. It was improved upon by giving it a different lining. This important step forward, known afterwards throughout France and Germany as the Thomas Process, was achieved by Sidney Gilchrist Thomas, aided by his cousin Percy Gilchrist, who through the good sense of his works' manager, was permitted to carry out certain physical tests at Blaenavon ironworks.

During the 1860s Bessemer steel, for rolling into rails, was being produced at Ebbw Vale, Rhymney and Dowlais, originally three ironworks. Ebbw Vale alone survived into modern times as an integrated iron and steel works and surprisingly on an inland site some distance from the point of import of raw materials and a greater distance from industrial areas in England which developed subsequently.

The use of the South Wales sea-board for the building of iron and steel works, and steel works—there is a distinction—began in 1888 when a new Dowlais works for the making of iron and steel was first developed on a site on East Moors, Cardiff. It was planned as a hot metal works to produce its own iron, which in its molten form with the addition of scrap steel, would be worked into steel in open-hearth furnaces. In time this works became

91

associated with an iron and steelworks at Port Talbot and with blast furnaces at Briton Ferry.

In west Glamorgan at the Landore steelworks, Swansea, William Siemens, from 1875 onwards, experimented in steelmaking by the open-hearth method. There was a growing need for a steel suitable for rolling into sheets which could be coated with tin for making tinplate. In previous times iron was hammered into a sheet for this purpose, but about 1720 John Hanbury, of Pontypool, first rolled iron into sheet for the making of tinplate. It would not be out of place at this point to say that this word is misleading, because the product is neither tin nor plate. Originally it was a thin iron sheet, now steel, coated with a thin layer of tin. The word tinplate, has however, been a familiar one for a very long time.

Iron sheets were coated with tin for the first time in Wales in Pontypool about 1665, followed by a works at Cydweli in 1719 and by a number of others near Newport, near Aberdulais and on the outskirts of Cardiff around the middle of the eighteenth century. About 1770 there were similar developments in north Pembrokeshire and in Carmarthen town.

The industry assumed a fairly even pattern of development in South Wales during the next 100 years, but towards the end of the nineteenth century there was a concentration of tinplate works in west Glamorgan and east Carmarthenshire where there developed a demand for suitable steel bar for rolling into sheets. The rolling of steel sheets for the market and of corrugated steel sheets was at times carried out in a tinplate works; it was also done independently by other works.

The demand for steel bar was met by the building of sixteen cold metal medium-sized steelworks. These were works which were supplied with iron for conversion into steel from blast furnaces outside their own locations. They were built at such towns as Swansea, Llansamlet, Gowerton, Gorseinon, Pontardawe, Briton Ferry and Llanelli. These towns and many others, were closely linked with the tinplate industry of the hand-rolling mills into which steel sheets were fed by hand by rollermen during the many preparatory hot and cold rolling processes before the coating of the sheets.

In a paper read to the South Wales Institute of Engineers in 1915 there appeared the phrase, 'a Welsh tinplate mill ... seems as unalterable as the laws of the Medes and Persians', one which was critical of the industry for its failure to achieve any decisive progress since the eighteenth century. The rolling process depended too much upon the skill of the worker and the industry could not produce tinplate of the uniform quality required by the progressive can-making industry. There were attempts at changes in mill lay-outs but they resulted in modifications rather than basic improvements.

The tinplate manufacturer seemed, at this time, reluctant to seek the assistance of the engineer, the chemist and the metallurgist. Ultimately the growth in foreign competitors forced upon the industry the formation of a special research team.

There were, however, improvements in the mill heating furnaces, gas firing replacing coal. Pickling machines and annealing furnaces were improved, the movements of raw materials between departments were streamlined and automatic tinning machines were introduced, turning a number of processes into a continuous operation.

Such improvements were as nothing compared with the forward strides in the United States of America where there were six strip mills in 1929 and twenty-eight by 1939, and when the cold-reduction process was mastered in 1929, the manufacture of tinplate in the form of strip by the electrolytic tinning process soon followed. In 1932 the British steel industry was granted the tariff protection it had been seeking, but for South Wales it brought only a new integrated iron and steel works to Cardiff. There were no plans for the tinplate industry. The reasons behind the industry's reluctance, its refusal to modernise at this time, have been described as 'smallness of mind'.

The steel industry in North Wales at the end of the nineteenth century and early in the present century developed at Brymbo and Shotton. At Brymbo a plant to produce basic open-hearth steel was built by John Henry Darby, a descendant of the Quaker family of Coalbrookdale, in 1885, and experiments towards continuous steelmaking by this method were attempted a few years later. In 1918 the works was acquired by Baldwins Ltd. The sheet making firm of John Summers and Sons, Stalybridge, Lancashire built an open-hearth steel plant and bar mill at Hawarden Bridge, Shotton and the firm's head-quarters was established there in 1908. By 1909 it was one of the largest makers of galvanised sheets and it then decided to establish a steelmaking plant for its own sheet bars and to enlarge its steelmaking capacity. The new sheet mills were known as 'Welsh' mills. In 1917-18 a second steel melting shop made up of eight open-hearth furnaces, and a bar mill were built there. The steelworks on the banks of the river Dee was destined for further expansion after the depression of the Thirties and war years of 1939-45.

COAL

Although coal was known to the Romans in Wales it was not greatly used by them nor the inhabitants of the country until the thirteenth century. By the fifteenth century it was being mined in Anglesey, Flintshire, Monmouthshire, Glamorgan and Pembrokeshire. It was used by blacksmiths, limeburners and to some extent in domestic fires. Attempts towards the substitution of coal for wood in ironmaking during the seventeenth century began to change the picture. When the difficulties encountered were mastered the use of coke from pit-coal was swiftly developed and the demand for coal increased in proportion. The iron industry's need for it became greater and greater as its own productive capacity increased.

Between 1830 and 1840 the coal industry began to abandon its subsidiary role. During the early years of the nineteenth century there had been expansion stimulated by the growing needs of the iron industry and by the demand from the copper smelting industry in the Port Talbot—Swansea—Llanelli region. There was also a domestic demand, which grew as the industrial areas became more populated, and other lesser requirements.

During this decade the tremendous potential of the industry as an exporter and supplier of coal for special needs was beginning to emerge. Over this period the amount of coal covered by these categories increased and shipments rose from just over 1 million tons to $1\frac{1}{2}$ million tons. After 1840 the major development in the South Wales coal industry was the growth in the shipments of coal, more particularly of steam coal to meet overseas demand. The production of coal in South Wales, including Monmouthshire, by 1874 had reached nearly $16\frac{1}{2}$ million tons, an increase of between three and four times since 1840. In that year the foreign shipments of coal amounted to 63,000 tons and by 1874 they had grown to nearly 4 million tons.

The South Wales Coalfield extends from Pontypool in the east to St. Bride's Bay in the west along a line roughly parallel to the Bristol Channel. Its appearance on a map has been variously described; for example as an elongated basin and as kidney-shaped. It has been regarded as an exposed coalfield with coal seams outcropping at the surface, this accessibility proving an important factor in its development.

It possessed coal of high quality principally of three varieties: it was amply supplied with bituminous coal, steam coal and anthracite. It cannot be simply stated that these different kinds have been nor are mined in defined areas because the upper seams in any locality are different from the lower seams. Generally, anthracite coal is found in the detached portion of the coalfield in Pembrokeshire and in the north-western area of the main portion from the river Gwendraeth to the head of the vale of Neath. Along the southern part of the coalfield between Swansea and Newport in the seams of the lower measures the coal is bituminous and in such areas as the Aberdare and Rhondda valleys steam coals of various qualities predominate. It has been estimated that on a broad basis the percentages are steam coals, 50; bituminous, 30; and anthracite, 20.

During the second half of the nineteenth century the development of the coal industry was rapid. Its swiftness was parallel to that experienced by the iron industry. In one sense the reason for it was similar—improved methods of production and the use of the steam engine for winding and pumping. The growth led to the opening up of the valleys of South Wales along their entire length. The iron industry had been confined to the heads of the valleys. The demand for steam coal for navies and mercantile shipping was enormous and maps indicating positions of collieries which had been sunk by 1913 present astronomic appearances.

In 1912 the export of coal from the ports of Cardiff, Penarth and Barry totalled over 20 million tons. The total amount of coal raised during this year in the whole of the coalfield was 50 million tons. During the years of development towards this peak of production the methods of working had progressed from hand operation to coal-cutting machines worked by compressed air and afterwards by electricity. Methods of raising coal improved in stages from the use of hand windlasses, horse whim gins, to various kinds of steam winding engines developed to meet new demands to reach the deeper coal measures. There were equivalent developments towards improvements in winding ropes. Transport of coal below ground was achieved through the use of various haulage systems; a coal-face conveyor was introduced in 1902; the shaker conveyor powered by electricity was used a great deal in South Wales and conveyor belts have been features of mine roadways for a considerable time.

A great deal of attention was given to mine drainage and ventilation, but there were many accidents and mishaps resulting in serious loss of life from flooding and explosions. Considerable progress was made in the use of personal lighting, and electrical-flameproof fittings were introduced for the lighting of main roadways. In parallel with these developments progress was made in the field of safety and health, in particular the deadly hazard of coal dust was being looked at by a research committee in 1939.

In 1841 Denbighshire had about 2,000 coal miners and Flintshire 1,700. In 1911 the figures were 10,500 and 4,000. During this period the numbers employed in the South Wales Coalfield rose from 11,000 to 214,000. These figures speak for the comparative sizes of the two coalfields. That of North Wales was contained within a narrow strip, at its widest point nine miles only, extending from near Oswestry to Point of Air. There was also a small coalfield in Anglesey.

Coal mining was more difficult in North Wales, the seams being thinner and deeper. An early source of demand for coal was the iron industry of the eighteenth-nineteenth centuries in Denbighshire and the chief coal-producing centres developed around Ruabon in the south of the county and Brymbo in the north. In the eighteenth century also there was a demand from the copper and lead smelting industries of north-east Wales. Farther north coal-mining at Hawarden was boosted by the demand of the potteries established in Buckley.

The new markets, better roads, canals and mineral railways brought rapid progress in coal mining in North Wales and technical progress such as the use of the steam engine was shared with the South Wales Coalfield. Mining villages developed at Bagillt and Mostyn in Flintshire, Brymbo and Rhosllanerchrugog in Denbighshire. They were the equivalent of Aberdare and Tonypandy in Glamorgan, Tredegar and Abertillery in Monmouthshire but even in 1829 there was a report of the 'gradual decline of the coal and iron works' in the north and these mining villages were never identified with huge production figures as were their counterparts in the south. Industrial developments in other fields did, however, provide a demand and the collieries 'held their own until after the Great War'.

After 1921 the South Wales Coalfield suffered marked industrial recession. There was a remarkable decline in the population of mining valleys such as the Rhondda and a migration to the new industrial centres of the Midlands and London. The basic industries of coal mining, iron and steelmaking were still regarded as the mainstay of the economy of the region but they failed to provide employment. Their recession had many repercussions and between 1925 and 1932 unemployment in Wales reached a peak figure of 234,730.

TRANSPORT AND COMMUNICATION

During the sixteenth and seventeenth centuries trade from Welsh ports was mainly coastal and communications from the small ironworks and coal mines were achieved along rough tracks and the navigable stretches of rivers. During the early years of the development of the modern iron industry Anthony Bacon, who was then the proprietor of the Cyfarthfa ironworks with an interest in the Plymouth ironworks, realised the importance of a good road linking Merthyr Tydfil and Cardiff. This was completed in 1767 and it ran through Caerphilly. Constant use and possibly poor construction soon made it a difficult road and it was followed by a turnpike road running along the floor of the Taff Valley. This was used to transport wagon-loads of iron to Cardiff.

The swift growth of the iron industry resulted in a need for a form of transport with a better capacity. Francis Homfray is said to have suggested the Glamorganshire Canal, authorised in 1790, and Thomas Dadford as its engineer-contractor. Dadford was already experienced in canal building in Shropshire and other counties. The building of the Glamorganshire Canal inspired the ironmasters and coal owners of Monmouthshire to promote the Monmouthshire Canal with a branch from Crumlin and, another from Pontypool to Newport. In a short time work began on the Brecon and Abergavenny Canal to link up with that already built to Pontypool. There was earlier canal building activity in the Neath area followed by the Neath Canal which was finished in 1795. The Swansea Canal, completed in 1798, opened up the Tawe Valley to industrial enterprise, particularly Ystalyfera and Ystradgynlais towards the head of the valley. In North Wales that most difficult part of the Ellesmere Canal, planned by the incomparable Thomas Telford from 1793 onwards, took it through the rugged country between the rivers Dee and Ceiriog, in the Vale of Llangollen. This resulted in the building of the Chirk and Pontcysyllte aqueducts described as being 'among the boldest efforts of human invention in modern times'.

Ironworks and coalmines were linked by hunderds of miles of narrow-gauge tramroads or tramways. This means of communication, using horse and tram, was in general use throughout Wales during the eighteenth and into the nineteenth century.

The canals failed to satisfy the needs of the populous, industrial south in the second part of the nineteenth century. They could not deal quickly enough with the mounting tonnages of the iron and coal industries.

Richard Trevithick had succeeded in building at Merthyr Tydfil a steam locomotive, the first to draw a load on rails, which pulled a train of trams on

96

the tramroad between Penydarren Ironworks and Abercynon in February 1804. There followed bigger and more efficient steam locomotives and railways, many of which followed the routes of early tramroads, which meant that the most complete networks of railways were in the industrial areas of the south and north-east.

The Taff Vale Railway between Cardiff and Merthyr Tydfil was completed in 1841. It was followed by many railways bearing the names of famous companies such as the Rhymney, Barry, Brecon and Merthyr, Rhondda and Swansea Bay, Manchester and Milford and the Vale of Neath. The relief of Wales made railway building in some instances difficult and expensive and in central and north Wales fewer railways were completed. The building of the Cambrian Railway, the line to Aberystwyth being completed in 1864, ran into many difficulties during its construction which owed much to David Davies, Llandinam, before he became a coalowner in the Rhondda Valley. Railway lines with England were given early priority, those running along the sea-boards of the north and south being the most important.

During the period of railway development the mania associated with it spread into Wales and small townships arranged public meetings at which there were loud calls for railway stations. They were regarded by the inhabitants as symbols which gave their towns an important status.

In 1922 these areas lost the familiar names of their original railways when the Great Western Railway took over the majority of the companies in the interest of rationalisation.

MINING FOR METALS AND SMELTING

Metalliferous mining as a subject is of special interest in the industral history of Wales because there were times when major contributions were made to the world's supply of metals and the development of processes of extracting metals from ores was pioneered in parts of the country.

The word ore, which has a commercial significance, is a rock or stone which contains metal. It can be assumed that there was an awareness of local sources of copper and lead in pre-Roman times and a stronger assumption of the awareness of iron, a metal already looked at in some detail, judged by the use made of local ores.

Every county in Wales has produced lead ore. The Romans used lead particularly in the form of water pipes and tanks and there are twelfth and thirteenth century references to churches having roofs of lead. During the sixteenth century the Crown was interested in the mines of Cardiganshire which produced lead ores rich in silver. They were known as Mines Royal and were administered by a society on behalf of the Crown. This monopoly caused bitter resentment, but it remained unbroken until the end of the seventeenth century. During this period, however, important contributions to the technical side of mining and smelting in Cardiganshire were made by Sir Hugh Myddleton, and Thomas Bushell who was granted permission to coin the silver at a mint in Aberystwyth. Sir Carbery Pryse and Sir Humphrey Mackworth were prominent during the period of the breaking of the royal monopoly and made important contributions to mining practice.

During the eighteenth and nineteenth centuries Cardiganshire and Montgomeryshire abounded with lead mines. There were many miles of leets taking water to waterwheels used in winding, pumping and ore crushing processes. The importance of the waterwheel to these areas, remote from coal supplies, cannot be overemphasised. Steam engines were introduced at a later date.

Despite the extraordinary spread of lead mines throughout Wales only a small number made big profits in the modern period. Amongst these were the Cardiganshire mines of Cwmystwyth and Fron-goch, and the Van mine in Montgomeryshire, one of the most prolific, which produced over 96,000 tons of lead ore, nearly 800,000 ounces of silver and more than 28,000 tons of zinc.

Flintshire and eastern Denbighshire were also important lead and zinc mining regions during the nineteenth century and between 1845 and 1909 produced nearly a million tons of zinc concentrates. The lead and zinc ores of South Wales had no great importance but a mine in Carmarthenshire—Nantymwyn—proved productive and profitable.

There is a history of lead mining in many areas into the 1920s and later, but it was punctuated by closures and re-openings and little success.

In common with lead mining, copper mining in Wales has an early history, but it was confined to Anglesey, Caernarvonshire and Merioneth. The remoteness of the sites, mostly on hills and mountains, and the visible evidence which they present today emphasise that the copper miners worked under difficult and often severe conditions. Many of them lived in stone 'barracks' near the mines during the working week.

In general, the output of the mines—again they were at their busiest during the eighteenth and nineteenth centuries—was not great apart from the phenomenal Parys and Mona copper mines in Anglesey which by 1768 were producing ore yielding about 3,000 tons of metallic copper yearly. The Parys Mine Company was formed by the Reverend Edward Hughes and Thomas Williams, a lawyer and the son of an Anglesey farmer. Williams became a prominent figure during the years when Britain moved into the industrial era. He cornered the greater part of the copper industry and his influence was felt even in Cornwall because he succeeded in controlling the sale and price of copper from 1787 to 1792. He owned copper warehouses in London, Birmingham and Liverpool and smelting works in South Wales and Lancashire.

In 1828 the annual output of copper ores was about 3,500 tons, most of it from Anglesey now in decline. By 1845 it had risen to 68,000 tons and thereafter fell rapidly to about 50,000 tons in 1847 and the downward trend continued so much so that the total amount produced during the next 65 years was not much more than 50,000 tons.

In Caernarvonshire the copper mines were located in Snowdonia, in the

Beddgelert district and in Cwm Pennant; in Merioneth at Glasdir, near Llanfachreth and on a small number of other sites. They were not great producers, but not for lack of endeavour by the early proprietors nor for the absence of persuasive prospectuses subsequently from companies usually having London addresses.

On the site of the Gilfach Copper Mine, in Cwm Ciprwth, above Cwm Pennant may still be seen the remains of a substantial cast-iron waterwheel in its stone housing and some distance away a T-bob pump at the mouth of a shaft and its rods descending into the depths below. The waterwheel which drove the pump and served as a winder for another shaft, still bears the name of the makers and its place of origin, Truro, in Cornwall. The site is about 900 feet above sea-level and the nearest port is Portmadoc about twelve miles away. These facts vividly illustrate the determination and tenacity of the people in the industry. A huge cast-iron stamper from the Britannia Copper Mine, which has been lying on the shore of Glaslyn, for many years, because it proved too heavy for scrap merchants to take it away, tells the same story.

In the modern period the only county concerned with gold mining was Merioneth. Discoveries were reported as early as 1843. Mining for metals did not produce the same intensive industrialisation as the iron, steel and coal industries of South Wales, but great ingenuity was shown in the attempts to extract the metal from the ore. This was not always successful 'and much current coin of the realm was expended and very little bullion obtained by smelting'.

Only about ten mines were successfully worked for a number of years, but there were more than 150 levels, trial levels and shafts. Mines developed around Clogau mountain provided valuable finds in 1860 and 1861 which culminated in production valued at more than £43,000 between 1863 and 1865, and under the name of the St. David's Gold and Copper Mines Ltd. between 1891 and 1894 produced gold worth over £17,000. The Gwynfynydd Mine ranked in importance with the Clogau group. It was discovered along with other mines in 1864 and gave good yields in 1888, 1893, and from 1901 to 1904. Other mines which were partially successful were Bedd-y-Coedwr, Voel, and Carn Dochan and Prince Edward which were outside the Dolgellau Mineral Belt.

Many photographs have survived which show how dependent was the gold mining industry, as were the other metalliferous mines, on water power for driving their prime movers. The sizes of the remains of a number of water-wheel pits indicate that some of these wheels were of great diameters and widths.

Neath, Port Talbot, Swansea and Llanelli developed into important smelting centres from the beginning of the eighteenth century, but as far back as 1584 copper ore from Cornwall was being smelted at Neath. This was an early example of taking the ore to the area where fuel was available. The ships returned to Cornwall laden with coal. Early in the eighteenth century Sir

Humphrey Mackworth was sending lead ore from Cardiganshire for smelting, also at Neath.

These beginnings laid the foundations for the world-wide reputation that the Swansea Bay region was to acquire for non-ferrous metallurgy. During the last quarter of the nineteenth century Swansea was regarded as the greatest metallurgical centre in the world.

Copper smelting began in the Swansea area in 1717 at Llangyfelach, and other works followed rapidly in the lower Swansea valley developed by companies run by Vivian and Son, William Foster and Company and the English Copper Company and others. Copper ore was imported from Cornwall, Anglesey and Caernarvonshire but by the 1880's the effect of copper smelting abroad began to be felt and the home industry began to decline. The area was also engaged in smelting lead, silver, spelter and zinc and in producing sulphuric acid for the tinplate industry.

QUARRYING

The demand for stone for industrial and domestic building stretches back a very long time. Stone, and its crushing and grading to appropriate sizes, for road building and other uses, has always been available in all parts of Wales so generous is the distribution of quarries. Limestone quarries on the other hand have been mainly confined to the margins of the coalfields; their production has for a considerable period been in demand for ironmaking, agricultural uses, mortar and cement, and road-making.

Slate quarrying has been aptly described as 'the most Welsh of Welsh industries'. The principal rocks of the slate industry are in Snowdonia where the terrain determined that the slate industry should not develop early and on a large scale for lack of good transport facilities.

Rock formations, the vastness of the slate quarries and slate mines suggest that the winning of slate has a long history and again the activities of the Romans can be invoked. In the commercial sense, however, slate was not worked until the second half of the eighteenth century when small ventures were developed until eventually they grew into large productive units.

Slate was won by open quarrying and mining. By the first method, generally used in Caernarvonshire, the rock was worked from the outside in galleries which in some quarries were from 60 to 70 feet high and of similar widths. The Penrhyn and Dinorwig quarries provide good examples of this method of working. At first this method was also followed in Merioneth, but between 1845 and 1850 it was realised that as quarries became deeper much worthless rock had to be removed to reach the good slate beneath. This was not profitable and underground mining was adopted at quarries in Blaenau Ffestiniog where slate was worked in underground chambers simultaneously at different horizons.

The qualities important in the selection of slates for roofing were straight and uniform cleavage, imperviousness to water and unaffected by frost, attractive colours and absence of mineral content. The durability of this form of roofing has been proved by time under many different conditions. The slates were trimmed to required sizes at the quarries and many and various were the tools of the quarrymen, some bearing interesting and attractive names. Slates had other uses such as the covering of walls and in the districts where slate was abundant it was used for window cills, steps, dry walling and in many other ways. Slabs of slate were used as bases for billiard tables and other boards related to games, for electrical switchboards, in vats, tanks and benches. Many generations of Welshmen used a writing slate framed in wood and a slate pencil before they graduated to notebooks, pens and ink.

The slate industry grew in importance during the second half of the nineteenth century, reaching its heyday just before 1900. In 1860 fifty-one slate quarries and mines were officially listed and sixty-five in 1938, sixteen of which were not working. The highest output of slate in Britain, 662,000 tons, was reached in 1898, North Wales providing about 70 per cent. By 1913 there was a significant fall and in 1938 it was only 284,000 tons, 77 per cent from Welsh sources.

The persistent decline continued after 1945 until between 1969 and 1971 three of the biggest quarries, the Dinorwig at Llanberis, the Oakeley at Blaenau Ffestiniog and the Dorothea at Tal-y-sarn were forced to close.

DIVERSIFICATION AND DEVELOPMENT

The degree of diversification reached by industry in Wales during the second half of the twentieth century is startling and the swiftness of this achievement equally so. Between 1930 and 1932 the staple industries, coal, iron and steel, had reached their nadir. It was the time of an appalling depression which can, however, now be looked upon as a watershed in the history of Welsh industry. It began the diversification and was also the reason for the beginning of improved techniques in the heavy industries.

Planning for new industries began in 1934 when the Treforest Trading Estate came into being on a site two miles south of Pontypridd and within easy reach of the stricken Rhondda and Taff valleys. In its early days people were employed in the manufacture of gloves, leather straps, textiles, toys, knitwear and chemicals. By 1943 it was geared to wartime manufacture and employed about 16,000. Other trading estates (now called industrial estates) followed, some on re-converted ordnance factory sites at Bridgend and Hirwaun, others as part of a pattern of industrial development, the Fforestfach estate near Swansea being one of these. Others have appeared at such places as Caerphilly and small groups of factories have been established on many sites throughout Wales where unemployment problems had to be met and in order to provide manufacturing facilities and labour for firms outside Wales which needed to expand. Within the coalfields and in quarrying districts new skills were perfected to meet the manufacture of intricate goods. The Welsh Industrial Estates Corporation now has 400 factories under its administrative control.

101

Oil refining, first planned at Llandarcy for strategic reasons in 1917, has developed swiftly in recent years. There are three refineries owned by international companies at Milford Haven, the building of a fourth started in 1971, where there is a natural harbour capable of handling crude oil tankers of over 200,000 tons. Oil is piped a distance of 60 miles from Milford Haven to Llandarcy. In Wales, as elsewhere, there is a growing dependence on oil as a source of energy; the traditional dependence upon coal is being eroded. There is an increased use of oil in Welsh industry. Oil used by the gas industry at the expense of coal has increased dramatically during the last decade, but it is expected that the availability of natural gas from the North Sea will now slow down this rate. In the field of personal consumption more use is being made of motor spirit, domestic heating oil, wax, plastics and detergents which derive in one way or another from the crude oil imported through Milford Haven. In 1969 the total amount of crude oil imported into this port amounted to 23 million tons, about 25 per cent of the whole amount imported into the United Kingdom.

The petrochemical industry, which is closely associated with oil refining, has already made its impact on the field of traditional materials through plastics and is now going through a phase of rapid expansion towards a long-term growth industry at Milford Haven, Baglan Bay and Barry.

Factories to produce man-made fibres have been built at Pontypool in Monmouthshire and at Greenfield in Flintshire. The manufacture of electronic components for radio, television and many other uses has been in progress at Abercynon and Dinas, Rhondda for a number of years. At these factories workers are assembling transistor circuits which are so minute that the work can only be done under magnification. The list of new industries is as long as it is diverse—it includes watchmaking in the Swansea Valley, glass engraving in mid-Wales, precision grinding controlled by closed circuit television at Europe's largest diamond stylus works in Denbighshire, motor-car axles at Swansea and Cardiff, washing machines at Merthyr Tydfil, excavating machines at Rhymney, motor-cars and money.

Modernisation and rationalisation have brought a new look to the original basic industries. In ironmaking the sizes of blast furnaces have increased and during the last twenty years there have been important developments in steelmaking; the Bessemer Converters were abandoned in favour of oxygen-blown converters and these were followed by L.D. converters and at Port Talbot within the last year the old open-hearth system of steelmaking has finally been abandoned for oxygen supply converters of 300 tons capacity. In the iron and steel industry technical improvement began in 1938 when the first hot strip mill was built at Ebbw Vale. In post-war years hot strip mills have been built at Shotton, Port Talbot and Llanwern. The art of cold reduction rolling of steel was mastered and at Ebbw Vale, Trostre and Velindre tinplate is made in strip form by the electrolytic process. The old-type hand mills of the tinplate trade survived until 1957. Most of the sheet steel and all the tinplate produced in Britain now comes from the computerised mills in Wales and a works near Swansea is producing the first wide colour-coated steel sheet to be made in Europe. Appreciable tonnages of stainless steel are produced at Griffithstown, near Pontypool and large steel re-rolling works have been developed at Cardiff for the production of rods, bars, sections, wire and nails, and steel tubes are made at Newport.

Since 1947 the coal industry has undergone re-organisation and development under the National Coal Board which included the sinking of new pits to meet the urgent demand for fuel during the after-war years. In 1950 there was only one power loader for cutting the seams and loading the coal into conveyors mechanically. By 1968 there were 196 mechanised faces producing three-quarters of the saleable output of the coalfield and new pits were sunk at Cynheidre and Abernant in Carmarthenshire. But the industry has been beset with difficulties, not always of its own making, and general re-organisation of its administration was also necessary.

Other industries which installed new and costly plant include the cement industry centred at Aberthaw, Rhoose and Mold, the aluminium industry at Rogerstone and Resolven, and the nickel industry outside Swansea. The service industries have developed on modern lines and have reached high points of efficiency. Electricity is generated at coal-fired and oil-fired power stations, at two nuclear reactors, and at Ffestiniog and Cwm Rheidol, in Cardiganshire there are hydro-electric schemes in operation. Electric power transmission has kept pace with the developments in generating. The gas industry now produces gas by modern methods at new works at Llandarcy and Wrexham, and 'it emerges triumphantly from the complex and enormous task of converting the entire Principality to North Sea natural gas'.

Two decades have seen a continuous transformation of the industry of Wales in new and sometimes unexpected directions. In looking at the diversification and development which have taken place it would be wrong to forget the workers at all levels, whose adaptive skills and abilities to absorb new ideas have made all this possible. It has been said that in the iron and steel industry 'men are the most important raw material of all—priceless assets that make great achievements possible'. This is equally true of other industries in Wales.

SELECT BIBLIOGRAPHY

William Rees, *Industry Before the Industrial Revolution* (Cardiff 1968).

H. Scrivenor, *A Comprehensive History of the Iron Trade* (London 1841).

John Lloyd, *The Early History of the Old South Wales Ironworks* (London 1906).

H. R. Schubert, *History of the British Iron and Steel Industry from 450 B.C. to A.D. 1775* (London 1957).

Arthur Raistrick, *Quakers in Science and Industry* (Newton Abbot 1968).

J. C. Carr and W. Taplin, *History of the British Steel Industry* (Oxford 1962).

T. S. Ashton, *Iron and Steel in the Industrial Revolution* (Manchester 1963).

W. E. Minchinton, *The British Tinplate Industry* (Oxford 1957).

F. J. North, *Coal and the Coalfield in Wales* (Cardiff 1931).

J. H. Morris and L. J. Williams, *The South Wales Coal Industry 1841-1875* (Cardiff 1958).

F. J. North, *Mining for Metals in Wales* (Cardiff 1962).

W. J. Lewis, *Lead Mining in Wales* (Cardiff 1967).

George Grant-Francis, *The Smelting of Copper in the Swansea District* (London 1881).

A. H. Dodd, *The Industrial Revolution in North Wales* (Cardiff 1951).

F. J. North, *The Slates of Wales* (Cardiff 1946).

D. S. Barrie, *The Taff Valley Railway* (Oakwood Press 1950).

Charles Hadfield, *The Canals of South Wales and the Border* (Cardiff 1960).

Margaret Davies, *Wales in Maps* (Cardiff 1958).

D. Morgan Rees, *Mines, Mills and Furnaces* (London 1969).

THE FIRE IN THE THATCH
RELIGION IN WALES

PENNAR DAVIES

VI

SPEAKING of an outburst of religious fervour that disturbed the sleepy tranquillity of an out-of-the-way border region of Wales, Walter Cradoc proclaimed to the House of Commons in 1646 that the Gospel had 'run over the mountains between Breconshire and Monmouthshire as the fire in the thatch'. The expression is as vivid as it is homely; and it may point to something not uncharacteristic of our Welsh condition, that something which has led to the adoption of the phrase 'Land of Revivals' as one of the descriptions of Wales passed around in some quarters until comparatively recent years. It does not tell us the whole truth about Welsh religious history; but it does link up with the undoubted fact that a people deprived of their own government, law, administration and indigenous leadership will frequently feed their fantasies with religion. I once suggested that Cradoc's 'fire' was the first of the Welsh nonconformist revivals. Perhaps it might be so described; but it was certainly not the first Welsh evangelical movement. The Welsh people (as distinct from the 'Roman' Britons of whom they are the most articulate descendants) were born to nationhood more than a millennium earlier, comrades of the Brythonic resistance who even as they sought to 'turn to flight the armies of the aliens' were being won to the new religious allegiance that was centred in the unique figure of the historical divine Son and saw their dearly bought land yielding the harvest of *llannau* which betokened the Galilean's conquest of Wales.

The 'christianisation' of the Cymry did not, of course, mean the total repudiation of their Brythonic heritage. It was a process of mutual assimilation —as had been the so-called 'expansion of Christianity' from Pentecost onwards. Brythonic habits of thought had already prepared them to accept a 'trinitarian' version of supernal reality with the conception of an enchanted otherworld and, in myths of Brân and others, the dependence of the people on the bounty of a suffering sacral king, a native mystery cult which I take to be the primal source of the Grail legend. But the Brythonic sense of the unity and fluidity of life prevented the Welsh from giving a welcome to the Augustinian emphasis on the moral helplessness of fallen humanity. The teaching of Pelagius probably reflected the moral zeal of his fellow-Christians in his native island and certainly found a welcome among them after it had been officially rejected at Rome. The later church traditions which picture the saints Garmon and Dewi as anti-Pelagian preachers are a gross libel on two strenuous political activists. In any case, Pelagius was very far from thinking that man could be good without God. What he resisted was not the doctrine of grace but the growing perversion and mechanization and stultification of it in the world-denying piety of a Jerome or an Augustine. Grace for him was not merely a remedial intervention necessitated by the Fall: it danced in the activity of creation itself. Its benefactions were sealed, but not conditioned, by the sacraments. Pelagius's stress on what might now be called the priority of the relationship between God and man has impelled some modern interpreters to hail him as a champion of justification by faith; and his emphasis is relevant here because it is an expression of an enduring reluctance within the Brythonic-Welsh Christian tradition to institutionalize the life of praise.

There was therefore a difference of theological outlook between the Christian life of Wales and the Rome-centred organization which confronted it in the person of Augustine of Canterbury at the beginning of the seventh century. Christianized Wales was a variant of the 'Celtic Christianity' which Toynbee has designated 'Far Western Christian Civilisation', one of his 'abortive' civilisations which were engulfed by others more powerful and aggressive. Our modern denominational divisions have ensured that the character of the 'Welsh Church' in the 'Age of the Saints' should be much disputed. Welsh Anglicanism has seen in it a primitively noble anticipation of the Church of England; Welsh Nonconformity has sometimes liked to think that it was a free evangelical movement with Dyfrig and Dewi and Beuno among its *hoelion wyth*; Welsh Roman Catholicism has sometimes argued that it was a docile and pious branch of the Catholic Church in the west and never broke away from the Roman obedience. It is no wonder that others have slyly suggested that its Christianity was the thinnest of thin veneers over an old pagan tribal culture and that the imprecations of its saints echoed the spells of the Druids. A considered and emancipated judgement would, I think, be that it was no more and no less pagan than other versions of Christianity in that age; that it felt itself to be a part of a world-wide Church at a time of accepted variations of the over-all pattern, a time when western Christendom was only beginning to emerge, when east and west were still unseparated and when the medieval Papacy (itself very different from the post-Tridentine phenomenon which is now changing into something else) was still only feebly kicking in Time's womb; that it differed completely from traditional episcopacy in that the episcopal and priestly functions were subordinated to the missionary and monastic activities of the 'saints' and that the pattern was not diocesan but connexional in the freest sense. And it could be added that the whole movement was politically aware and vigorous, that many of its leaders were of princely families, that it was constantly seeking to challenge and to direct the secular powers and that it had humanitarian concerns and contributed a freedom-loving idealism to the making of Welsh law and custom.

That the Brythonic-Welsh evangelism was the main fountain-head of 'Celtic' Christianity admits no doubt. The notion that it was isolationist springs from propaganda that sought to magnify the achievements of the Roman mission launched by Gregory through the timid company of monks headed by Augustine. There is evidence that Brythonic Christian witness was maintained even in the eastern parts of what is now England until the eve of Augustine's arrival in Kent and that Edwin of Northumbria was converted not by Augustine's assistant Paulinus but by the northern Cymro Rhun. There can be no manner of doubt that it was among the Irish that the Celtic Christian culture came to its finest flowering in such matters as missionary enterprise, stone monuments and manuscript illumination, but many of the roots were in Welsh soil; and when this phase of Christian history, with its strange libertarian asceticism and penitential mysticism, came to an end it was principally from Wales that much of its virtue was transmitted into the chivalric romance of the Middle Ages.

Of all the branches of the Celtic Church it was that in Wales that held out longest against the Roman method of calculating Easter. The ecumenist who gave the lead in at long last accepting it was Elbodugus of Gwynedd in the latter half of the eighth century. Other Celtic 'peculiarities' must have remained for centuries. The Normans, when they arrived, found a 'Church' so laicized as to be almost unrecognisable—'almost independent and autonomous', as the unsympathetic Gougaud admits, contrasting it with the Anglo-Saxon Church which was so wholly bound to Rome. Even after the loss of this independence by the passing of the sees of Llandaff, St. David's and Bangor under Norman control early in the twelfth century, the Welsh did not allow the authority of Rome and Canterbury to interfere unduly with their inherited ways. For a few generations there seemed to be strong hope that the yoke of Canterbury might be broken and that Welsh Christians might under the guidance of their own archbishop make their own *modus vivendi* with the Papacy. The first Norman bishop of St. David's, Bernard, though in some ways typically Norman in his restless ambition, had the uncommon imagination, sympathy and courage to declare for the Christian integrity of the Welsh people. He showed respect for Welsh life, claimed metropolitan authority for his see, got the Pope to canonize St. David and welcomed to Wales the Cistercians whose simplicity and fervour infused new life into the Welsh Christian tradition. He was much more of a statesman than Giraldus Cambrensis whose revival of the metropolitan claim about the turn of the century is so much better known. The hope returned once more under Glyndŵr and then faded for ever. It is sometimes oddly claimed that the disestablishment of the Church of England in Wales during our own century was the fulfilment of the hope. In the fragmented Christianity of Wales and the world in 1920 it was a grimly comic caricature of what might have been.

With the help of what is left to us of the rich Welsh literature of the period let us try to savour the quality of religious devotion in the age of Welsh kings and princes. The core of it was the worship of the *Gwledig*—the Sovereign Lord—of the creation, God. What has been called the earliest extant Welsh hymn, 'Gogonedawg Arglwydd, hanpych gwell', sees the marvels of earth and heaven, nature and history, art, learning and religion as uniting to bless the Lord of glory. He is King, Wizard, Pope, keeping his heavenly court, Rex

Regum. The Trinity is a cheerful mystery and not a quasi-philosophical doctrine. The emphasis is Sabellian: it is our Creator, says Cynddelw, who suffered on the cross, and so the poet gives Christ the divine titles, as another calls him 'Creator, Emperor, joyous Governor'. Into God's world the corruption of human sin has entered. Adam and Eve are ready to hand as symbols, but the stress is on the responsibility of the person and the need for moral endeavour. In a line of Meilyr, influenced perhaps by the Waste Land symbol in Celtic myth, we learn how human sins have laid waste the earth. It is God who delivers his children from plague and sorrow. Christ's wounds plead to us to follow him. It is for us to do good and to see in the poor 'the image of the Trinity'. For earthly loves, even the love taught by Ovid, says the poet-prince Hywel ab Owain, there is hope of mercy. For all sinners the Day of Judgement must come, and the climate of hell, varying from scorching heat to freezing cold, must at all costs be avoided. For Meilyr heaven is an island of rest for which Bardsey with its long-buried saints provides a potent symbol.

Since God is Chieftain, sin is treason—like the betrayal of Christ in a poem of Elidir Sais. In the Welsh Middle Ages heroic paganism, romantic chivalry, christian penitence and christian exultation are interwoven. While religious verse like the pieces I have mentioned was being produced the courts of princes were being roused by old-time eulogy of warriors and entertained by story-tellers with their tales of destiny and tragedy and romantic journeyings and magic metamorphoses, tales of slain god-kings and waste lands and cauldrons of re-birth and blissful otherworlds, tales which as they were re-told from court to court and from generation to generation tended to cluster more and more about the figure of Arthur, the *rex quondam rex futurus* with his knights and ladies and the quest for the Grail, originally the quest for the deliverance of the stricken land by the healing of the mortally wounded patron-monarch, but later—under Cistercian influence, Welsh and continental, I imagine—transmuted into a kind of parable of the quest of the soul and of chivalric Christendom for the ultimates of Christian devotion. The persistence of such a wealth of pagan lore influencing and influenced by a Christian system of belief has no strict parallel elsewhere in Europe. It is so spectacular that we may say of the Welsh Christianity of the ninth to the twelfth century what Toynbee implied of the Celtic Christian civilisation in the preceding centuries, namely that if it had been allowed to develop unhindered it would have been entirely different in character from the Rome-centred Church of western Europe. We can savour its idiosyncrasy in certain peculiarities of Welsh law like the privileges enjoyed by women and the startling provisions about divorce. And what is most extraordinary is that these strange liberalities are accompanied by an almost Hebraic urge to communal repentance and national messianism. Think of what the *Brut* tells us of the way the Welsh greeted an invasion by William Rufus—fasting, praying, charities, austerities, hoping not in themselves but entirely in God. Think of the hopes that gathered around

109

the names of Cadwaladr, Arthur, Owain. Think of the 'Deuteronomic' view of Britannic history reflected in 'Gildas' and reappearing from time to time in later historical interpreters. Think of the magnificent words of the Old Man of Pencader, affirming the national identity of the Welsh under a providence that sweeps all men and nations to judgement.

Although in the fourteenth and fifteenth centuries we see a quickening in the process of assimilating Welsh Christianity to that of western Europe, the process was still uncompleted when Wales suffered the simultaneous impact, under the second Tudor king of England, of full political and administrative incorporation in the English state and a politically engineered sub-Protestant Reformation. In the fourteenth century, the century of the joyous genius of Dafydd ap Gwilym, it is still possible to say that Welsh Christians thought their own thoughts in their own distinctive way. Some critics are at pains to insist that although he laughed at the life-denying admonitions of repressive monastic asceticism and took the woodland as his true cathedral Dafydd was in truth an obedient son of Mother Church; but they overlook the fact that the Mother Church of which they speak, presumably the august ecclesiastical organization headed by the Pope at Rome and under him in England by the Archbishop of Canterbury, was inevitably for the Welsh still something of a stepmother. This is the true difference between Dafydd and his contemporary Lorenzo Valla who of all the Italian humanists of his day had the most penetrating mind and who like Dafydd flung out a challenge to the traditional cult of virginity. Valla, though patronised by the first of the Renaissance popes, Nicholas V, was consciously undermining the structure of the medieval Church of the west; Dafydd was reasserting a Welsh-Christian delight in God's largesse against an alien ecclesiasticism which was still felt to be an intruder. Even in the fifteenth century it was possible for an inspired follower of Dafydd's to produce a superb poem in which he commends a course in Ovid to an over-zealous nun and draws a contrast between the *crefydd* of the monks of Rome and the more glorious *crefydd* of the woodland and the cuckoo. In Wales the absence of a hierarchical authoritarianism made the distinction between orthodoxy and heterodoxy so fluid as to be virtually non-existent. That is why the history books that speak of the blameless 'orthodoxy' of the Welsh 'Church' and give the impression that the only Welsh ecclesiastical aberration was the fondness of priests for their wives are so hopelessly wide of the mark: they bring to the study of Welsh history the presuppositions that are relevant only to a religious system that remained alien. The disciplining of Walter Brute, medieval radical, pacificist, leveller, and believer in the divine mission of the Brython to destroy the papal antichrist, serves only to show how alien the sytem was. The Welsh were remarkably immune from two endemic afflictions of the late medieval and early modern psyche: heretic-baiting and witch-hunting. This is not to deny the genuineness or the fervour of their devotion. The Dafydd ap Gwilym who could mischievously trace the descent of Hiraeth from Adam the son of Serch—Amor—could also

110

write with imaginative intensity of the agony—and the vomit—of Christ on the cross.

But although the Cymric Christianity was never entirely eradicated there can be no doubt that the last phase of the Middle Ages witnessed a well-planned operation, through the appointment of English churchmen to Welsh sees, to incorporate the church life of Wales into the system controlled by Canterbury and Rome. Between these men and the common people of Wales there yawned a great gulf. This alienation of the upper hierarchy was one of the factors that conditioned the Welsh to receive with comparative passivity the changes in religion under the Tudors. It also helped to bring about the theological degeneracy and feckless superstition that were to appal John Penry. At the same time Wales was more open than hitherto to outside influences. In a notable expression of mystical devotion, *Y Gysegrlan Fuchedd*, it is possible to trace the influences of Anselm, Bernard, Bonaventura and the *devotio moderna*; and in the aesthetic philosophizing of Einion Offeiriad we have a delectable attempt to interpret the old Welsh tradition of poetic praise according to the pattern of scholastic 'realism'. Likewise Wales could now yield scholars and thinkers to the universities of Europe, such as the John of Wales who sought to give moral inspiration to Christians by citing examples of pagan virtue and the Thomas Wallensis who suffered imprisonment for maintaining against the Pope that the pure in heart can see God without having to await the Last Judgement. It is arguable that John represents a reversion to Pelagius and that Thomas's view of the Beatific Vision has something in common with the royal hall of Gwales in *Branwen* and with the romantic cult of the Grail.

It is a far cry from these idealisms, classical and romantic, to the state-managed 'Reformation' that added to the bewilderment and dividedness of the Welsh in Tudor times—a 'Reformation' that must be distinguished in our histories from certain doctrinal and devotional movements which constitute the real Reformation in its varied forms, 'Catholic', 'Protestant', 'Humanist', 'Radical'. The disunity proclaimed in these epithets is the tragedy of modern 'Christendom' and was in a special sense the tragedy of Tudor and Stuart Wales. The evils consequent upon this disunity within Wales and without are not to be exorcised by ecclesiastical compromises and ambiguous formulae and organisational mergers; but a beginning may be made of abolishing them by a more generous and less sectarian understanding of the Welsh patriots and martyrs and visionaries of the age of religious conflict. Protestant humanists like William Salesbury, Richard Davies and William Morgan chose to do what they could within the Establishment and produced a rich and inestimably influential Welsh version of the Bible and the Protestant theory of a noble and ancient British Church free (in the early centuries) from Romish corruptions. One Roman Catholic, Gruffydd Robert, wrote the first grammatical description of the Welsh tongue; another, Rhosier Smyth, surprisingly advocated universal toleration in a free republic; others preached, administered, founded seminaries, suffered martyrdom. John Penry—who seems to have been a dandy, more colourfully and dashingly so than the Welsh-descended Puritan theologian John Owen, who also liked fine feathers—eagerly advocated the evangelization of Wales, became daringly involved in the activities of a hunted Puritan press, escaped to Scotland, rashly joined the London Separatists and was seized and hanged before he could return to his native land. I take the perhaps minority view that he was the satirist of genius who had the chief hand in the Marprelate lampoons. Welsh puritanism did not become a movement until later in the time of Cradoc, Erbery, Morgan Llwyd and Vavasor Powell, those libertarians of the spirit who in their different ways all exhibited the radical streak in Welsh religious leftism; and although one of the most promising products of Puritan exuberance, a venturesome Welsh Quakerism, was lost to Wales by emigration to America, the whole phenomenon—a leaping and exulting 'fire in the thatch'—was of great moment for the future of the Welsh.

Of course, Puritan radicalism is not the whole of 'Welsh Nonconformity', and Nonconformity is not by any means the whole truth about 'the Welsh way of life'—to use a painful phrase which has been no aid to clarity. In the eighteenth century the Evangelical Revival, in addition to giving us Methodists, Calvinistic and Wesleyan, fruitfully watered the dryness of much of the older Dissent, while the 'Rational' portion of Nonconformity passed into Arminianism, Arianism and eventually Unitarianism, producing in Iolo Morganwg the wayward genius who begat the bardic Gorsedd. It was Evangelical Nonconformity that expanded remarkably in the nineteenth century, helped by movements of population with which the Anglican parochial system could not cope swiftly enough and stimulated by waves of godly excitement of which the last (of significant dimensions) was the revival of 1904-5. The dominant Evangelicalism of the two centuries that have preceded our own century of growing Secularism can at many points be contrasted with the more varied and more adventurous phenomenon of the Puritanism of the mid-seventeenth. It is more pietistic and less political, directed rather to the salvation of the trembling soul than to the hastening of the coming of the New Jerusalem among men (although it is possible to cite exceptions and modifications on both sides of the contrast). From it have sprung movements of social welfare and education and mission and humanitarianism, but its energies have served amelioration rather than dynamic change. While the more radical wing of it in the last century sought to enfranchise the common people and to enlarge the liberties of mankind, the more conservative was preoccupied with saving souls for heaven. To say this is not to disparage the prodigious grace-gifts of the leaders of the Evangelical Revival. The more revelations we get of the tortuosities of the inner life of Howel Harris, the more vivid the relief into which his courage, vigour and magnanimity are thrown; and the more we learn of all aspects of the mind and work of Williams Pantycelyn, the more we feel compelled to marvel at the height and depth and breadth of his meditation.

112

It would be wrong to forget that these men and others who worked with them were Anglicans as well as Methodists. The part played by Welsh patriots within the Anglican tradition has been a potent factor in the making of the Wales we know—from the time of Richard Davies and Edmwnd Prys to the time of G. O. Williams and Euros Bowen. In truth, to the English trichotomy of High, Low and Broad Church Welsh Anglicanism has added a dichotomy of its own: its Church has been both the 'old Mother' and the Church of *Lloegr*. For centuries it enjoyed wealth, influence and prestige—in comparison with any of its rivals in Wales—and all this rested upon the victorious aggression of Norman and English kings and archbishops and upon English Acts of Uniformity. Even after Disestablishment—and the bitterness of the preceding controversy (although no bones were broken) reflects no credit on either side—there are some in the Church in Wales who still cling to the trappings—titles, precedence, rings and royal recognition—a foible which inevitably frustrates the good intentions of its most earnest ecumenists. Yet nothing is more unthinkable than to detach the work of the clerical and other Anglican lovers of Welsh learning and letters from the history of Wales since the Reformation. Ellis Wynne and Theophilus Evans and Goronwy Owen stand among our classics as securely as Morgan Llwyd and Charles Edwards— and so do the Silurist and the George Herbert who sang of the mild glories of the 'British Church'. I am prepared with Gwenallt to see a genuine social concern among the Welsh royalists in the Civil War (though he is less than just to the element of social radicalism in the Puritan movement) and I have wept with Henry Vaughan over the loss of the flower of young Welsh manhood at Naseby. I confess also to a warm liking for the distinctive quality of the work of such disciples of the Tractarians as Glasynys and Nicander; and I find Welsh High Churchmanship since their time much more hopeful than it had been before. I hope most Welsh 'churchmen' find Glyn Simon's contribution to a Welsh *aggiornamento* as encouraging as I do.

The 'Free' or 'Evangelical' denominations of Wales have like Welsh Anglicanism exhibited the symptoms of a split mind though in varying ways and degrees. They too have not been innocent of *Prydeindod*, and in some instances have resembled extensions into wild Wales of English denominations. Unlike some of their counterparts in England they have since the eighteenth century revival flourished among the working classes, rural and industrial, but at different periods they have been hindered by a too 'otherworldly' evangelical-ism or by a too facile theologically liberal optimism from rousing the people to capture the 'kingdom' that was the theme of the original *kerygma*. They have sometimes prided themselves, not without reason, on the 'democratic principle' embodied in various ways in their own polities and on their contribution to the growth of democracy in the state; but their failure to implement the principle with the delicate fervour necessary to transmute democracy into theocracy has unfitted them to cope with modern secularism and reduced their fellowships to spiritual clubs. Not once or twice have they

113

compromised with the abomination of desolation, beguiled by the vision of a Puritan state church or bribed by a *regium donum* to abandon or postpone their quest for liberty; or allowed the weighty things of their law to be shelved for the sake of some wretched particularism, making a fetish of a particular external observance or of a particular ethical scruple. Despite professions of a cordial catholicity of the Spirit they show all too often how 'denominationally minded' a Free Churchman can be. And yet when all this has been said it must be added that it was through their Bethels, plain and shy or vulgar and ostentatious or (here and there) dignified and tasteful, rather than through our cherished *llannau,* that an awakened *gwerin* became articulate and (whatever the limitations may be) creative. Gwilym Hiraethog, Islwyn, Michael D. Jones, Daniel Owen, Emrys ap Iwan are but five names to represent the expansive Nonconformity of the last century; and the stream of cultural vitality has by no means dried up.

Rome's opportunity to win the Welsh was lost in the days of the first Elizabeth. Our history might have been very different if Welsh Romanist exiles like Morys Clynnog had been able to convince the Curia and the Jesuits that Wales was to be considered apart from England. In our own time Roman Catholicism is becoming a naturalised Welsh phenomenon and is being accepted with surprising sweetness: its distinguished converts no longer worry anybody outside the Roman communion (except perhaps a Church in Wales bishop or two) and the fluent Welsh of an Irish-born, Spanish-trained priest no longer seems to be sinister. It is possible that within their communion one or two of the distinguished converts may not fully agree with those of their priests who rejoice in the new direction initiated by Pope John. We need, of course, no prophet to tell us that unchecked progress in that direction will lead Rome to the edge of a precipice from the bottom of which there will be no return. In the meantime, the presence in Wales of some admirable and lovable Romanists serves two useful purposes: it exposes the sinful folly of our acquiescence in the secularisation of education and gives us a picture of the only feasible alternative we have to Morgan Llwyd.

Much of the energy of the Welsh zealots of the Ecumenical Movement is misdirected towards amalgamating disparate ecclesiastical traditions on the basis of some temporary compromise located somewhere between those two alternatives. Fortunately, there is another side to ecumenism—fraternisation. When fraternisation blossoms into brotherly love we shall be as united as we are meant to be. That we shall need all the brotherly love that we can muster becomes disturbingly evident when we consider the theological cleavages which partly cut across the denominational divisions. We have, and must not forget that we have, a fine plethora of literalist, apocalyptist, revivalist and faddist sects (all save one imported, the indigenous specimen being in origin an offshoot of the Evan Roberts revival); but in addition we have an assortment of theologies and occasional skirmishes between conservative and liberal or humanist and neo-orthodox. The pendulum has been swinging very much as on the continent, though rather more timidly and with the clock lagging behind. Miall Edwards innocently provided us with a rounded statement of liberalism when it was already being demolished among the German theologians. Our neo-Calvinists have been either hesitant or naïve or inconsistent or too moderate to make a decisive impact; some have gone into a huddle with the literalists. Later influences were best mirrored in the brief but powerful utterances of J. R. Jones—the religionless Christianity of Bonhoeffer, the self-absenting God of Simone Weil, Tillich's Ground of Being. Only a few were even mildly influenced by the theologies of the 'Death of God' and these were content to use the phrase, as J. R. Jones did, to mean the discarding of an inadequate conception of God or some agonizing experience of estrangement or loss. The idea that the Church has to come to terms with secularism—'The world supplies the agenda'—has not swept the country: we are not sure whether it implies a take-over bid or a sell-out.

Contemplating the whole vista of Welsh history from our vantage-point we see that the Christianity that developed in Wales, a beam of light in the 'Dark Ages', combined a strenuous ideal of moral endeavour with certain social graces and liberties which gave it a different character from that of any other Christian *milieu*. We see too that through myth and romance which were the matrix of the Arthurian legend it contributed spiritual and moral ardours to the making of medieval chivalry; and we also see that despite many changes it retained its distinctive flavour so persistently that the more rigidly hierarchical Rome-centred 'Western Church' could not fully assimilate it or be fully assimilated by it. The completion of the process of annexation by which Wales was subjected to English government took place at the time when Europe was plunged into religious conflict, and the Welsh found themselves lost and benighted in their brave new world. Their subsequent history shows on the one hand that their religious life has reflected the doctrinal controversies of Europe and on the other hand that some strange fires have run over the thatch during the generations, fires akin to those that burned in the age of the 'Saints' and in national acts of penitence like that which greeted Rufus' invasion and in the welcome given to the Cistercians and, I make no doubt at all, in other ways and in other periods unrecorded in the extant documents of our pre-Reformation history. These visitations of the frolicsome numen—the Paul who spoke of 'the joy of the Holy Ghost' knew all about it—indicate contact with a source of power that is free of all our ecclesiologies.

It is not part of my purpose to disparage other ingredients in our heritage. In a *koinonia* both free and united—and I find it undeniable that the *ecclesia* of the apostles and even the *eglwys* (or *eglwysi*) of Dewi and Elfoddw and Sulien were nearer that unspotted and unwrinkled messianic community than any existing denomination—the walls of partition between catholic sacramentalism, humanist ethicism and evangelical solafideism melt away: I see no reason why the universal priesthood of believers should not delight in colour, sound and symbol, or should not see Christ in one of the least of his brethren in the

115

Third World. But to find the renewal without which all our synods and assemblies cannot save us we must meet the *Iesu* who claimed nothing and gave all and who eludes all our systems and even the marvellous and marvelling hints towards a theology strewn all over the New Testament itself. There is still none other name under heaven given among men.

SELECT BIBLIOGRAPHY

E. G. Bowen, *The Settlements of the Celtic Saints in Wales* (University of Wales Press, Cardiff 1954).

E. G. Bowen, *Saints, Seaways and Settlements* (University of Wales Press, Cardiff 1969).

Nora K. Chadwick (ed.), *Studies in Early British History* (Cambridge University Press, Cambridge 1943).

Nora K. Chadwick (ed.), *Studies in the Early British Church* (Cambridge University Press 1958).

Nora K. Chadwick, *The Age of the Saints in the Early Celtic Church* (Oxford University Press, London 1961).

Pennar Davies (ed.), *Rhyddid ac Undeb* (Gomer, Llandyssul 1963).

E. Lewis Evans, *Morgan Llwyd* (Brython, Liverpool 1931).

Louis Gougaud, *Christianity in Celtic Lands* (Sheed and Ward, London 1932).

J. W. James, *A Church History of Wales* (Arthur Stockwell, Ilfracombe 1945).

R. T. Jenkins, *Hanes Cymru yn y Ddeunawfed Ganrif* (University of Wales Press, Cardiff 1928).

R. T. Jenkins, *Hanes Cymru yn y Bedwaredd Ganrif ar Bymtheg* (University of Wales Press, Cardiff 1933).

D. Gwenallt Jones, *Y Ficer Prichard* (Church in Wales Press. Printed Caernarvon n.d. [1946]).

J. R. Jones, *Ac Onide* (Dryw, Llandybie 1970).

R. Tudur Jones, *Hanes Annibynwyr Cymru* (John Penry Press, Swansea 1966).

R. Tudur Jones, *Vavasor Powell* (John Penry Press, Swansea 1971).

Saunders Lewis, *Williams Pantycelyn* (Foyle, London 1927).

Saunders Lewis, *Braslun o Hanes Llenyddiaeth Gymraeg* (University of Wales Press, Cardiff 1932).

J. E. Lloyd, *A History of Wales* (Longmans, London 1912).

Prys Morgan, *Background to Wales* (Christopher Davies, Llandybie 1968).

Geoffrey F.Nuttall, *The Welsh Saints 1640-1660* (University of Wales Press, Cardiff 1957).

Geoffrey F. Nuttall, *Howel Harris* (University of Wales Press, Cardiff 1965).

R. Ifor Parry, *Ymneilltuaeth* (Gomer, Llandysul, 1962).

Gwynfryn Richards, *Ein Hymraniadau Annedwydd* (Church in Wales Press, Penarth 1962).

W. J. Rhys, *Penodau yn Hanes y Bedyddwyr* (Ilston, Swansea 1949).

Gomer M. Roberts, *Portread o Ddiwygiwr* (Darlith Davies, Caernarvon 1969).

David Williams, *History of Modern Wales* (Murray, London 1950).

Glanmor Williams, *The Welsh Church from Conquest to Reformation* (University of Wales Press, Cardiff 1962).

Hugh Williams, *Christianity in Early Britain* (Clarendon Press, Oxford 1912).

[Some of the views of the author of this essay are developed in his *Y Ddau Gleddyf* (Brython, Liverpool 1951), *John Penry* (Independent Press, London 1961) and *Rhwng Chwedl a Chredo* (University of Wales Press, Cardiff 1966)].

WELSH POLITICS
CYMRU FYDD TO CROWTHER

KENNETH O. MORGAN

VII

THE outstanding feature of Welsh politics in the past hundred years has been its continuity. No part of the British Isles has been more consistently a stronghold of the political Left, or more consistently a graveyard for the hopes of the Conservative Party. Since the first world war, the domination of the Liberal Party has given way to that of Labour; yet the pattern of Welsh politics remains basically much the same. In the 1970 general election, which saw the Heath government returned and a national swing to the Conservatives of roughly 4.8 per cent, the Conservatives' share of the Welsh vote was actually lower than that obtained in any election since 1950. They also lost no fewer than eight deposits in Wales. In 1970, as in 1890, the only areas of real Conservative strength in Wales were on the periphery—eastern Monmouthshire, the vale of Glamorgan, southern Pembrokeshire, coastal Denbighshire and Flintshire; the anglicized suburbs of Cardiff and Swansea in the south, the residential calm of Llandudno and Colwyn Bay in the north. For the rest, the heartland of Wales, in agricultural and industrial areas alike, remained apparently as firmly in the control of Labour in the early 1970s as in that of the Liberals of the 1890s. Tom Ellis and Lloyd George would have instantly recognised the face of Welsh politics as revealed at the polls in June 1970. Just as the party balance has remained remarkably constant, so too the substance of political debate has followed a well-worn path. For a hundred years, Welshmen have pondered and dissected the problem of sustaining a national community without a national state. Incidental achievements such as the passage of Welsh disestablishment in 1919 or the creation of a Secretaryship of State in 1964 have not eliminated the basic issue, though they have helped to re-define it. In the 1970s, as in the 1870s, Welsh politicians are (or, at least, ought to be) preoccupied with their countrymen's ambivalent relationship with their English neighbour. While remaining a source of jobs and of investment, England continually threatens to engulf what remains of the native culture of Wales, as it has long since undermined its social structure. The very achievement of Welsh politicians, Liberal and Labour, in winning recognition and equality for themselves and their nation in the wider political unit of which Wales forms a part has simply made the issue more acute. Only on very few occasions have Welsh politics moved in an overtly nationalist direction: the *Cymru Fydd* movement in 1894-6, the resurgence of Plaid Cymru in 1966-8, stand out by their rarity. But the essential difficulty of defining the Welsh political presence, of ensuring that Wales is recognised as a distinct unit, more than a mere region, yet less than a sovereign state, still remains undiminished. The problem of our 'special relationship' with England is still

118

with us, as it was with our great-grandparents. In 1972, with the report of the Crowther commission on constitutional arrangements in Wales and the English regions eagerly awaited, Welsh politics retain all their complexity and charm, appropriate for a nation most dedicated to radical change yet most hidebound by immemorial tradition.

I

Modern Welsh politics fall conveniently into three clear chronological periods —the Liberal ascendancy from the mid-1860s down to the first world war; the Labour ascendancy from the end of that war down to the mid-1960s; and the nationalist upsurge of the years since 1966. The first of these periods, the years of almost unchallenged Liberal hegemony heralded by the 1867 Reform Act and the 'great election' of 1868 is in many ways the most significant of all. Certainly, it is a period which has most obviously left its mark on the political pattern and institutions of Wales today. It followed a revolution in the location of political power. The Reform Bills of 1867 and 1884, the Redistribution Bill of 1885, the Local Government Act of 1888, gave political power to the majority of the people. Within two decades, the entire face of authority in Wales was transformed. The old Anglican squire-archy, Tory and Whig, which had governed the land nationally and locally during what Henry Richard termed the years of 'feudalism' down to the mid-1860s, was rudely displaced by a new élite, a new nonconformist middle-class with massive working-class backing. In every general election from 1868 to 1918 Liberals captured the overwhelming majority of seats in Wales, rural and industrial. They were as impregnable in the industrial metropolis of Merthyr Tydfil as in the pastoral uplands of Merioneth. In that year of radical jubilation, 1906, the Conservatives failed to win a single seat in the principality. Even more important in some ways in its implications for Welsh society, was the 1888 Local Government Act. As a result of its passage, popularly-elected county councils totally supplanted the gentry who had ruled, perhaps terrorized, the countryside for centuries at the Quarter Sessions, as justices of the peace. No longer was the nonconformist Welsh-speaking majority in any sense a second-class citizenry. It was the heir to a political revolution which it had itself largely created.

Further, the political leaders of this revolution were not merely orthodox Liberals but assertive radicals distinctly on the left of their party, a thorn in the aged Anglican flesh of Gladstone himself. By the mid-1880s, the generation of Whiggish Liberals of twenty years earlier—cosmopolitan, elderly spokesmen like Henry Richard, George Osborne Morgan, Hussey Vivian and Lewis Llewelyn Dillwyn—were giving way to a new kind of Liberal—younger, assertively Welsh, much more outspokenly radical. Tom Ellis, the son of a Merioneth tenant farmer, combined ardent Welsh patriotism with a Fabian

119

urge for social reconstruction. Llewelyn Williams, another farmer's son and also an Oxford graduate like Ellis, sought to revive the national tradition of sixteenth-century recusant Catholicism. By contrast, D. A. Thomas, the industrial tycoon who owned the Cambrian collieries, demonstrated that the mercantile bourgeoisie of the coalfield could respond to the same ardent national consciousness that fired a tenant farmer's son in the rural hinterland. There were other remarkable radicals also emerging—Sam Evans, the hammer of the Anglican Church and the searching critic of the Jameson Raid; Ellis Griffith, a brilliant, wayward man whose career turned out to be an immense disappointment; William Jones, whose 'silvery tones' captured the imagination of *Punch*. Above all, there was David Lloyd George, elected for Caernarvon Boroughs in 1890. Lloyd George's career in Welsh, as in British, politics was in many ways an ambivalent one. In Wales, too, he was something of an outsider, out of sympathy with the joyless puritanism of the chapels and the bitter sectarianism which they generated. Yet, until he entered the Cabinet in 1905, Lloyd George's political reputation was almost entirely based upon his record as a vehement crusader for Wales: he viewed the world at Westminster as a foreigner. Lloyd George's rise to executive power is testimony to the vitality and passion of Welsh political life during these years. It shows also how Welsh radicalism was able to provide new life and inspiration for the British Liberal Party with which it was so intimately associated.

By the mid-1880s, Welsh politics was polarized by a clearly-defined radical programme—disestablishment of the Church, popular education, land reform, temperance reform, perhaps a modified form of local devolution. These were the supreme objectives of Welsh Liberals in rural and urban areas alike, and of the overwhelming majority of the political nation. Left in desperate resistance to change were the beleaguered gentry who sustained the tattered flag of Welsh Toryism throughout countless electoral reverses—with the assistance of the Unionist party in England. The Welsh radical programme made somewhat uneven progress in the decades down to 1914. There were separate laws for Wales—the 1881 Sunday Closing Act and the 1889 Welsh Intermediate Act. There was some departmental autonomy, as with the Welsh Department at the Board of Education in 1907 and the separate Welsh National Insurance Commission (of which Thomas Jones was the secretary) in 1912. Welsh disestablishment made steady progress also, despite the apathy of most English Liberals and a perceptible decline in enthusiasm among younger nonconformists in Wales itself. Against the odds, disestablishment was placed second on the Liberals' Newcastle Programme in 1891, despite Gladstone's Anglican hesitations; Welsh disestablishment bills were introduced in the Commons in 1894, 1895, 1909 and 1912-14. On the eve of war in August 1914, disestablishment and disendowment of 'the alien Church', for decades the obstacle to what Welsh nonconformists revered as 'religious equality', was on the verge of fulfilment. By contrast, other radical demands made little permanent headway. A Welsh Land Bill failed to be passed in the 1890s, and after the turn of the century the land question somewhat lost its priority for Welsh radicals as agricultural prices improved. The 'Welsh revolt' against the 1902 Education Act, which 'put Rome on the rates', also petered out. Yet it is in education that can be found perhaps the most glorious legacy of the years of Liberal hegemony down to 1914. In the creation of the new 'county schools' after 1889, in the formation of the university colleges at Aberystwyth, Bangor and Cardiff, and in the national, federal University of Wales of 1893, the Welsh Liberals (for it was largely their work) created the finest of monuments to nineteenth-century radicalism. It revolutionised social opportunity and social mobility for Welsh boys and girls: it set the seal on the new élite that the Welsh Liberals wished to create and perpetuate. Nothing in Welsh life today more clearly evokes the optimism, pride and dignity of those golden years at the turn of the century. The official historians of the university of Wales, two nonconformist Liberals, writing in 1905, were justified in writing that 'the history of learning in Wales is the history of the nation itself'.

The years of Liberal ascendancy were marked by an intense pride in nationhood. Welsh periodicals in the years up to 1914 extolled thirty years of national achievement, symbolized by the rise to supreme authority of Lloyd George. National institutions like the *Eisteddfod* were never more flourishing. Welsh literature was never more vigorously creative, with Owen M. Edwards and John Morris-Jones to supply it with a 'soul' and a 'body', with creative inspiration and a technical discipline, in the view of W. J. Gruffydd, one of their younger disciples writing in 1911. Welsh industry and commerce had never been more thriving; even in the previously impoverished countryside of north and mid-Wales the new prosperity was having its effect, with the growth of railways and new credit institutions. On all sides, it seemed, Liberal Wales brought a time of unparalleled national progress, one that unified the land from Barry to Braich-y-pwll. Pride in nationhood was as equally marked in remote rural communities which had collected their pence to further the new college at Aberystwyth, as in the growing city of Cardiff which expressed its civic pride and its Welshness in the neo-baroque structures now surrounding Cathays Park. Nationality was everywhere proclaimed, not least in the world of sport. After the triumphant victories of Wales over the 'all black' New Zealand rugby team in December 1905 and in 'triple crown' successes in subsequent years, local journalists dilated on the precise aspects of the Celtic genius displayed by Dickie Owen or Gwyn Nicholls, often with the Darwinian emphasis fashionable at the time.

Yet the high noon of Liberal Wales was not an era of nationalism. Despite the national emphasis prevalent in Welsh politics at the period, despite the patriotic currents suffusing Welsh literature, Welsh Liberals basically did not seek self-government. Unlike the Irish, they sought equality within the United Kingdom, not severance from it. Only for one brief interlude, did

121

Welsh Liberalism show a tendency to turn in a nationalist direction. This was the *Cymru Fydd* (Young Wales) movement of the 1894-6 period, a disastrous episode which has poisoned movements for national devolution ever since. Originally a body started by emigré Welshmen in London and Liverpool, the *Cymru Fydd* League in 1895 was taken over by David Lloyd George. Disillusioned at the failure to get disestablishment and other Welsh issues taken seriously by the Rosebery government at Westminster, Lloyd George attempted to fuse *Cymru Fydd* with the Liberal Federations of North and South Wales. But at a tumultuous meeting at Newport in January 1896 Lloyd George was howled down by the Liberals of the South Wales Federation, headed by D. A. Thomas, previously a partisan of *Cymru Fydd* himself. The delegates cheered a Cardiff Englishman who declaimed that the cosmopolitan population of Cardiff, Barry, Newport and Swansea would never submit to Welsh domination. *Cymru Fydd* promptly collapsed and nothing like it has ever re-emerged. Lloyd George himself attempted for a time to float the idea of 'home rule all round', in the hope of winning the support of English radicals, but this came to nothing. The failure of *Cymru Fydd* has often been misunderstood. Frequently presented as a simple division between north and south Wales, it was rather a schism between the Welsh hinterland, rural and industrial, and the coastal ports on the southern fringe. But the collapse of *Cymru Fydd* was more than this. It was basically undermined by divisions within every Liberal Association in Wales, divisions which Lloyd George's short-term euphoric triumphs tended to conceal. After two decades of achievement within the orbit of the British Liberal Party, after centuries of isolation and neglect, why should Welshmen now opt for the impotence of separatism? The years 1900-14 showed that home rule had little appeal in Wales, and the Liberal government after 1906 did nothing to further it. Lloyd George's eyes were now fixed on far wider and more attractive objectives. When an earnest Middlesborough ironmaster, E. T. John, tried to revive the Welsh home rule movement in 1910-1914 and introduced a bill in the House of Commons, he attracted little attention. The attachment of Welshmen to established Liberalism still stood secure.

The only real challenge to the ascendancy of the Liberals in the period between 1867 and 1914 did not arise from internecine turmoil over self-government. Nor, of course, did it come from the somnolent ranks of Welsh Conservatives in their rural fastnesses. Rather did it come from the upsurge of Labour. Wales had been largely insulated from the socialist and trade union movement in Britain generally down to the late 1890s. But a new phase was heralded by the mighty six-months coal stoppage in South Wales in 1898 that threw 100,000 men out of work and left a legacy of growing class bitterness. In 1900, in two remarkable elections, Keir Hardie was returned for Merthyr Tydfil, while John Hodge almost defeated a local Liberal employer in the intensely Welsh constituency of Gower. Henceforth, the ILP made steady progress in South Wales, spurred on by the stubborn resistance of

Liberal Associations to working men as candidates. When the Miners' Federation affiliated to the Labour Party in 1909, it meant that Wales now had five Labour members; even William Abraham, 'Mabon', the apostle of industrial peace and of the old nonconformist values, sat on the Labour benches, under protest. By 1914, there were prospects of direct conflict between Liberal and Labour candidates in most South Wales constituencies. Even more significant was the growing militancy in industrial relations. By 1912, 'Mabonism', the creed of conciliation and class harmony, was out-of-date: it had perished at Taff Vale and Tonypandy. The Cambrian coal stoppage of 1910-11 brought a new generation of miners' leaders to the fore, young Marxists like Noah Ablett. The *Miners' Next Step*, published by the Miners' Unofficial Reform Committee at Tonypandy in 1912, foreshadowed overt class conflict and the use of 'direct action' or syndicalist methods to overturn the structure of capitalist private ownership. Further, the major targets of the miners' rank-and-file movements were frequently Liberals. Judge Bryn Roberts, for twenty years Liberal M.P. for Eifion, symbolized judicial hostility to the miners' demands. 'Mabon', the very epitome of 'Lib-Labism', was being urged by belligerent younger men like Charles Stanton to 'move on or move out'. Above all, D. A. Thomas, the Liberal apostle of *Cymru Fydd* in 1894, for over twenty years a radical member of parliament, was now reviled as the 'czar of the coalfield', the hated coalowner of the collieries of Tonypandy. The bitter assaults on D. A. Thomas's reputation by the miners—and his own intemperate response to them—seemed to foreshadow an era of class warfare which would sweep the old Liberal ascendancy away.

Yet the challenge of Labour did not basically undermine the Liberals' position prior to 1914. In North Wales, even in the impoverished slate-quarrying areas of Gwynedd, the Labour Party made little headway. In the mining valleys, the Labour members seemed almost more obviously victims of the new industrial militancy than were the Liberals themselves. In any event, the 'direct action' doctrines of the Plebs League and of the Central Labour College were limited in their appeal. Outside the Rhondda and Aberdare valleys, the 'Lib-Labs.' were still firmly in control of the South Wales Miners' Federation. Even in its areas of strength, industrial militancy was distinctly on the wane in 1913-14: by the outbreak of war, the Unofficial Reform Committee had virtually dissolved, and moderate men like William Brace were again being returned to the South Wales Miners' Federation executive. It could even be argued that the industrial militancy of the years before 1914 was as much a tribute to the old Liberalism as a reaction against it: the classes of the Central Labour College were obviously modelled on the traditional Welsh Sunday School, while young militants like Ablett, Frank Hodges, Arthur Horner and A. J. Cook were deeply influenced by the mystique of the chapel and by the religious revival of 1904-5. Labour, then, had not fundamentally displaced the older Liberal élite by 1914. If Keir

123

Hardie's *Merthyr Pioneer* could ridicule 'the little Bethel stage of Wales for the Welsh', an attitude which stressed Welsh radical values rather than the international creed of working-class solidarity, most Welshmen were still devoted members of that little Bethel and the triumphs that it enshrined from the years since 1867.

II

The first world war brought about a transformation in the character of Welsh politics. It inaugurated a period of Labour ascendancy which remained without serious challenge from 1918 until after the general election of 1966. In some ways, this was the product of the collapse of the Liberals. The Liberal Party was a supreme casualty of total war, symbolized by the bitter division between supporters of Lloyd George and Asquith after December 1916. The 1918 general election offered deceptive evidence that the Liberals still retained their former primacy despite the vast expansion of the franchise. Liberals won twenty-one seats out of thirty-six in Wales, while Lloyd George himself received intense national adulation as 'the man who won the war'. One embittered critic saw the 'coupon' election as a 'national ceremony of congratulation' for Lloyd George in the aftermath of victory. Equally, when Lloyd George's political position began to be undermined in the period 1920-22, the Liberal Party collapsed with him. It was notable that the Liberal Party organisation in Wales, by contrast with the rest of Britain, was overwhelmingly Lloyd Georgian after 1918, while Lord St. David's kept the Welsh National Council loyal to the Coalition. Accordingly, when Lloyd George fell from power in October 1922, the consequences for Welsh Liberalism were wholly disastrous. Eight seats were lost to Labour in the 1922 election, and a steady erosion continued throughout the twenties and thirties. Welsh Liberalism seemed increasingly conservative and stagnant: even the inspiration of Lloyd George's new radical policies of the later 1920s to deal with unemployment and industrial recession failed to promote any revival. Lloyd George was discredited and defeated, and so was the party with which he was identified.

The decline of Welsh Liberalism, however, was rooted in causes far more profound than the personal standing of Lloyd George. Basically, Welsh Liberalism declined because the society which gave it birth was passing away. Welsh society was no longer dominated by the parson and the squire: the radicals of pre-1914 had done their work too well. Welsh disestablishment was achieved in 1920 amidst monumental indifference, while the Welsh gentry rapidly sold up the bulk of their estates to their tenants. Liberalism no longer had the same objectives for which to strive. Nor perhaps did it have the same inspiration and morale. The first world war was an intense crisis of conscience for nonconformist Liberals all over Wales. The obscene tragedy of 1914-18 seemed to mock at every value for which Liberalism traditionally contended. There were a few overt and courageous pacifists—men like Principal Thomas Rees of Bala-Bangor and Dr. J. Puleston Jones, who wrote in journals like *Y Wawr* and *Y Deyrnas* and who were persecuted in consequence. Other Liberal intellectuals went through a more private torture—writers like T. Gwynn Jones and W. J. Gruffydd, for instance. Others joined the Union of Democratic Control, or found a new outlet for their energies and beliefs in the League of Nations Union after 1920. Many went out of politics entirely— like D. R. Daniel, an old friend of Lloyd George back in the 1880s, but now appalled by the Welsh Premier's strident bellicosity and intolerance of dissent. And many Liberals went over to the Labour Party. When George Maitland Lloyd Davies was returned as Christian Pacifist and Socialist member for the University of Wales in the 1923 general election, it seemed to symbolize the disillusion with the Liberal tradition among the Welsh intelligentsia. The Liberal ethic and the Liberal Party had parted company, some time between the Tonypandy riots and the atrocities of the Black and Tans.

In rural Wales, the Liberals retained their foothold until after the second world war. Lloyd George sat in the House as member for Caernarvon Boroughs until 1 January 1945. He led a family group of four in rural Welsh constituencies in the thirties. Even in 1945 the Liberals still retained eight seats in Wales. But after the second world war, more than ever they seemed the party of the past, a glorious past perhaps, but one with little direct relevance to the postwar world of the welfare state and a dissolving empire. After 1945 the few remaining Liberal bastions gradually submitted to Labour. Anglesey and Merioneth were lost in 1951; Carmarthen also fell in a famous by-election in February 1957 just after the Suez invasion, with Lady Megan Lloyd George as the Labour candidate. The Liberal revival of the late 1950s and early 1960s made little impact in Wales: there were no Torringtons or Orpingtons there, while Welsh Liberals now tended to appear well to the right of the new radical programmes proclaimed successively by Jo Grimond and Jeremy Thorpe. In 1966, Cardiganshire, one of the two seats still in Liberal hands, was also lost to Labour. It was a remarkable result that may have owed something to the former Liberal member's pact with the Conservatives throughout the fifties, as well as to the charismatic appeal of the Labour candidate, Elystan Morgan (until 1964 a vice-president of Plaid Cymru). This result meant now that only one constituency in Wales remained in Liberal hands, Montgomeryshire, the seat of Emlyn Hooson. It was a tragic comment on a once-great tradition. In Arthur Schlesinger's words, the Welsh Liberals had become a party of memory, not a party of hope.

The obverse of the relentless decline of the Liberals in Wales was the new dominance of the Labour Party. As has been seen, Labour was already mounting a formidable challenge to the Liberals prior to 1914. Many local authorities had a strong Labour representation: Enoch Morrell had been a Labour mayor of Merthyr as early as 1905. But the first world war transformed the Labour

Party in Wales as elsewhere. It was then that took place the 'strange death' of Liberal Wales and of Liberal England, so misleadingly ante-dated by an older generation of historians. During the first world war, Labour became a national party, with a new organizational structure at constituency level. The expansion of the trade unions during the war years gave it a new mass following, while the strains in the economy during wartime made the conflict between capital and organized labour the outstanding feature of social life. The old battles between church and chapel became absurdly out-of-date. Further, Labour in Wales was advancing rapidly to the far left. The success of the Bolshevik revolution in Russia deeply influenced the mining valleys: the red flag flew at miners' lodges in Maerdy and elsewhere. A new generation of Marxist miners' agents—Ablett and Cook, Arthur Horner and S. O. Davies—showed that 'Mabonism' was dead and almost forgotten. As the immediate post-war boom led by 1921 to widespread unemployment and the grim legacy of industrial stagnation throughout the coalfield, the Labour Party was the inevitable beneficiary. Eight seats were won from the Liberals at the 1922 election. In the 1923 election, Labour claimed 21 seats in Wales; by 1929 this had risen to 25. Even in the débâcle of 1931 (which aroused particular stress in South Wales since Ramsay MacDonald had until recently been member for Aberavon) most of the Welsh mining seats, like those in Durham, held firm to Labour. Throughout the grim days of the thirties, Labour's position in South Wales was consolidated, reinforced by the years of unemployment and misery, by the emigration of over 400,000 Welshmen to England in search of work, and by the class polarisation that marked the later years of the National government in the 1930s. Every major development in the coalfield in the inter-war years—the crisis of 'Black Friday' in 1921; the agony of the general strike; the 'stay-down stoppages' in protest against company unionism; the emotional appeal of the Republicans in the Spanish Civil War—all served to unify and consolidate the Labour movement in Wales. It drew its political and industrial wings ever closer together.

The only real challenge to Labour in South Wales, indeed, came from its leftward flank, from the Communist Party. The Communists made much headway in South Wales (and Scotland also) in the twenties, especially through the Minority Movement which claimed to be the heir of the old Unofficial Reform Committee. In the thirties, the Popular Front movement after 1935, and especially the cause of Spain and of the International Brigade there, reinforced the appeal of Communism, apparently the most unequivocal opponent of the government and of the capitalist system that had been crucifying South Wales for fifteen years past. A decisive trial of strength between Labour and the Communists came in Rhondda East, perhaps the most radical constituency in the British Isles. In a by-election in 1933 and again in the 1935 general election, W. H. Mainwaring, the Labour candidate and once a joint-author of the *Miners' Next Step*, narrowly beat off the challenge first of Arthur Horner and then of Harry Pollitt. But the victory was decisive.

126

The Welsh Labour movement chose to stay within the mainstream of national party politics, as the Welsh Liberals had done in 1896. Although Pollitt cut down Mainwaring's majority in Rhondda East to a mere 972 in 1945, it no longer carried significance. The permanence of Labour rule was long since assured.

With South Wales so overwhelmingly secure a Labour stronghold, Welsh Labour leaders began to play an increasingly major role in the party nationally. The Central Labour College after 1919 generated a new stream of talented young miners who were to play decisive roles in the history of Labour in the inter-war period and subsequently; Ness Edwards, James Griffiths, Morgan Phillips, and, above all, Aneurin Bevan, were prominent among them. They represented a new generation of leadership just as surely as did Tom Ellis and his compatriots in the Wales of the 1880s. When Aneurin Bevan entered parliament in 1929 and launched his career there with a scathing attack on Lloyd George, the old radical hero of South Wales, it seemed to symbolize the birth of a new political era. The élite of the small towns, the chapel and the Sunday School were being displaced by the products of the industrial slums, the WEA and the miners' lodge. Welshmen stamped their personality firmly on the Labour Party as it emerged to full authority in the later thirties and during the second world war. Aneurin Bevan's vehement onslaughts on Churchill's war leadership after 1940 did not perturb the native populace who still recalled the brutalities of Tonypandy (for which Churchill was somewhat unfairly given the responsibility). Welshmen inevitably figured prominently in the Attlee government after 1945, with two great ministers, James Griffiths at the Ministry of National Insurance and Aneurin Bevan at the Ministry of Health, superbly renewing a Welsh connection with social welfare, first forged by Lloyd George before 1914. In Transport House, another Welshman, Morgan Phillips, was the supreme *apparatchik*. And at wider, more sub-terranean levels, Welshmen poured into the English Labour movement in the thirties and forties, rhetorically swaying many a local constituency Labour Party into a new radical direction. It is not too fanciful, perhaps, to compare the role of the Welsh in English Labour politics in the thirties to that of the Irish in Liberal politics a generation and a half earlier. In each case, an outside ethnic minority permeated the British political structure, rejecting many of its values and challenging the comfortable conventions of Anglo-Saxon parliamentarianism. In Slough, in Oxford, in many London and Birmingham constituencies, after the coming of the Welsh, constituency politics were never to be the same again.

Until the 1945 general election, Labour's strength had lain, however, essentially in the mining valleys. In the rural fastnesses, Lloyd George's writ, not Aneurin Bevan's still ran. But in the post-war period, despite the vicissitudes that the Labour Party underwent nationally, Labour's strength in Wales became a nation-wide one. Until 1945, Labour had little durable strength in the north: a brief triumph in Caernarvonshire in 1922 and the

127

occasional success in Wrexham were temporary phenomena. But after 1945, Labour rapidly assumed the mantle of the older radicalism. Caernarvon was decisively won by Goronwy Roberts in 1945; in 1951, Anglesey was won by Cledwyn Hughes, and Merioneth by T. W. Jones: in each case, a Welsh-speaking nonconformist Labour candidate was able to outbid the Liberal in his own territory. The climax of Labour's progress came with the general election of 1966, when thirty-two seats out of thirty-six were won. Four seats were captured in Wales—Monmouth and Cardiff North in south Wales, Cardiganshire and Conway in the rural areas. Significantly, all four victorious Labour candidates were young professional men, three of them lecturers, the fourth a solicitor, very much the kind of candidate who would have been a Liberal, two generations earlier. Labour, it seemed, had not only retained its hard-core working-class vote in the mining areas; it was now expanding its appeal across the whole spectrum of society. In 1966 the Labour Party looked more like the national party of Wales than at any other time in its history. Its complete supersession of the older Liberalism, and the absorption of its radical traditions, seemed finally confirmed.

During much of this period of Labour dominance, Welsh politics had apparently little that was nationally distinctive. The Labour Party emphasized the ties that unified the working-class and socialist movement throughout the British Isles. Still dominated by the centralist ethos of the Webb tradition, it looked with suspicion on anything at all redolent of Welsh separatism. Certainly, the Labour Party before 1914 had been sympathetic to local home rule: Keir Hardie had included Welsh home rule on his programme at Merthyr Tydfil. In 1918 Ramsay MacDonald, George Lansbury and other national Labour leaders proclaimed their sympathy with federalism and local self-determination, so recently upheld in President Wilson's Fourteen Points. But, with the cohesive effects of the depression in the inter-war period, Labour soon lost interest in Welsh home rule. Aneurin Bevan in particular regarded the social and economic issues of the socialist movement as ones that transcended national boundaries. He used the first 'Welsh day' debate in the Commons in 1944 as the occasion for a fierce tirade of ridicule directed against utopian dreams of self-government.

Nor did the other political parties offer much for Welsh devolutionists in this period. Lloyd George's administration after 1918, headed as it was by the apostle of *Cymru Fydd* of twenty years earlier, provided nothing for Welsh separatist feeling. The Speakers' Conference in 1919-20 proposed rival schemes of regional parliaments and of grand councils, neither of which excited much concern. Otherwise, Lloyd George took no apparent interest in Welsh self-government: after all, Ireland was already trouble enough. He did hint to the Welsh Liberal members that they might press for a Welsh Secretaryship of State, but this seems to have been merely a mischievous distraction. For the rest, moves for local devolution achieved little between 1918 and 1945. There was some administrative reform. The Welsh Board of

Health was created in 1919, a unique devolution of authority by a government department at that period. There was further decentralization during the second world war, with regional commissioners being set up, and functions being devolved to Welsh permanent officials in Cardiff by the Board of Trade, the Ministry of Labour and other departments. But none of this entailed any transfer of *power* from Westminster to Wales. Nor is there much evidence to suggest that Welsh opinion wanted such a change to occur.

Nevertheless, there was a series of extended devolutionary moves after 1945. In 1948 the Labour government set up a twenty-seven man Council for Wales and Monmouthshire, a well-intentioned body whose eighteen years were marked by a growing frustration at the failure of successive administrations to pay heed to its varied proposals. In 1951, when the Conservatives returned to power, Churchill unexpectedly went further, and set up a Ministry for Welsh Affairs. It was invariably merged with another government department, until 1957 with the Home Office. A Minister of State was appointed to assist the Welsh Minister in 1957; unfortunately, he was attacked as an obscure peer. But none of this made much impact on Welsh opinion, and the results of successive general elections between 1951 and 1964 confirmed that the suspicion of Toryism in Wales was too deep-rooted to be so easily overcome. Symbolically, Huw T. Edwards, chairman of the Council for Wales, resigned in 1958. In any event, the Ministry for Welsh Affairs soon became the scapegoat for some unpopular government decisions. In particular, the plans to drown the valley of Tryweryn in Merioneth and allow the Liverpool corporation to sell its water at great profit brought intense odium on the Welsh department, and particularly on Henry Brooke, its maladroit temporary occupant.

In fact, the 1950s did see some indications that, after decades of quiescence, Welsh politics were again resuming a national aspect. In 1950, a new Parliament for Wales campaign was inaugurated. It had inter-party support on a wide scale. Lady Megan Lloyd George (still a Liberal) was its chairman, and Elwyn Roberts (later general secretary of Plaid Cymru) its organizer. Five Labour M.P.s also supported the campaign—Goronwy Roberts, Cledwyn Hughes and T. W. Jones in north Wales, Tudor Watkins and S. O. Davies in the south. S. O. Davies introduced a bill in March 1955 which proposed to create a Welsh parliament: 250,000 signatures were presented in support. But the measure got nowhere. The Conservatives were as uncompromisingly unionist as ever, while the five Labour rebels were publicly rebuked by their party's national executive. By 1957 the campaign was dead: in any case, issues such as Suez, Hungary and the Rent Act were absorbing popular attention. However, the Parliament for Wales campaign left some important legacies. It led to a Grand Committee being set up in 1960, including all thirty-six Welsh M.P.s, with the theoretical power to interrogate ministers on their Welsh policies. More important, the Labour Party quite unexpectedly placed the creation of a Secretaryship of State for Wales on its election

129

programme. The reasons for this shift are obscure, but they probably owed much to James Griffiths's new role as deputy leader of the Labour Party and chairman of its Home Affairs Committee. When Labour was returned in 1964, a Secretaryship of State was duly set up. The veteran, James Griffiths became the first occupant of the post and inaugurated some searching inquiries into the machinery of government in Wales. In 1966 he was succeeded by a much younger man of proven ability, Cledwyn Hughes. Labour in 1964 had on paper an undeniably attractive programme. In addition to the new Welsh Office, it proposed a more active regional policy for industry, a Welsh Water Board and local government reorganisation. In addition, the plan for leasehold enfranchisement, long championed by George Thomas and other South Wales members, was massively popular in Cardiff, Swansea and other towns. Leasehold was believed to have helped throw votes in Llandudno behind the Labour candidate for the Conway division in 1966. The first Wilson administration of 1964-66, therefore, seemed a climax of nearly half a century of Labour ascendancy. It remained to be seen, however, whether the Secretaryship of State really heralded a new phase of Labour sympathy with rising national sentiment in Wales, or whether it would merely arouse expectations that could not possibly be fulfilled.

III

The pattern of Welsh politics unexpectedly entered a third and totally different phase on 14 July 1966. On that day, in a by-election in Carmarthen brought about by the death of Lady Megan Lloyd George, Gwynfor Evans, president of Plaid Cymru, captured the seat from Labour with a 2,431 majority and a swing of 17 per cent. It was a major sensation. Nothing in Plaid Cymru's forty-year history had suggested so dramatic a triumph. The party had been formed in 1925 at the Pwllheli national eisteddfod by the merger of two smaller groups of intellectuals headed by the poet Saunders Lewis. Their main objective was to ward off the new threats to the Welsh language and culture looming up in the post-war world: almost incidentally, they came also to advocate self-government for Wales, and their programme included a demand for dominion status within the British Commonwealth. The party was rich in intellectual and cultural talent, but meagre in numbers and political expertise. It attracted distinguished figures like the novelist Kate Roberts, the scholar G. J. Williams, and the administrator Ben Bowen Thomas, all of them anxious at the way in which the native culture was being eroded. But the party found very little mass support outside limited circles of writers and university teachers. It first began to contest parliamentary seats in 1929 when the Rev. Lewis Valentine fought Caernarvonshire, but its performance here and elsewhere was feeble. Valentine polled only 1·6 per cent of the vote in 1929. The Blaid achieved more general prominence in 1936 when Saunders

Lewis, Valentine and D. J. Williams were imprisoned after deliberately setting fire to an R.A.F. bombing school in Penrhos, Caernarvonshire. The decision to transfer the case from a local court to the Old Bailey infuriated Lloyd George and many others not normally sympathetic to the Blaid. But in general Plaid Cymru was a small and struggling body in the first twenty years of its existence, an enthusiastic pressure-group of amateurs rather than an organised party. The angular and uncompromising personality of its first president, Saunders Lewis, also added to the party's problems. Lewis's vehement Catholicism (the mainspring of his nationalist faith) antagonised many nonconformist sympathizers. Indeed, with Professor J. E. Daniel (the party's second president, 1939-43) and Ambrose Bebb also prominent in the Blaid, its Roman Catholic element was unusually influential. In addition, Saunders Lewis's alleged enthusiasm for Italian totalitarianism, for Mussolini's corporate state and for the 'distributist' economics of Fascism also alienated other possible supporters (for instance, the writer W. J. Gruffydd and the members of the quasi-socialist 'Gwerin' movement). During the second world war, Lewis was freely accused of Fascist sympathies; very unfairly, the Blaid was tarred with the same brush. In addition, the war added new difficulties. The party, inheriting as it did the pacifist tradition of Victorian radicalism, advocated non-involvement; several of its leading members were conscientious objectors. Saunders Lewis himself left political life in disgust in 1943 after a fiercely-fought by-election in the University of Wales, in which he was defeated by his former supporter, W. J. Gruffydd, running as a Liberal. The personal bitterness unleashed by this by-election, in the journal *Y Llenor* and elsewhere, continued to distract the meagre band of Plaid followers for many years to come.

The first fleeting signs that Plaid Cymru might be winning more widespread support among working-class electors came in two by-elections at Ogmore and Aberdare in 1946, when the party won 30 per cent and 20 per cent of the poll in these respective contests. But this was illusory: the polls were probably a protest against local post-war unemployment. Presided over now by Gwynfor Evans, a Welsh-speaking nonconformist in the traditional radical mould (who had succeeded Abi Williams as president in 1945), the Blaid struggled to make much impression on the political scene in the twenty years that followed. The performance of its candidates in the general elections of 1950, 1951, and 1955 was consistently disappointing; nor did the party gain much strength from its involvement in the 'parliament for Wales' campaign or the protests against the drowning of Tryweryn valley. In 1959 it fought Welsh constituencies on a broad basis for the first time, when twenty candidates were put up, but the total of 77,571 votes was a meagre reward. The Blaid was still very far from winning a single parliamentary seat. In the 1964 election, its performance was even worse: twenty-three candidates were put up, obtaining only 69,507 votes. Only two of them (one being Gwynfor Evans in Carmarthen) saved their deposits. In these depressing circumstances, the Blaid did well to hold on to its share of the vote in the March 1966 general election, a mere eighteen months after a contest which had severely strained the party's finances. At this election in 1966, the twenty Blaid candidates polled 61,000 votes, and Gwynfor Evans himself notably improved his position in Carmarthen. But it was still a poor return for forty years of political agitation. In March 1966, Plaid Cymru was still very far from being a credible challenge for political power. To the leaders of the major parties, it had nuisance value but posed no real threat.

The by-election at Carmarthen in July 1966, then, brought about a complete transformation. Exactly how and why Gwynfor Evans captured the seat from Labour is still open to debate, although enthusiasm for Welsh home rule seems to have played very little part. Undoubtedly the contest took place in uniquely favourable circumstances for the Blaid. Labour had recently been returned by a very large majority; in no sense was the standing of the Wilson ministry on risk. A protest could safely be lodged at the current economic measures of the government; 'blown off course' by a run on the pound according to its leader, the government shortly introduced the draconian 'July measures' that could only further depress the Welsh economy. In addition, there was widespread local criticism that Labour had not selected a new candidate at the general election four months earlier. Lady Megan Lloyd George, the former Labour member, was known to be a dying woman then, and the unfortunate Labour candidate in July, Gwilym Prys Davies, himself a most able and idealistic man, was the inevitable scapegoat for the inadequacies of his constituency party. And, of course, Gwynfor Evans himself, intelligent, dignified, courteous, charismatic, a member of the Carmarthenshire county council for many years past and resident at Llangadog, was in all respects the best candidate that the Blaid could possibly bring forward. As a result of these and other factors, the landslide vote in favour of the Blaid at Carmarthen revolutionized the whole pattern of Welsh politics.

For the next three years the aftermath of the Carmarthen triumph was traumatic. For the first time, Plaid Cymru emerged as a real threat to the Labour Party, able to attract a wide range of votes that the Conservatives or the Liberals could never command. Two more sensational by-elections followed, significantly enough both of them in solid industrial constituencies, the hard core of Labour strength for over forty years. In Rhondda West in March 1967, there was an immense swing of 27·1 per cent to the Blaid. In a constituency where their candidate, the trade Unionist Vic Davies, had lost his deposit in March 1966, the Blaid polled now 39·9 per cent of the vote, and cut the Labour majority to a mere 2,306. In Caerphilly in July 1968, the Blaid did even better. The swing to it soared to 28·1 per cent, and the Labour majority collapsed dramatically from over 21,000 to only 1,874. The Plaid candidate in this last contest, Phil Williams a young university teacher, won high praise for the intelligence and force with which he expounded his party's economic and fiscal programmes. In the aftermath, Plaid Cymru seemed a party transformed. Its membership reached new heights, climbing to over 40,000. The party made particular inroads amongst students and other younger voters, posing a contrast with an apparently ageing and inert Labour Party. The whole Nationalist party seemed to be going through an upheaval at this period. Instead of being a small, amateurish pressure-group, largely confined to Welsh-speaking rural areas, the balance of strength in the party was swinging to industrialized, anglicized south-east Wales, symbolized by Phil Williams's remarkable performance at Caerphilly. Meanwhile in west Wales the veteran James Griffiths was persuaded to stay on at Llanelli, to forestall another possible by-election disaster at the hands of Plaid Cymru's prospective candidate, the rugby star, Carwyn James. The Blaid's economic policies were being overhauled, too. Instead of clinging to a traditional regard for small, decentralized co-operative units and for economic isolationism, the party's Research Group, headed by Phil Williams and Dafydd Wigley, now elaborated a sophisticated programme which emphasized planning, *dirigisme* and the economic ties which bound Wales to England. At a period of deflation and depression, and the running down of the staple coal industry in the valleys, these schemes had an obvious appeal. On a far wider basis, a new mood of nationalism, political and cultural, seemed to be sweeping the land as it had not done since the 1890s. The victory of the Scottish Nationalist, Mrs. Winifred Ewing, at a by-election in Hamilton in 1967 lent new heart to nationalist sympathizers in Wales. In 1967 and 1968 there seemed few obstacles to the new nationalist tide. The Independents and other religious bodies lent it open support. Non-political movements like the all-Welsh schools campaign and the league of youth, *Urdd Gobaith Cymru*, were now suffused with nationalism. Welsh pop culture found a folk-hero in the nationalist singer, Dafydd Iwan. Not even a series of alarming bomb explosions in government offices in Cardiff and elsewhere (apparently the handiwork of the 'Free Wales Army', an extremist group) failed to halt the Blaid's progress in all these fields. For the Blaid seemed all too obviously moderate, constitutional and responsible— without having lost its crusading appeal or its radical mystique. The effective performances of Gwynfor Evans in parliament lent it further momentum.

In the face of these strange developments, the response of the Wilson government was strangely inert. Its economic policies seemed hardly calculated to revive its strength in the valleys. The stringent deflationary 'squeeze' imposed by James Callaghan and then Roy Jenkins at the Exchequer (the former a Welsh M.P., the latter a native of Abersychan) had a grave effect on the prospects of industrial growth in Wales. In some mining areas (notably in parts of the Caerphilly constituency) unemployment soared to over ten per cent, while the subsidiary industries that the valleys tended to attract were the first to be cut back in the aftermath of the squeeze. The more specifically Welsh policies of the Labour government aroused scant enthusiasm either. Admittedly, the passage of leasehold reform was widely welcomed in south Wales towns, while the new redundancy payments eased the growing

133

burden of unemployment in mining and other areas. For the rest, there was little enough to report. The Welsh 'Economic Plan' of 1967, the last of the regional plans to appear, was an inadequate document; its facile over-optimism about employment prospects in Wales (in a decade when the Welsh male labour force fell by over 64,000) was widely criticised. The local government reorganization proposed by Cledwyn Hughes in 1967 also failed to meet with much approval, not only amongst local authorities (always notoriously suspicious of reform) but also amongst specialists in local government. For the massive industrialized counties of Glamorgan and Monmouth were left largely undisturbed, while immense boundary changes were to be imposed on the sparsely-populated rural counties of north and mid-Wales. Nor was it clear how these plans would fit in with the Maud proposals for England. Above all, the joint council proposed would be merely a nominated body. It was widely believed that Cledwyn Hughes, backed up by Richard Crossman, had fought hard for an elective council in the Cabinet, but that his colleagues, led by James Callaghan, voted him down. It was a decision that cost the Labour Party in Wales dear, faced as it was with a rising nationalist challenge.

Above all, in the period of Labour government up to 1970, the performance of the new Secretaryship of State failed to arouse much enthusiasm: perhaps too much had been claimed for it by its advocates in 1964. Its initial powers were varied—housing and local government, roads and aspects of economic planning; agriculture and health were added in 1969. But the Welsh Office was slow to evolve new or independent functions, inevitably perhaps since government in Wales and in England had been so intermeshed. Even so, the gap between the scope allowed the Scottish Office in Edinburgh and the modest activities of the Welsh Office was notable: it made the latter resemble not much more than a somewhat high-powered rural district council. Certainly, the Welsh Office had very little power: it was a co-ordinating department, carrying out in a Welsh context policies made elsewhere. It had little executive authority, while the new Economic Council which took over from the old Council for Wales in 1966 was again, inevitably perhaps, an advisory body whose recommendations might or might not be given attention. In short, the Secretaryship of State for Wales aroused much disappointment, and indirectly fanned the flames of nationalist protest. Its limitations were clear enough. While it could supervise the detailed application of government policies in Wales along a wide area, it could seldom inititate. Its budget was dictated by Whitehall and hedged about by treasury control. The Welsh Office could not receive a global sum annually to be expended as it wished on a variety of purposes in Wales. Its status was in this sense colonial. Somehow the inadequacies of the Labour administration seemed to be symbolized in the amiable figure of George Thomas, Secretary of State since April 1968. Thomas had been an effective and highly popular constituency member: he had made the leasehold issue his own. But at the Welsh Office he seemed somewhat miscast, as well as unexpectedly thin-skinned. His fierce suspicions of the nationalist movement (perhaps reinforced by his own inability to speak much Welsh) made the gap between the Labour Party and the new nationalist mood in Wales somewhat wider.

The difficulties confronting the Labour Party were reinforced by the appointment of the Crowther Commission to inquire into the British constitution—a direct result of the Nationalist polls at Hamilton and Caerphilly. When the Crowther Commission visited Wales in January 1970, the Liberals and Plaid Cymru made known their familiar proposals for a Welsh parliament. The Conservatives, for some curious reason, offered no evidence at all. The Labour Party, however, attracted most attention for the disarray into which it lurched. There were disagreements amongst the Welsh members of parliament and on the Regional Council of Labour, while Transport House also intervened lest the Welsh proposals lean too far in a nationalist direction. In the event, however, the Labour Party did formally propose a two-tier scheme, crowned by an elected Council for Wales, with some executive as well as advisory powers. Although far from being a legislature, this was a notable advance in Labour's ideas. It was as if Keir Hardie had come again. At the cost of much internal turmoil and agonised debate, the Labour Party had at last begun to break free from the shackles of Sidney and Beatrice Webb and to acknowledge the value of decentralized power being accorded to small local communities. An elected council for Wales figured, somewhat inconspicuously, on Labour's election programme in 1970.

In reality, the Crowther Commission coincided with a period when the nationalist resurgence in Wales seemed to have passed its peak. As the Labour Party gradually climbed upwards in the opinion polls and recovered from the nadir of Dudley, Meriden and Caerphilly, Plaid Cymru was falling on somewhat harder times. Since there were no further by-elections, it was hard to sustain the euphoria of Carmarthen, Rhondda West and Caerphilly. The party had in any case been much embarrassed by the investiture of Charles as Prince of Wales at Caernarvon in July 1969. This meaningless pageant obviously put the nationalists at an emotional disadvantage, and the party cut a somewhat embarrassed figure throughout. More important, the Blaid was now being gravely embarrassed by the Welsh Language Society, *Cymdeithas yr Iaith Gymraeg*. This body had been formed in 1962 after the famous B.B.C. lecture by Saunders Lewis, 'Tynged yr Iaith' (The Fate of the Language) in which the speaker advocated direct action and civil disobedience, and urged that all political action be subordinated to the campaign to save the language. At first, the young student members of the Society (for it was very much a movement of the youthful, educated middle class) lent immense support to Plaid Cymru, as canvassers and local activists. But by 1969 its increasingly militant methods were difficult to reconcile with Plaid Cymru's role as a constitutional and responsible body. In the latter months of 1969 the Society's tactics became increasingly daring in their attacks on road signs and other visible symbols of English predominance. There was widespread

135

resentment expressed in the Welsh press in January 1970 when a group of young members of the Blaid, among them Gwynfor Evans's own daughter, interrupted a High Court case in London, and were briefly imprisoned. This kind of action, unrelated to any obvious practical objective, was counter-productive and merely alienated potential voting support.

Another indication of weakness in the Blaid was its failure to make headway in local government. It put up its most significant effort so far in the county council elections in April 1970, when 56 officially-endorsed candidates were put up, eighteen of them in Glamorgan. Labour was challenged on a broad front for the first time. But in fact in the whole of Wales only seven official Plaid candidates were returned (although, of course, many more got in as Independents in the rural areas). The Blaid lost one of its two seats on the Glamorgan County Council and one of its three seats in Carmarthenshire. The Blaid polled well only in a few scattered areas where its local organisation was strong—in Treorchy in the Rhondda West constituency; in Llanfabon (in Caerphilly division); and in the Gadlys ward of Aberdare. In general, South Wales's traditional loyalty to the Labour Party was confirmed. The local elections were another blow to the Blaid and a renewed encouragement to Labour.

In the light of the tumultuous changes in Welsh politics since July 1966, the June 1970 general election aroused much expectancy in Wales. For the first time, the Blaid's resurgence would be put to an adequate test, and the party put up candidates in all thirty-six seats in Wales. Labour had several marginal seats to defend—Cardiff North, Conway, Cardiganshire and Monmouth. In addition there was local conflict in two other constituencies. In Pembroke-shire, Desmond Donnelly's defection to found a right-wing 'New Democratic Party' had split the local constituency party to its foundations, and his official Labour opponent faced a difficult task. Again, in Merthyr Tydfil, the 83-year-old S. O. Davies, a veteran of the Unofficial Reform Committee during the first world war, had been turned down by the constituency party and was to be opposed by Tal Lloyd of the AEU, the official candidate who was selected only three weeks before polling day. These developments suggested that there might be some Conservative gains in Wales this time. Nevertheless, it was the conflict between Labour and Plaid Cymru that attracted most speculation in June 1970 as the election campaign dragged on its slow and inexpressibly dreary course.

The election results in the event were tantalising, leaving all parties somewhat dissatisfied. For the Liberals, who put up nineteen candidates, the evidence of decline continued. Emlyn Hooson held on to Montgomeryshire, and there was a good Liberal poll in Cardiganshire, but the general results were depressing. Nor could the Conservatives derive more than a limited satisfaction from the returns. True, they did gain four seats in Wales, Cardiff North, Monmouth, Conway, and Pembrokeshire (the last by courtesy of Desmond Donnelly who split the Labour vote). On the other hand, they polled badly elsewhere in Wales, lost eight deposits and failed to remove their stigma of being an English (and, indeed, Anglican) party in Wales. Labour yielded ground compared with 1966, but their marginal seats were lost by only the narrowest of majorities, while Elystan Morgan held on to Cardiganshire with an increased majority. To counter the defeat of the official Labour candidate at Merthyr who was routed by the aged S. O. Davies by over 7,000 votes, there was the victory of Gwynoro Jones (Labour) over Gwynfor Evans in Carmarthen by a majority of nearly 4,000. Despite losing the election, Labour had retained twenty-seven seats out of thirty-six in Wales, and its ascendancy there had been emphatically confirmed. For Plaid Cymru the results were most tantalising of all. Its 36 candidates polled the creditable total of 175,016 votes, 11·5 per cent of the Welsh total. In three constituencies, Caernarvon, Aberdare and Carmarthen, it gained over 30 per cent of the vote; in four others, over 20 per cent. Yet the party finished up with no seats, twenty-five lost deposits and the shattering loss of Gwynfor Evans at Carmarthen. It had in many ways been a sad election for the Blaid—its veteran secretary J. E. Jones dying after a heart attack during the election campaign, Gwynfor Evans himself much weakened after a severe operation. The saddest feature of all for the Blaid was the confirmation that, in spite of the brave revival of 1966-68, it was still a small fringe party, at a fundamental disadvantage when it came to competing at general elections when the rise and fall of governments were at stake. Perhaps, after all, the massive Plaid polls in 1966-68 really reflected a protest by disillusioned Labour voters, voting (or voting with their feet) against their own party when it was in office? Perhaps, with the Conservatives again in government, Labour would resume its natural role again as the party of protest? No-one could tell at this stage. All that was clear was that the events of June 1970 suggested that the nationalist resurgence had so far been transient and limited in its impact. The 1970 general election was a turning-point at which Welsh politics obstinately refused to turn.

IV

In the eighteen months following the election, the fundamental trends in Welsh politics were hard to discern. The new Secretary of State, Peter Thomas, who sat for Hendon South, had a difficult passage from the outset. Although he was given wider powers by the Heath government, with education now added to his concerns, it was a most unhappy augury that Thomas was expected to combine his office with the chairmanship of the Conservative Party. Inevitably, he became a scapegoat in both capacities, particularly in Wales where unemployment mounted alarmingly throughout 1971, to levels unknown in peacetime since before 1939. Again, the powerlessness of the Welsh Office significantly to influence decision-making and economic planning was underlined, while Peter Thomas's own performance as a minister was criticised as severely as was that of his Labour predecessor. It was a matter of surprise when in December 1971 it was announced that the government had agreed to a Welsh Water Board being set up (including the Wye valley in its ambit though not the Severn). This at least was one notable triumph for Peter Thomas, making good a curious omission by the previous Labour administration. For the rest, 1971 was a dismal year for the fortunes of the Conservative Party in Wales: in the borough elections in May there were massive losses even in such unlikely areas as the affluent Cardiff suburb of Whitchurch (which Labour was to win again in the May 1972 elections).

At the same time, Plaid Cymru was curiously inactive in the eighteen months after the 1970 general election. As in the past, it made no impression in the 1971 borough elections, and only an unexpected county council by-election victory at Aberdare later in the year brought the party much encouragement. The party seemed somewhat in suspense between an older generation of leaders in the mould of Gwynfor Evans, mainly Welsh-speaking and from rural areas, and the new anglicized technocrats in the south-east and the Cardiff suburbs. More important, the initiative was being stolen largely by the Welsh Language Society, whose methods became increasingly daring (fanned in some cases, perhaps, by fleeting sympathy with the activities of the IRA in Northern Ireland). By the end of 1971, the Welsh Language Society seemed to be passing beyond immediate practical targets such as road signs, birth certificates or road fund licences (where several victories had already been won over bureaucratic inertia) towards more ambitious and perhaps unrealisable objectives such as an all-Welsh channel on the B.B.C. or an all-Welsh college at Aberystwyth. This kind of campaign was not calculated to widen the appeal of Plaid Cymru amongst the eighty per cent of the population who were monoglot English. As the young supporters of the Welsh Language Society sat in university libraries or climbed up radio transmission masts, noisily proclaiming their zeal for martyrdom, it boded ill for the future political prospects of Plaid Cymru. 'Expressive politics', devoted to personal liberation and self-emancipation rather than to realising specific short-term objectives, could turn into the politics of despair. The pattern of Welsh politics in the period up to the next general election would rest in part on whether the responsible leaders of the Blaid could restrain this mood, without alienating the idealism of their younger supporters.

Superficially, it was the Labour Party which could look forward to the immediate future with most optimism at the beginning of 1972. As has been seen, Labour had immense success in the May 1971 borough elections: eleven seats were gained in Cardiff, nine in Newport, three in as unlikely a town as Aberystwyth. With unemployment rising and industry stagnating, Labour could again seize the moral initiative. Again, when Mrs. Thatcher terminated the free distribution of milk to children at primary schools, it was the Labour mayor and councillors of Merthyr Tydfil who were in the van of resistance.

Labour also was ideally equipped to voice widespread Welsh apprehensions about the entry of Britain into the Common Market, scheduled for January 1973. Like the Welsh Liberals and Plaid Cymru, the Welsh Council of Labour fiercely attacked the implications of the Common Market for regional economic policies. Those four Welsh Labour M.P.'s who voted for the Common Market in October 1971 were severely censured by their constituency parties. Labour, it seemed, could face the future months or years of the Heath government with every confidence, in its traditional Welsh strongholds. Even so, there were several indications that the Labour Party had areas of frailty, evidenced in constituencies such as Aberdare where Plaid still launched such a vigorous challenge, or in Merthyr where S. O. Davies had easily (and ominously) overcome the official machine. Labour in Wales in early 1972 was something of a contracting and certainly an ageing party. Party membership had fallen well away from a peak of 44,000 in 1950; while young socialist branches were in distinct decline as young Welsh men and women turned to more direct forms of communal involvement, or simply lost interest in politics altogether. This suggested that perhaps the hazards faced by the Labour Party in 1966-68 might not have evaporated completely by the next general election, as the Merthyr by-election in 1972 confirmed.

One new factor that would undoubtedly operate then would be the redistribution of seats. This could mean the Conservatives improving their position at last. They could perhaps, share two of the four new seats in Cardiff; hold on to Monmouth (where the Bettws housing estate was being transferred to swell the Labour majority in Newport); and make headway in Swansea West) with the addition of tiny fragments of the Gower to the constituency). Labour had already lost one of its two seats in the Rhondda as a result of redistribution; this was another blow to the waning political power of the Welsh miners, which was likely to wane still further as a result of the national miners' strike which began on 10 January 1972. In addition, the Blaid would surely remain a threat in constituencies such as Caernarvon and Merioneth in the north, and Aberdare in the south: Labour's decision to nominate a West-country trade unionist in the last-named constituency was almost incredible in the light of the nationalist challenge. Again, the re-drawing of local government boundaries, as foreshadowed by Peter Walker's new measure in 1971, could lead to a further redistribution of parliamentary constituencies in the late seventies, again perhaps to Labour's disadvantage. All this, however, still lay in the realm of speculation in early 1972. On the other hand, there was still vitality and vigour in the Welsh Labour Party, symbolized by younger professional men like Elystan Morgan(Cardiganshire), John Morris (Aberavon), Alan Williams (Swansea West) and Ted Rowlands (nominated as prospective candidate for Merthyr in late 1971). If one of these could be appointed shadow spokesman on Welsh affairs, and George Thomas transferred to a more congenial niche (for example housing, or alternatively Home Office affairs with which he had already been fruitfully associated in 1964-6), it could

139

herald a more lively and creative phase for a party for which historic milestones tended to become millstones. If such a change did not occur, then the speculation by the present writer in June 1967 that the Labour Party in Wales might go the same path of ossification and decay as the Liberals in the past could yet be fulfilled.

The outstanding prospect in the immediate future in 1972 was the coming report of the Crowther Commission. Obviously, it can only be guessed what that body might propose for Wales. But it was striking that virtually all the evidence presented to Crowther urged an extension of devolution and popular participation. Sir Goronwy Daniel, then permanent secretary at the Welsh Office, explained how the functions of the Office could easily be extended into the social, medical and educational fields, in line with its Scottish counterpart. All the major parties save the Conservatives advocated some kind of representative assembly on an all-Wales basis, with appropriate remodelling of the structure of local government beneath it. Meanwhile every indicator of public opinion in Wales suggested a considerable demand for a greater range of decision-making to be located in the principality. Since administrative devolution alone would not meet this demand, it followed that some kind of modified legislature or at least elective council should be created, perhaps with the Secretaryship of State lapsing. It would cause much disappointment amongst most sections of opinion if Crowther did not propose a new leap forward towards Welsh self-government. Undoubtedly a proposal of this kind would generate much dispute in Wales, notably within the Labour Party. But it would surely be an indication of the strength and representative character of the Labour Party in Wales that it should conduct an open dialogue along these lines. Certainly, as Welsh politics are constituted at present, there is no other institution which can debate the issue so fruitfully.

The main justification of some kind of representative assembly being installed in Wales is that there are specific issues here upon which the Welsh alone can ultimately deliberate and decide. The existence of a Welsh political and cultural presence has long been established; indeed it is a glorious legacy of the Liberal ascendancy before 1914. No longer can English politicians or periodicals mindlessly reiterate that 'there is no such place as Wales'. Some of these facets of Welsh distinctiveness can be resolved harmlessly enough. One example is the Welsh Sunday Closing issue which was partially defused by local referenda in 1961 and 1968, and which has lost its capacity to frighten or enrage large sections of the community. But far more dangerous and divisive is the language question. The limited and confused nature of student 'protest' on behalf of the language should not conceal its potentially damaging implications. It would be absurd to imply that Wales might be a prey to the violent communal upheavals of Belfast or Bangla Desh: fortunately, it has little in common with those unhappy, divided societies. Nevertheless, the twentieth century is littered with examples of how local frictions can escalate and disrupt social harmony; we may not yet have seen the more disturbing results of

140

internal conflict between Welsh- and English-speaking Welshmen. All the political parties, including the Blaid, could be its victims. What is transparently clear is that the machinery of government—that is, English government— has failed adequately to respond to Welsh pleas for greater status and protection for the native language, in the 1960s as in the 1860s. The most modest of appeals for recognition—a road fund licence or a street sign—have for years foundered in the face of insensitive hostility from Whitehall officialdom. Not until the report of the Hughes-Parry committee in 1966 was the Welsh language even accorded 'equal validity' in the courts. Even now this is very far from being satisfactorily implemented. The conflict that the partisans of the Welsh Language Society have unleashed is a symptom, not a cause of the inadequacies of the governmental response. What is surely required here is a new set of institutions located in Wales itself where the Welsh themselves can deliberate on the language issue and where conflict can, if possible, be reconciled. Welshmen will be very far from unanimous in their conclusions; but they will be capable of a sensitivity and an understanding denied to all but the most patient of outsiders. It may be hoped that some institutional means of lessening tension on the language issue (which still obsesses many Welshmen almost to the exclusion of other priorities) may be a by-product of Crowther. Otherwise, Wales may yet be a prey to a species of nationalism that may rent the nation asunder as surely as the nationalism of the Liberal years before 1914 unified it.

The alternative, of course, is that nothing whatever will result from the Crowther report. It may well be totally shelved by the Heath government, as an embarrassing legacy from days of nationalist by-election successes long since over. The next general election may turn entirely on issues such as the Common Market, national economic policies and the cost of living. Any form of Welsh home rule may be set aside or forgotten as surely as it was in 1896, 1920 or 1955. The record of the movements pressing for greater self-government is one of constant non-fulfilment. Perhaps Crowther will be yet another milestone in this saga of disappointment. Perhaps the Welsh have really little interest in the issue anyhow, and schemes for local participation in government are the pet preserve of remote, ineffectual dons in their ivory or cupro-nickel towers. Perhaps there are no Welsh politics any more. Perhaps they perished with the dreams of the Welsh Liberals in August 1914 or with Lloyd George in his traumatic decline and fall in 1922. Perhaps the satirical claims of English critics in the last century have been finally given substance by the centralism, conformism and concentration of the twentieth century, and Wales really has little more distinctive a political personality now than has Norfolk or Northumberland. Perhaps Wales itself has merged into the politics of memory, too. Somehow one feels (as well as hopes) that this conclusion is a superficial one. The past hundred years of politics in Wales—the politics of democracy inaugurated by the 1867 Reform Act—is shot through with consciousness of nationhood. It has, fortunately, assumed a different form from that in Ireland, more subtle, less strident. But its existence is undeniable to anyone who contemplates the alternating strands of national awareness that have woven themselves so intimately into the socio-political fabric of Wales for over a century. This awareness has not led to a self-governing Wales—possibly it never will. But it has produced a valuable and significant series of by-products—the Welsh educational structure; separate legislation and departmental autonomy; the Secretaryship of State. All of them, whatever their inadequacies, have contributed to a skein of aspirations that Plaid Cymru and others have been able to exploit in the recent past.

The historian, we are often told, should never turn prophet, never utilize the past to explain the present, let alone try to discern the future. Nevertheless, scholastic purists will surely not object if this historian humbly suggests that all the indications of the past hundred years are that the Welsh political problem will not disappear, but that it will continue to torment and fascinate us for decades, perhaps generations to come. This may be in part because of the very unifying factors in the modern world that are usually supposed to be eroding national consciousness in Wales. In fact, they could strengthen it, and make it more acute. After all, the Welsh Language Society learnt many of its techniques from Berkeley and the Sorbonne: the 'Welsh extremist' is Cohn-Bendit with a Caernarvon accent. But the basic reason for the enduring nature of the Welsh political problem is rooted in the restless genius of the Welsh themselves. In *Under Milk Wood* the Rev. Eli Jenkins gave praise that his people were a musical nation. In some respects, this may still be so. There are those who believe that we are still a religious nation. Undoubtedly we are also a sporting nation, on the rugby field especially, always competitive, sometimes chivalrous, endlessly inventive. But the making of modern Wales ultimately lies not with choirs, chapels or stand-off halves. Its battles will not be won on the playing-fields of Llandovery, but rather within its institutions and the earthy, democratic culture that gives them life. Here there is still much room for hope in the later twentieth century. For, in our innermost being, and let praise be given for it, we are in very truth a political nation.

SELECT BIBLIOGRAPHY

The literature on modern Welsh politics is extremely patchy. For a general treatment see the later chapters of David Williams, *Modern Wales* (London, 1950); Sir Reginald Coupland, *Welsh and Scottish Nationalism* (London, 1954); Kenneth O. Morgan, 'Welsh Nationalism: the Historical Background', *Journal of Contemporary History*, Vol. 6, No. 1 (1971); and Sir Frederick Rees, *The Problem of Wales and Other Essays* (Cardiff, 1964). For stimulating general ideas, see Glanmor Williams, 'The Idea of Nationality in Wales', *Cambridge Journal* (1953); *idem*, 'Language, Literacy and Nationality in Wales', *History* LVI (February 1971); and Gwyn A. Williams, 'Twf Hanesyddol y Syniad o Genedl yng Nghymru', *Efrydiau Athronyddol* XXIV (1961).

The Liberal ascendancy is covered in Kenneth O. Morgan, *Wales in British Politics, 1868-1922* (Cardiff, 1963; second edition, 1970). The second edition takes the account up to June 1970. Henry Pelling, *The Social Geography of British Elections, 1885-1910* (London, 1968) has a chapter on Wales. Also valuable is E. T. Davies, *Religion in the Industrial Revolution in South Wales* (Cardiff, 1965). For biographies of some of the leading figures of the period, see Watkin Davies, *Lloyd George, 1863-1914* (London, 1939); Kenneth O. Morgan, *David Lloyd George: Welsh Radical as World Statesman* (Cardiff, 1963; second edition, 1964); E. W. Evans, *Mabon* (Cardiff, 1961); T. I. Ellis, *Thomas Edward Ellis* (Liverpool, 2 vols., 1944-8); K. Idwal Jones (ed.), *Syr Herbert Lewis* (Cardiff, 1958); Viscountess Rhondda and others, *Life of D. A. Thomas, Viscount Rhondda* (London, 1921); Kenneth O. Morgan, 'D. A. Thomas: the Industrialist as Politician', *Glamorgan Historian* III (1966); E. Morgan Humphreys, *Gwŷr Enwog Gynt* (Aberystwyth, 1950); *idem, Gwŷr Enwog Gynt: Yr Ail Gyfres* (Aberystwyth, 1953); Eluned E. Owen, *The Later Life of Bishop Owen* (Llandysul, 1961). Aspects of politics are covered in Kenneth O. Morgan, 'Democratic Politics in Glamorgan, 1884-1914', *Morgannwg* IV (1960); *idem*, 'Liberals, Nationalists and Mr. Gladstone', *Trans. Hon. Soc. Cymm.*, 1960; *idem*, 'Cardiganshire Politics: the Liberal Ascendancy, 1885-1923', *Ceredigion* (1967); *idem*, 'The Liberal Unionists in Wales', *Nat. Lib. Wales Journal* (Winter, 1969); and *idem*, 'Wales and the Boer War— a reply', *Welsh History Review* IV, No. 4 (December 1969). For the rise of Labour, see Frank Bealey and Henry Pelling, *Labour and Politics, 1900-6* (London, 1958); chapters V and VI of Morgan, *Wales in British Politics*; Glanmor Williams (ed.), *Merthyr Politics: the making of a Working-Class Tradition* (Cardiff, 1966); Kenneth O. Fox, 'Labour and Merthyr's Khaki Election of 1900', *Welsh History Review* II, No. 4 (Dec., 1965); Cyril Parry, *The Radical Tradition in Welsh Politics: a study of Gwynedd politics, 1900-1920* (Hull, 1970); Wil John Edwards, *From the Valleys I Came* (London, 1956); and W. W. Craik, *The Central Labour College* (London, 1964). There is a chapter on South Wales in Roy Gregory, *The Miners and British Politics, 1906-14* (London, 1968). There is little in print on Welsh politics during the first world war. Edward David, 'Charles Masterman and the Swansea By-Election of 1915', *Welsh History Review* V, No. 1 (June 1970) admirably discusses one episode. Kenneth O. Morgan, 'Wales and the Great War', *Welsh History Review* III, No. 3 (June 1967) offers some general comments. Peter Stead, 'Vernon Hartshorn', *Glamorgan Historian* VI (1970) is a most interesting discussion.

The years of Labour ascendancy since 1918 have still to find their historian. English historians are invariably 'little Englanders' and ignore Wales completely. Even C. L. Mowat's *Britain between the Wars* (London, 1955), a superb book, has practically nothing on Wales. A. J. P. Taylor's *English History, 1914-1945* (Oxford, 1965) makes a virtue of the omission (see a most perceptive review of it by Henry Pelling in *Past and Present*, April 1966). Attempts by English political scientists to apply their models to the Welsh scene are generally derisory. At least Welsh election results are available in F. W. S. Craig, *British Parliamentary Election Results, 1918-1949* (Glasgow, 1969), while the Nuffield general election surveys for 1964 and 1966 have small sub-sections on South Wales constituencies. For the decline of the Liberal Party after 1918 see Trevor Wilson, *The Downfall of the Liberal Party, 1914-1935* (London, 1966); Kenneth O. Morgan, 'Twilight of Welsh Liberalism: Lloyd George and the Wee Frees, 1918-35', *Bulletin of the Board of Celtic Studies*, XII (May 1968); *idem*, 'Lloyd George's Stage Army: the Coalition Liberals, 1918-22', in A. J. P. Taylor (ed.), *Lloyd George: Twelve Essays* (London, 1971); C. P. Cook, 'Wales and the General Election of 1923', *Welsh History Review* IV, No. 4 (Dec., 1969); and W. Hughes Jones, *Wales Drops the Pilots* (Caernarvon, 1937). For the Labour Party, there is something in Arthur Horner, *Incorrigible Rebel* (London, 1960); Michael Foot, *Aneurin Bevan*, Vol. I (London, 1962); and James Griffiths, *Pages from Memory* (London, 1969). Two

143

admirable pioneer studies are Hywel Francis, 'The Welsh Miners and the Spanish Civil War', *Journal of Contemporary History*, Vol. 5, No. 3 (1970); and David Smith, 'The Struggle against Company Unionism in the South Wales Coalfield, 1926-1939' (to be published in the forthcoming Labour History number of the *Welsh History Review*, June 1973). For Communism, see Lewis Jones, *We Live* (London, 1939). Goronwy Jones, *Wales and the Quest for Peace* (Cardiff, 1970) is valuable on the League of Nations Union.

The outstanding scholarly treatment of the recent nationalist resurgence is Alan Butt-Philip, 'The Political and Sociological Significance of Welsh Nationalism since 1945' (unpublished Oxford D.Phil. thesis, 1971): it is much to be hoped that this most excellent study will soon be published. For the rest, material on the development of Plaid Cymru and the Welsh Language Society has invariably to be gleaned from members of those bodies. Among the most helpful sources for the Blaid are Gwynfor Evans's chapters in *The Historical Basis of Welsh Nationalism* (Cardiff, 1950); Gwynfor Evans, *Rhagom i Ryddid* (Bangor, 1964); Huw T. Edwards, *Hewn from the Rock* (Cardiff, 1967); Gwynfor Evans and Ioan Bowen Rhys, 'Welsh Nationalism' in *Celtic Nationalism* (London, 1968); and J. E. Jones, *Tros Cymru* (Swansea, 1970). Helpful for the language movement are Gerald Morgan, *The Dragon's Tongue* (Cardiff, 1966), which prints a translation of Saunders Lewis's famous 1962 BBC lecture; Robyn Lewis, *Second-Class Citizen* (Llandysul, 1969); and Ned Thomas, *The Welsh Extremist* London, 1970). The journal *Barn* is also most informative. There is a thoughtful discussion in Ednyfed Hudson Davies, 'Welsh Nationalism', *Political Quarterly* (July-September 1968). For developments in Welsh government since 1950 see an excellent summary by Ivor Gowan, 'Government in Wales in the Twentieth Century', in J. A. Andrews (ed.), *Welsh Studies in Public Law* (Cardiff, 1970); R. Borthwick, 'The Welsh Grand Committee', *Parliamentary Affairs* (Summer, 1968); J. E. Trice, 'Welsh Local Government Reform—an Assessment of Ad Hoc Administrative Reform', *Public Law* (Autumn, 1970); and E. L. Gibson, 'A Study of the Council for Wales and Monmouthshire, 1948-1966' (unpublished Aberystwyth M.A. thesis, 1968). There are contemporary comments in Kenneth O. Morgan, 'Inaction for Wales', *Socialist Commentary* (June 1967). A most interesting short discussion is Rhys David, 'The Future of the Welsh Office', *Planet* 1 (August-September, 1970). It is much to be hoped that the evidence submitted before the Crowther Commission will be made available to historians in the future. A recent perceptive work is Ioan Bowen Rees, *Government by Community*, London, 1971).

POSTSCRIPT (May 1972)

Since I wrote the above, Lord Crowther, chairman of the commission, has sadly died. In February 1972, the Welsh Labour members overwhelmingly endorsed an elected council. In the same month, S. O. Davies died at the age of 85. Five candidates (Labour, Conservative, Liberal, Plaid Cymru and Communist) contested the subsequent by-election at Merthyr held on 13 April. Here, Ted Rowlands re-gained the seat for Labour with a 3,710 majority; but the most remarkable feature was Plaid Cymru's capturing 37 per cent of the poll (11,852 votes). However, Labour again dominated the borough elections on 4 May, with over fifty net gains, notably in Cardiff, Newport and Barry.

THE EDUCATION OF WELSHMEN

R. BRINLEY JONES

VIII

WHEN the Romans entered Wales, they found the country occupied by Celtic tribes who, in race, culture and language, differed little from those who dwelt in other parts of Britain. In Anglesey, a centre of Celtic ritual practice, they found the Druids whose learning impressed and frightened them. For three centuries Rome dominated and through its legionaries and auxiliaries representing at first and second hand the culture of a great empire, one might have expected enormous influences in the field of education. There is little doubt that the culture which they brought prepared the ground for later exercises of the mind, but evidence is sparse for claiming any immediate influence on the indigenous inhabitants. Those who eked out a living in the shadow of the Roman villas may well have caught a glimpse of this new culture and early Welsh borrowings such as *ysgol* (schola), *llyfr* (liber), and *myfyr* (memoria) may have significance. It was Rome, too, that first brought the story of Christ to the land; there were probably Christian 'pockets' by about 180-200 A.D. and there may have been a Byzantine church at Caerwent—but it was by another route that Christianity really entered Wales.

Traditionally the abandonment of Wales by the Romans is associated with the usurpation of Magnus Maximus (383-8), but there is evidence that, in places, Roman habits lingered long. Maybe some people regarded themselves as Roman citizens until as late as the middle of the sixth century, and there is evidence of intellectual involvement in Latin culture well after the date of the Roman withdrawal. But these contacts were few and it was with the new invasion by a Church whose language was Latin that a further and more lasting bond was forged.

Christianity entered Wales mainly from the west and directly from the continent; its early character was predominantly monastic. Christianity came via the western sea-routes which brought messages and messengers from Gaul or Northern Spain or from the Eastern Mediterranean. There was considerable contact too between Wales and Ireland. There is reason to believe that Christianity had made some impression in South-East Wales before the end of Roman rule and so it is not surprising that here the new missionary zeal found a ready place and it was here that learning first flourished. But the labours of the missionaries reached out all over Wales. It is possible that the final conversion of Wales may well have been completed by the end of the sixth century. The larger monastic establishments at Llantwit Major, Nantcarfan, St. David's, Llandeilo Fawr, for example, were missionary centres generating energy which exercised considerable influence. So considerable

146

indeed, that the age has been called 'the Age of Saints'. These saints were great travellers and though one must beware not to overstate their educational impact, here was the spoken word, the contact with a teacher, a reference to events in history and an overspill from other cultures. We normally recognise two generations of the saints; the first, the more intellectual represented by Illtud (noted for his knowledge of the Old and New Testament and other arts) and the second typified by David/Dewi who tended to see the dangers of too much learning and who came under the influence of Eastern asceticism. But both generations had respect for learning.

Two hundred years after the demise of Rome, the picture of Britannia had changed. The Anglo-Saxon invaders had arrived and held most of what we now call England, but in the north, the west and the south-west the Britons remained and it is among those that the Welsh language, as we know it, was born. Indeed its earliest poetry may well belong to the latter part of the sixth century and was written by the poets Aneirin and Taliesin who lived in the old kingdom of the North. The late fifth and early sixth century witnessed the isolation of the Welsh from the other Celtic kingdoms. From then on, Wales strengthened its language and its faith; both became inextricably bound together and were to be two dominant features in the story of Welsh education.

The Church was the custodian of learning but from the eighth century on, for almost three hundred years it suffered sadly from Scandinavian attacks and many of its manuscripts were destroyed but the existence of Welsh entries in a Latin paraphrase of the Gospels by Juvencus, dating from the eighth or ninth century and others in a copy of the *De Nuptiis Philologae et Mercurii* by Martianus Capella dating from the late ninth century show that the lights of learning were not entirely extinguished. But such learning was very much the preserve of those associated closely with the Church.

We know very little about the organisation of education in these early centuries. The three ways in which pupils could acquire some measure of formal education would be from the teaching of the parish priest, the monastic schools (intended for those who wished to become monks) and the grammar schools attached to large churches and cathedrals though these later freed themselves from such ties. There were song schools maintained at cathedrals, at collegiate and some parish churches, and later there were chantry schools (though evidence suggests that only few of the chantry priests fulfilled their teaching obligations). Grammar, meaning Latin grammar, was basic and the text book was the *Donatus*; the fact that this word was borrowed into Welsh as *dwned* (first recorded in the fourteenth century) showed that it took root in Wales. Apart from this and scriptural knowledge and teaching, some secular learning was transmitted. The two real divisions of medieval education were the *trivium* consisting of grammar, rhetoric and logic; this formed the basis of school education, and the *quadrivium*, consisting of music, arithmetic, geometry

147

and astronomy, the more advanced study.   The texts in which these subjects were studied dated from the fifth and sixth centuries and were the compilations of Martianus Capella, Boethius and Cassiodorus. We have already mentioned the Welsh entries in the copy of a work by Martianus Capella.

For the majority of laymen there was little call for formal education; the lowest would learn the crafts associated with his work.   Indeed education was proscribed for some.   The laws of Hywel the Good had stated that, "There are three arts which a villein may not teach his son without his lord's permission, scholarship, bardism and smith-craft;   because if his lord permits the scholar to wear a tonsure, or a smith to enter a smithy, or a bard to sing, then no one can afterwards enslave them".   The freeman however might wish to learn some of the refinement and manners of the court and follow arms (*dwyn arfau* is recorded early in Welsh).

But society was now demanding other expertise—there was training for the lawyers and storytellers and for the poets. Such training was long and arduous and required knowledge of history and genealogy and language. Though the bardic schools had but a relatively small following, they are of such importance in the history of the language and literature of Wales that their contribution to Welsh education cannot be overemphasised. There were the schools which trained musicians too, otherwise how could Giraldus Cambrensis have paid such tribute to companies of singers, or poets refer to organ playing? And one needs only to recall the buildings and frescoes and remnants of an artistic past to realise that there were 'schools' here, too. All was not to be learned in what we understand as schools. There was a folk-learning and exchange; there were those who could afford pilgrimage and who met those on their way to the shrines in Wales. It was all education of a kind.

The twelfth century is regarded as a turning-point in the history of western education. It was a period of extraordinary intellectual curiosity, of mental energy and of religious revival. Earlier the monasteries had been the treasuries of learning and the manuscripts produced in their *scriptoria* proved to be of inestimable value to later scholarship. One needs only to think of the manuscripts copied in Strata Florida, the Cistercian house, to realise what a contribution they made. It was there that Giraldus Cambrensis deposited his manuscripts for safe keeping when he left for Rome. And of Strata Florida the poet Guto'r Glyn said that its learning was so distinguished that an Oxford training was superfluous. But the monasteries were to exercise less general influence in the field of education than the friaries which grew with the religious awakening of the century. The harmonization of 'faith' and 'reason' brought about by the remarkable fusion of Christian and Aristotelian teaching is the supreme achievement of the intellectual Middle Ages. It produced the scholastic theology of the later Middle Ages and at its best the finest flower of intellectualism exemplified in the work of Thomas Aquinas; it is interesting to find a John de Monmouth bequeathing a treatise on Aquinas to Merton College, Oxford. The works of Einion Offeiriad, Siôn Cent and Ieuan ap Rhydderch show that the teachings of the medieval schoolmen in the forms of 'realism' and 'nominalism' had reached Wales. The beginning and end of the later Middle Ages are marked by the rise and fall of scholasticism and the history of the Welsh word *dilechtid* (dialectica) mirrors the change. From signifying the dialectic of the schools it translates *astutia* in the meaning of 'wiliness' by the middle of the sixteenth century.

The universities were the intellectual exchanges of the Middle Ages and Wales shared much of the vigour to be found in them. Normally students entered university at the age of fourteen or fifteen. Welsh students are to be found at Oxford, Cambridge, Paris, Bologna, Perugia and Rome, but it was to Oxford that most of them turned and some four hundred are to be recognised in the records of medieval Oxford. The university had been granted its charter in 1156 and as early as 1238 there is reference to a certain clerk *de confinio Wallie* who shot a cook there. Indeed, there are several references to their riotous behaviour though in 1436 they are described as being good and diligent students . . . and there is good reason to conclude that some made a mark. As early as 1335 Oxford had been named as the centre to which Cistercians should be sent for their education. The friars were early to recognise the value of university training and one, John Wallensis, was regent master of the Franciscans at Oxford before proceeding to Paris where he became regent master of the order and was known as *Arbor Vitae*. A secular priest, Thomas Wallensis, became a regent master of Paris and one of the earliest readers to the friars in Oxford; his very considerable learning earned the admiration of Robert Grosseteste and Roger Bacon. The reputation and learning of Geoffrey of Monmouth are known; Henry de Gower became Chancellor of the University. Others make fleeting appearances in the records —Robert, monk of Margam took part in theological discussions at Oxford in 1314, and Lewis ap Howel, rector of Trawsfynydd was concerning himself about his doctorate of Civil Law in 1373. Indeed it would appear that many Welshmen specialised in Law and among their number, one of the most interesting was Adam Usk (1352-1430), a doctor of laws, teacher at the university and a scholar befriended by two popes. By the fifteenth century Welshmen were numerous at Oxford. Of those who proceeded to university, some returned to Wales to serve state as well as church. Perhaps it was for the purpose of training men to serve the 'state' of Wales that Owain Glyn Dŵr, himself trained at the Inns of Court, in 1406 requested a faculty from Pope Benedict XIII to found two universities, one in North Wales and one in South Wales. But such a dream took centuries to be realised.

The students referred to were privileged and the majority of the priests were ill-educated and possessed little Latin. Archbishop John Pecham had said of

149

Wales that "the clerk of the country is scarcely better lettered than the layman". This probably accounts for the considerable corpus of vernacular religious literature found in Wales at this time.

The devastation, disease, depopulation and social unrest of the fourteenth century stunted the growth of learning and the education of the clergy declined. There was a marked drop in the number of students at the universities and the influence of the monasteries and friaries diminished. Later the rebellion of Owain Glyn Dŵr wrought destruction in some places. But by the middle of the fifteenth century there were signs of change. In 1450 the bards tried to put their house in order by examining the rules of their craft and the training of their apprentices. And Welshmen were distinguishing themselves in other fields; Robert Jones (1485-1535) is regarded as a pioneer of polyphonic music. The gentleman-poet, Ieuan ap Rhydderch of Cardiganshire, displays his talents in grammar, civil law, sophistry, Biblical knowledge, history, geography, the black arts—and the works of Aristotle. He was proud of his knowledge of French:—

> Dysgais yr eang Ffrangeg,
> Doeth yw ei dysg, da iaith deg.

Knowledge of French was nothing new, of course. The earlier Norman incursions and contacts with French religious houses had introduced the language into Wales and French literature, too, had been much in vogue. The first abbot of Margam was Welsh but he was succeeded by William de Clairvaux. And Giraldus Cambrensis must have spoken Welsh, French and Latin. In England, where French was the language of high society for a considerable time, French was also the medium of teaching grammar until the middle of the fourteenth century. Maybe this was the case in Wales too. By the fifteenth century, French was again a foreign language and Ieuan ap Rhydderch may well have acquired his French at university.

In many ways Ieuan represents two worlds, the medieval and the modern. He is on the threshold of a new age which heralded the new humanism and a new generation of scholar-gentlemen. Now, though the Church retained some of its influence, it was not the force which it had been, previously, in education. The political changes which culminated in the Acts of Union (1536-1543), made London an attractive centre for aspiring Welshmen and together with the new spirit of enquiry which was abroad, created a new influx into the universities and a new demand for a pre-university education too. More was required now than training for the Church; the resurgence of trade and the emergence of new industries required literate merchants and craftsmen; there was a new middle class, new dimensions for the mind, a new and wider purpose for education. The distinguished Elizabethan Welshman, Sir Roger Williams (*c.* 1540-1595) who sought and found fame and fortune in the European wars was "from his childhood more given to military than scholastical matters, yet for forms sake he was sent to the university" (as Anthony à Wood said of him); education was beginning to have claims of its own. The authority of the Church had also been called into question. The religious changes sent refugees, Protestant and Catholic to seek asylum in the cultural centres of the continent: Richard Davies was at Frankfurt, Gruffydd Robert was at Milan. Others roamed for other reasons. Siôn Dafydd Rhys had been to Venice, Crete and Cyprus, having graduated in Medicine at Siena and having taught at Pistoia; in 1569 he published his *De Italica Pronunciatione*. Morris Kyffin served as Surveyor of the Muster Rolls in the English army in the Low Countries and in 1591 was with the forces in Normandy. The universities and inns of court once again saw a crop of men who proved to be servants of Wales—John Prys, Richard Davies, Gruffydd Robert, Thomas Huet, Morys Clynnog, Siôn Dafydd Rhys, Henry Salesbury, Henri Perri, Huw Lewys, Edward James, Richard Parry, John Davies and Thomas Wiliems at Oxford; William Morgan, Richard Whitford, Edmund Prys, Eubule Thelwall, Robert Holland at Cambridge; John Wynn, George Owen at the inns.

The one device that revolutionised education was the invention of printing with movable type, devised by a Mainz goldsmith, Johann Gutenberg in the middle years of the fifteenth century. Printing presses were established in quick succession in Switzerland, Italy, France, Spain and England. Suddenly dependence on manuscripts was over (not that copying them was past in Wales; the sixteenth and seventeenth centuries were the golden era of manuscript-copying—but this was of restricted interest). Protestantism, with its concern for Biblical authority was to see particular relevance in the printed word . . . and in the polemical writings that followed, both sides recognised its power. More than four thousand copies of Martin Luther's address *To the Christian Nobility* were sold within five days in 1520 from a small Wittenberg press. There was a hunger for knowledge and this new means of dissemination was available to assuage it. It was to educate the new gentry and the new clergy of Wales and, with time, the whole of Wales. The Welsh language was also to gain; the first Welsh book was published in 1546 and by the end of the seventeenth century almost two hundred Welsh titles had appeared.

Not that events augured well for the Welsh language in education in the sixteenth century. Welsh was proscribed in official use; English was the language of government, administration, law and justice. It is not surprising, therefore, that those who looked for preferment should send their sons to Winchester, Eton, St. Paul's, Bedford, Westminster and St. Alban's, for example . . . and Shrewsbury and Hereford were naturally very popular. In 1527, William Jones, of Newport in Monmouthshire, wished to send his sons to Bristol "according to the manner and conditions of the nurture of England". (There were many Welshmen who distinguished themselves as

151

teachers; Hugh Lloyd from Llŷn who entered Winchester in 1560 became a master there from 1580 to 1587). Some were sent to noble families for fosterage and service, others went to private teachers—as did Richard Davies, bishop, who received his early education from his uncle who was well-versed in the language and literature of Wales; it proved to be a propitious tutelage. Sometimes the gentry employed private tutors for their sons—Sir John Wynn appointed the Reverend Lloyd, vicar of Llanrwst for the task. There were private schools, too, many of which had a short and chequered existence; there is the example of Alice Carter who turned her shop in Denbigh into a schoolroom in 1574. Some Catholics were persuaded to send their sons for schooling on the continent, doubtless to ensure the purity and strength of their faith and to prepare them for service in the Church. But the demand for education among the new classes was such that arrangements had to be made nearer home.

In consequence, grammar schools were established by the monarch, by clerics, by merchants, by gentlemen, by lawyers and by scholars—partly for reasons of philanthropy, partly for reasons of teaching wholesome doctrine, partly for reasons of state and partly to answer the demands of a new society. (The foundation of schools by laymen was not entirely new, of course; David Holbache founded one in Oswestry in 1407). Schools were founded at Brecon 1541, Abergavenny 1543, Bangor 1557, Carmarthen 1576, Ruthin 1595, Cowbridge 1608 and Monmouth 1614—in some cases on old foundations. The royal licence which gave being to Christ College, Brecon referred to the lack of learning where "not only are the clergy and laity of every age and condition rude and ignorant of their duty towards God and their obedience due to ourselves, but have no skill in the English tongue, so that they are unable to observe or to understand our statutes, which they are bound to keep." The school was provided with endowments to pay the salary of the schoolmaster and usher, of a reader in divinity and a preacher; it was their duty "to give instruction in letters, and to expound the gospels purely and freely."

At the Friars' School in Bangor, the pupils were taught Latin and Greek, and English was taught in the lower forms; there was also qrovision for religious instruction. The well-worn Donatus grammar of the Middle Ages gave way to William Lily's grammar. No place was given to the teaching of Welsh; indeed, at Ruthin, pupils who spoke Welsh "shall be deemed faulty and an imposition shall be given". (Such 'impositions', metaphorically speaking, created a dichotomy in Welsh society—the dichotomy between the Anglicised and educated Welshmen and those who acquired no English; the dichotomy was to remain for a very long time.) In many schools there was time for recreation and sport, as had been suggested by some of the great educationists of Tudor England; at Bangor archery was taught.

From such schools pupils proceeded to the universities and the Inns of Court. One college, the first to be founded in Oxford after the Reformation, deserves special mention. In 1571 Hugh Price, treasurer of St. David's

Cathedral, petitioned the queen to establish a new college. The petition was favourably received and the letters patent of 27 June 1571 laid down the purpose for which Jesus College was founded:—

"... to the Glory of God Almighty and Omnipotent, and for the spread and maintenance of the Christian religion in its sincere form, for the eradication of errors and heresies, for the increase and perpetuation of true loyalty, for the extension of good literature of every sort, for the knowledge of languages, for the education of youth in loyalty, moral- ity, and methodical learning, for the relief of poverty and distress, and lastly for the benefit and well-being of the Church of Christ in our realms and of our subjects of our especial grace and of our own sure knowledge and spontaneous motion, we have decreed that a College of learning in the sciences, philosophy, humane pursuits, knowledge of the Hebrew, Greek and Latin languages, to the ultimate profession of Sacred Theology, to last for all time to come, be created, founded, built, and established ..."

There was nothing in the original charter to suggest a Welsh foundation, but it would seem reasonable to assume that Hugh Price was particularly concerned about his fellow-countrymen. Indeed Anthony à Wood, the Oxford historian, claimed that it was Price's intention "to bestow his estate for the maintenance of certain scholars of Wales to be trained up in good letters". To that end, Price left land to the value of £60 per annum to the college. The number of "certain scholars of Wales" grew and during its four hundred years of existence Jesus College has played a very significant part in the life of the principality of Wales and made a notable contribution to the education of Welshmen.

It is essential to remember how little pre-university education was available in Wales. The schools described were small and most of the pupils in them were the sons of the gentry, the clergy and the merchants, with a sprinkling of poor scholars. For example, Cowbridge probably catered for some fifteen free pupils at the start. The majority of Welshmen remained untutored.

Puritanism laid stress on the value of popular education and the first attempts to provide schooling on a larger scale than hitherto came with the Common- wealth. The Act for the better Propagation of the Gospel, of 1650-53, and the Works of the Trustees for the Maintenance of Ministers, of 1653-1660, provided such schools. In that they were subsidized by an allocation from tithes, they represent the first state-aided system. Some sixty or more schools were established in Wales, mainly in the towns though some were founded in remote villages, probably as the result of the enthusiasm of a particular local person. The schools were to be found more on the eastern side than on the west; there was not one established in Carmarthenshire, though there were eleven in Denbighshire, eight in Montgomeryshire and nine in Breconshire.

153

The education given was similar to that of the grammar school though on occasions they prepared for a grammar school if one existed locally. Some of them were co-educational. The subjects taught were English, writing, reading, arithmetic and some Latin. No Welsh was taught and this may well account for the fact that the schools were short-lived. We know little of the quality of the education dispensed in them though it is probably fair to assume that they contributed to the success of Puritanism in Wales.

During the Commonwealth period, too, there was talk about setting up a university in Wales and Shrewsbury, Machynlleth, Aberystwyth and Cardigan were mentioned as possible sites. But due to lack of funds the enterprise failed.

The Act of Uniformity of 1662 required that no one could maintain a school without a bishop's licence but after much dispute by 1670 this was no longer enforced in the case of those who taught reading, writing and arithmetic. As a result, many nonconformist schools and academies were opened and the standard in them was reputedly so high that even Anglicans used them occasionally. One of the most interesting of these schools was the one founded by Samuel Jones (1628-97) at Brynllywarch in Glamorgan. Jones had been a Fellow of Jesus College, Oxford, and a lecturer there. He became vicar of Llangynwyd but was deprived because he refused to bow under the Act of Uniformity. He established his school at Brynllywarch and later attracted older students there. He was a man of considerable scholarship and culture and his academy was regarded as a 'university' for early Nonconformist ministers.

Another divine who refused to accept the Act of Uniformity of 1662 was Thomas Gouge (1605-81). He was a Londoner who became convinced of a missionary task in Wales. In 1674 he founded the 'Welsh Trust' described in retrospect in *Survey of London*, 1720:—

> "This favour of the Londoners toward poor children began diverse years ago in North and South Wales. When about the year 1670 the poverty and ignorance of those parts raised a compassion in the hearts of many good citizens . . . so that they and their interest contributed such sums of money as maintained a great number of poor Welsh children at school to read English, write and cast accounts. And schools for that purpose were erected and settled in many places in those countries . . . And this Charity extended not only to poor children but to the rest of the poor Welsh inhabitants to furnish them with Christian knowledge."

Gouge carried out his work in conjunction with Stephen Hughes (1622-88) another early Nonconformist (possibly educated at Carmarthen grammar school) whose main concern was to provide Wales with devotional books in Welsh. The Trust set up over a hundred places for the distribution of devotional literature and in the first year, 1674, eighty-seven schools were established though they had dwindled to thirty-one by 1678. Perhaps as many as two thousand children were taught each year but when Gouge died in 1681 the schools came to an end. They may have done so because he did not leave trained teachers to carry on his work, but his philosophy that "the younger generation could best be secured for the glory of God and service of man by an English education" may well have been the greatest stumbling-block to their continuing success. Welsh was still the language of the people. But the work of the 'Trust' was important; it had emphasised the need for educating the poorer classes and had distributed literature on a large scale.

The year after Thomas Gouge died, a young man of twenty-one, a product of Oswestry grammar school, went up to Jesus College, Oxford, and became assistant to Dr. Plot, professor of Chemistry in the university. He was Edward Lhuyd (1660-1709). As a botanist, geologist, antiquary and philologist he gained the respect of great scholars of the day. The Oxford antiquary, Thomas Hearne, later said of him, "what he does is purely out of love to the good of learning and his country". His immediate influence on the scene in Wales was small though his researches were to bear fruit later. And his vast correspondence reveals that he was helpful to many young Welshmen who went up to the university. No greater tribute exists of what a grammar school and university education could achieve for a Welshman than the case of Edward Lhuyd. But he was a rare bird of course, a man of genius.

The next provision for education on a large scale came from the Society for Promoting Christian Knowledge, founded in 1699, many of whose pioneer workers had been associated with the schools of the Welsh Trust. Its two main concerns were the provision of schools and of appropriate literature. The parent body in London wrote to clerics in each county in Wales inviting them to become corresponding members of the Society. The intentions were "for the instruction of such poor children in reading writing and in the Catechism . . . the most effectual method to train up the poorer sort in sobriety and the knowledge of Christian principles." But the schools also taught arithmetic to boys and needlecraft and allied subjects to girls; in addition, provision was sometimes made for tuition in agriculture and navigation. The language of the schools was generally English though there was some awareness of the value of teaching through the medium of Welsh (particularly in North Wales) and it would appear that the Society was tolerant in this respect. Dean John Jones of Bangor endowed some schools "for the instructing of poor children for ever to read Welsh." Ninety-six schools were founded between 1700 and 1740. Generally they were maintained by voluntary subscription, endowment and church collections. It was only in extreme cases that the Society gave financial aid though the schools were able to get school books and material free or at very little cost. There were private benefactors, too; a school was founded at Dolgellau in 1720 "at the charge of a lady of London." There was substantial support from industrialists like Sir Humphrey

155

Mackworth of Neath and landowners like Sir John Philipps of Picton Castle who gave liberally to the founding of schools and libraries—(the minutes of the Society for December 18, 1703 had considered "a proper method for erecting lending libraries in Wales, where they are extremely wanted")—and the printing and circulation of Welsh books "for the pious instruction and education of children as the surest way of preserving and propagating the knowledge and practice of true religion". The great number of schools established in Pembrokeshire is clearly attributable to encouragement from him. Realising that one of the problems facing the movement was the supply of teachers, Sir John Philipps even advocated the setting up of a training college but he found no response from the Society.

The success of the schools depended a great deal on local enthusiasm and support. There is reason to believe that the standard of instruction was high and the schools were subject to inspection. Teachers were required to be members of the Church of England, of sober life and conversation and possessing knowledge of the three 'R's.' It was not always easy to convince the poor people of the value of education and enticements were offered to make schooling attractive. In Haverfordwest in 1710, for example, the children were to "receive five shillings a quarter for their parents." In some schools the pupils were clothed, free of charge; there is reference to Pembrey in 1712 where the ten poorest scholars were to be clothed "and given dinner five days a week at a public house near the school."

There is no question about the valuable work done by the Society. Apart from the establishment of schools, the publication of books and bibles was a major factor in the religious and educational revolution of the eighteenth century in Wales. But no new school was founded by the Society after 1727. There were several reasons for this, among them the Schism Act of 1714, the struggle that developed between High and Low Church for the control of the schools and possibly the Jacobite Rising in 1715.

In 1719, Sir Humphrey Mackworth had suggested the wisdom of appointing "one of the best schoolmasters in London to begin the setting up of schools in Wales, who may be a sort of itinerant master". Sir Humphrey's dream of itinerant masters became a reality in the life and work of Griffith Jones (1683-1761), the incumbent of Llanddowror in Carmarthenshire. His mission was not to create "gentlemen, but Christians and heirs of eternal life . . . not to elate their minds, but to make them by the grace of God good men in this world and happy in the next." The curriculum was basic; it consisted of reading and of learning the Catechism. From Llanddowror (where he established his 'College' for training his teachers) circulating schools were organised in many parts of Wales. The schools would last for some three to four months at a time, mainly during the winter months, and they were held "in the parish church or chapel; sometimes well-disposed persons lend a school-room gratis . . . and where we are obliged to hire a house, it is on moderate terms." For those who could not attend during the day, there was evening instruction. Literature, Jones obtained through the S.P.C.K. (The magnitude of the Society's contribution at this time may be gauged by the fact that between 1717-1769 it published more than seventy-thousand Welsh bibles). The schools were well organized, "several of them having two, and some three masters, who are obliged to keep a methodical list of the names, places of abode, ages, quality, calling and condition in the world, disposition and manners, progress in learning etc., of all the men, women and children that are taught by them." The teachers were required to be members of the Church of England and loyal to the Crown. Basic to his whole idea and accountable for much of his success was that teaching was carried on through the medium of Welsh where that was the mother-tongue because "to them English schools must be the same as setting up French charity schools for the poor in England". Griffith Jones's main concern was for teaching children though in the event adults made up the great proportion of his scholars. He gives a moving account in one of his reports:—

"In most of the schools, the adult persons do make about two thirds of the number taught in them. In some places, several who, for old age, are obliged to wear their spectacles, come into them. I am informed of two or three women, aged about sixty, who knew not a letter before, did attend constantly every day, except sometimes when they were obliged to seek abroad for a little bread; and discovered a very hopeful disposition, often weeping, and lamenting, that they had not an opportunity of learning forty or fifty years sooner; but resolved not to be sparing in pains-taking to come at it now."

To achieve this end, Griffith Jones made collections of money and gained the support of patrons (such as Sir John Philipps and Madam Bridget Bevan). In order to keep up the interest of his supporters, he issued an annual report entitled *The Welch Piety*. (It is from these publications that the quotations used here are derived.) It is estimated that from 1737 to 1761, 3,325 schools were held in just under 1,600 places with 153,835 scholars attending. Jones met with some opposition from those who claimed that he was closely associated with Methodists. After his death, the work was carried on by his cultured and wealthy friend, Madam Bevan; she died in 1779. It is of some interest that by the year 1764 even Catherine the Great of Russia had heard of Griffith Jones's scheme—and she wanted to hear more.

Meanwhile those parents who could afford to do so, continued to send their sons to the English public schools—and Westminster seems to have been a particular favourite. David Jones (1663-1724), cleric, proceeded from there to Oxford, as did Peter Foulkes (1676-1747), scholar and divine, and Timothy Thomas (1694-1751), cleric and scholar. Others went from Westminster to Cambridge—Edward Jones (1641-1703), who became bishop of St. Asaph and Erasmus Lewis (1670-1754), government secretary and member of parliament. The Welsh grammar schools continued—there must have been thirty of them—and some of them produced leaders of the popular educational movements; mention has already been made of Stephen Hughes, probably educated at Carmarthen grammar school and Griffith Jones who certainly went there. New schools appeared, too; one of them was established at Ystrad Meurig in 1736 by Edward Richard (1714-77), another Carmarthen grammar school product, noteworthy because he combined an excellent knowledge of the classics with a keen interest in the Welsh literary scene. Edmund Meyrick (1636-1712), sometime Fellow of Jesus College, Oxford, had endowed a school at Tŷ-tan-domen in Bala (later to become Bala Grammar School). The Nonconformist Academies gained a good reputation and were patronised occasionally by churchmen. The curriculum in some of these academies was wide; although in later years they catered for the Nonconformist ministry, this was not always the case. Thomas Morgan (1720-99), Independent minister, describes some of his education:—

> "January 21st 1742. Came to Carmarthen and entered myself under the tuition of the Revd. Samuel Thomas. And there I read some in Virgil's, Horace's, Homer's and the Greek Testament. Afterwards read Watts's Logic, Ward's Algebra, Geometry . . . Watt's Astronomy and Geography, Keill's Natural Philosophy . . .
>
> October 19th 1743. Entered myself under the tuition of the Revd. Evan Davies who joined with Mr. Samuel Thomas to put up the Academy in Carmarthen."

It was as well that such varied education was available; the obligation to subscribe to the Thirty-Nine Articles virtually debarred Nonconformists (and Roman Catholics) from admission to Oxford and prevented them from taking a degree at both Oxford and Cambridge. The abolition of religious tests at the universities did not come about until 1871.

The next really powerful movement for the education of the masses—an education which eventually made them articulate, knowledgeable in their Bible, questioning and gradually politically aware—was the Sunday School movement. Its chief architect in Wales was Thomas Charles (1755-1814), educated at Llanddowror, the Dissenting Academy at Carmarthen and Jesus College, Oxford. At the age of twenty-nine he joined the Methodist movement. He realised early that a pre-requisite for evangelisation was to create a literate people. The circulating schools of Griffith Jones had ceased to be a force and Charles observed "that the country gradually reverted to the same state of stupor and ignorance in which Mr. Jones found it when he first thought of these institutions." Jones's schools had never gained much ground in North Wales. Charles set up his own charity school movement, training its itinerant teachers at Bala. In 1785, when he started, there was one master; by 1794,

158

there were twenty masters. His intention was clear, "Our point is to diffuse knowledge and promote piety among all ranks"—and his teachers were selected for having those qualities. One of the essential differences between his and Griffith Jones's schools was that Charles intended his schools' visitation to be the start of a continuous education; by 1789 his charity schools were being succeeded by Sunday schools. (The movement was not new—they had already appeared in England and Wales but nothing had existed to compare with the scope and organised system of Thomas Charles). The schools met with great success first in North Wales, then in the South. They catered for all ages and both sexes and in order to educate them properly, Charles set about to prepare school books. He was also chiefly instrumental in establishing the Bible Society in London which, in 1804, became The British and Foreign Bible Society. In that year, 20,000 copies of the Bible and 5,000 copies of the New Testament were distributed throughout Wales. At last the country at large was being educated—the hymns of the Methodist Revival put fine poetry on the lips of the people and the Sunday schools taught them to read and write and analyse passages of Scripture. At the same time the Eisteddfod was gaining ground and bringing a new cultural occasion into the life of the people. The beginning of the nineteenth century heralds a new era in the education of Welshmen.

To appreciate fully the problems confronting those who attempted to educate Welshmen at the beginning of the nineteenth century it is essential to remember the part that religion played; in the Sunday school movement it showed great success but in the bitter sectarian dissensions that emerged, it did much to hamper the progress of education. It is well to remember, too, that in Wales religion became a matter of 'class', where the master was usually Anglican and English-speaking and the workman increasingly Nonconformist and Welsh-speaking. For the master and the new rich of the industrial revolution, there were the English public schools—but what remained for the Welsh at home? True, they were being educated by the increasing number of books published and by the proliferation of periodical literature but the provision that existed for every-day education was meagre indeed. A number of grammar schools, the property of the established church, remained, though some had disappeared and others deteriorated. Often they prepared for the priesthood. In 1828 a further provision was made for clerical training, when Saint David's College, Lampeter, was founded as a result of the generous efforts of Thomas Burgess, bishop of St. David's from 1803 to 1825. Originally intended to provide priests for his own diocese, it later gave great service to the rest of Wales. By 1852 it was granting the B.D. degree and by 1865 the B.A. degree. It was the first time for university degrees to come out of Wales. Training for the church was also the aim of Thomas Phillips, London-born surgeon, who founded Llandovery College in 1847; by stipulating that the Welsh language should be used in the classroom he made it a unique educational establishment in Wales. There were also some 'genteel' schools like the one advertised in the *North Wales Gazette* in July, 1826:—

> "Miss Norris respectfully informs the Gentry of Carnarvon and its vicinity, that her school will re-open on Monday, July 24. Terms for boarders under nine years of age, 20 guineas per annum; to include Reading, Writing, Geography, Arithmetic, Works, etc. Washing, two guineas per annum; French and Italian, one guinea per quarter each. Music on the usual terms.
>
> Above nine years of age, 25 guineas per annum. Each young lady to bring a silver spoon, four towels, and a pair of sheets."

And there were the 'private adventure schools' organized by individuals for their own profit and varying much in competence and standard.

Two voluntary societies turned to help. One, the *British and Foreign Schools Society*, was founded by Joseph Lancaster in 1808; the society was non-sectarian. The other, the *National Schools Society* was founded by Andrew Bell in 1811; it embraced the doctrine of the established church and its schools were managed by the laity in cooperation with the parochial clergyman. At first the National Society made greater headway in Wales because of the support it had from the church; the British Society lacked its organisation and support. By 1870, however, there were more than 300 British schools in Wales. Something of the nature of the early schools established by the societies can be gleaned from excerpts from the rules of the 'Llantwit National School' established on 6 June, 1831:—

> "The children are divided into classes, and each class has two teachers, who instruct it by turns . . .
>
> Every child is expected to attend Church on the Sunday, unless his parents wish him to attend some other place of worship, in which case the Minister of the place of worship which he attends is requested to furnish him with a certificate . . .
>
> The school is open to all children (above four years of age) of this and the adjoining parishes, on payment of one penny a week for each child . . .
>
> It is hoped that corporal punishment will be found altogether unnecessary, or at least that it will only be inflicted when every other mode of punishment has failed."

Both societies adopted the monitorial system whereby the teacher trained monitors and they in turn taught the rest of the class. It was economic tuition and it is estimated that the education of a child might cost a shilling a year. The learning imparted was basic. In 1833 the government voted its first grant of £20,000 to be shared between both societies; this was to rise to £100,000 by 1846. Such grants showed that government was beginning to realise the necessity of encouraging educational activity. Not all were pleased with state subsidy however, and the Voluntaryists, particularly active among the Independents and Baptists of South Wales refused such aid and attempted to set up their own schools independently. They were most active between 1844-1854 but the schools did not meet with much success.

One who realised that sectarian differences were hampering progress in education and who saw that parents were keeping their children away from the National schools because of church teaching was Hugh Owen (1804-81), clerk in the Poor Law Commission in London. In August 1843 he wrote an open letter to the Welsh people asking the Nonconformists to join forces to establish British schools in all areas and explaining how necessary it was to accept government aid; in March 1847 he published another letter setting forward the advisability of British schools for Wales. His letters received attention . . . and eventually many British schools were established first in North and later in South Wales. In 1856 he was one of the chief supporters of the movement to establish the Normal College at Bangor, and later he was largely responsible for securing a similar college for women at Swansea. (The National Society had already established a training school at Caernarvon in 1846 and had extended it into a college in 1849; in 1848 the Society had established the Carmarthen Training College to answer the needs of South Wales). It was Hugh Owen who first mooted the idea of the University College of Wales, at Aberystwyth, established in 1872. Owen was a superb organiser of education.

In the meantime, others were organising schools to meet specific needs—providing for the rapidly expanding industrial communities. Here the proprietors of works established schools for the children of their employees. It was not a new idea—but it was revolutionary in scope. Most of the works schools in Wales date from after 1833. At the start they were independent of outside help but after 1850 most of them sought government grants through the two voluntary societies. The schools were established in connection with all the major metallurgical industries, with the collieries and in the quarrying districts. In consequence their preponderance was in the South. They made a considerable contribution to education in Wales; they appeared spasmodically to 1840 but by 1870 they were familiar landmarks in the industrial areas. All in all, 134 works schools were established (45 connected with ironworks, 15 with non-ferrous metal industries, 12 with tinplate works, 47 with collieries, 12 with slate quarries, 2 with textile industry and 1 with a stone quarry). The workmen were compelled to pay towards their maintenance though attendance was voluntary. The most ambitious school scheme was the one devised in the Merthyr district by Sir Josiah John Guest (1785-1852). It was the largest complex of its kind in the country; the earliest Guest school dated from 1828. His wife, Lady Charlotte, took a keen interest and by 1849 the Guest education scheme consisted of infants, junior and senior day-schools, adolescent evening-schools and adult day and evening schools. The existence of the works schools in the industrial areas relieved considerably the pressure on the two voluntary societies. After 1870 they were not closed but transferred into the care of the newly elected school boards.

In 1845 the National Society proclaimed the inadequacy of educational opportunity in Wales. It spurred William Williams, a Carmarthenshire man and member of Parliament for Coventry to ask for an inquiry to be made into the state of education in the Principality. As a result, three commissioners were appointed to carry out an investigation—J. C. Symons, R. R. W. Lingen and H. Vaughan Johnson. The object of their Commission was to ascertain "the existing number of schools of all descriptions for the education of the children of the labouring classes and of adults, the amount of attendance, the age of the scholars, the character of the instruction given". It is generally agreed by now that whatever their competence as investigators, their ignorance of the Welsh 'scene' was a serious disadvantage. The report which was published in 1847 is a substantial volume of 1,183 pages. The remarks which they made about the moral standards of the people and their lack of sympathy with the Welsh language provoked an outcry; it was so intense that the exercise was labelled 'the treachery of the Blue Books'. But the reports are interesting in the information they give about educational provision. There were parishes without schools and where they existed, many were in very bad state of repair. The teachers and teaching were often grossly inadequate and the attendance at school was lax. The following excerpts reveal something of the spirit of the report (and the bias of the reporters):—

(a) "This school is held in a ruinous hovel of the most squalid and miserable character; the floor is of bare earth, full of deep holes; the windows are all broken; a tattered partition of lath and plaster divides it into two unequal portions; in the larger were a few wretched benches, and a small desk for the master in one corner; in the lesser was an old door, with the hasp still upon it, laid cross-ways upon two benches, about half a yard high, to serve for a writing desk! Such of the scholars as write retire in pairs to this part of the room, and kneel on the ground while they write. On the floor was a heap of loose coal, and a litter of straw, paper and all kinds of rubbish. The Vicar's son informed me that he had seen 80 children in this hut. In summer the heat of it is said to be suffocating; and no wonder."

(b) "The extreme youth of the teachers, is a fruitful source of ignorance and disorder in many schools. Many youths who are themselves fresh from school, some not 18 years of age, being entrusted with the charge of large schools, containing scholars who are wholly undisciplined and ignorant.

On the other hand, still worse results are occasioned by employing aged persons and cripples, who are yet more numerous among the class of Welsh teachers."

(c) "Whether in the country, or among the furnaces, the Welsh element is never found at the top of the social scale, nor in its own body does it exhibit much variety of gradation. In the country, the farmers are very small holders, in intelligence and capital nowise distinguished from labourers. In the works, the Welsh workman never finds his way into the office. He never becomes either clerk or agent. He may become an overseer or subcontractor, but this does not take him out of the labouring and put him into the administering class. Equally in his new, as in his old, home, his language keeps him under the hatches, being one in which he can neither acquire nor communicate the necessary information. It is a language of old-fashioned agriculture, of theology, and of simple rustic life, while all the world about him is English."

The fact that "all the world about him is English" was to be a theme in Welsh education for some considerable time. Economic growth and improved communications were to emphasize the value of knowledge of the English language for getting on in the world. As a result of Robert Lowe's Revised Code of 1862, all grants to schools were to be based upon attendance and competence in the three "R's", such competence to be measured by an Inspector; the system was known as "payment by results" and by its nature it did nothing to promote the status of the Welsh language in the school system. Earlier, in the 1847 Blue Books, there is recorded evidence of the punishment meted out to the pupil who spoke Welsh :—

"My attention was attracted to a piece of wood, suspended by a string round a boy's neck, and on the wood were the words, 'Welsh stick'. This, I was told, was a stigma for speaking Welsh."

Lowe's Code did nothing to remove the 'stick'. It was later educators like Thomas Powell, Dan Isaac Davies and O. M. Edwards who saw the injustice of it and who acknowledged the importance of the native language. The contribution to education of Sir O. M. Edwards, sometime Fellow of Lincoln College, Oxford and later Chief Inspector of Schools for Wales was very considerable. In 1909 he said, "Every H.M.I. will see that Welsh is put in its right place in the curriculum of every school". This was the command of the Chief Inspector. The local education authorities, the creation of 1902, were to be presented with new possibilities in respect of Welsh.

163

By the middle of the nineteenth century interest in popular education was growing. The Reform Act of 1867 had granted the right to vote to a large number of town workers and there was a realisation that education might make such a vote worth-while. The result was W. E. Forster's Education Act of 1870. By this, grants to the voluntary schools were increased and new schools were to be built where there was need. School Boards were convened and such Boards were to build schools which would be supported by government grant, local rates and school fees. The old voluntary schools were allowed to retain their rights in religious teaching but the new Board schools were to be undenominational. In consequence, hundreds of Board schools were built in Wales. Forster's Act also gave Boards the right to institute bye-laws making school attendance compulsory between the ages of 5 and 13; but not all took steps to enforce this. It was A. J. Mundella's Act of 1880 which made attendance compulsory. In 1891 school fees, which had been 2d. or 3d. a week, were abolished.

Interest in higher education was growing too. As has already been shown, Oxford and Cambridge had attracted their share of Welshmen and the nineteenth century continued such a tradition. The Scottish universities also played their part in educating Welshmen—David Daniel Davies (1777-1841) distinguished physician who attended at the birth of Queen Victoria, had been to Glasgow as had Sir William Milbourne James (1807-81) who was Lord Justice, and John Jenkins (1808-84), a barrister; others had gone to Edinburgh—John Evans (1767-1827), Baptist minister, and Abraham Rees (1743-1825), editor of *Chambers's Encyclopaedia* from 1781 to 1786 and Fellow of the Royal Society. David Lloyd Morgan (1823-92), naval surgeon was at St. Andrews. Others went to London, like Timothy Richard Lewis (1841-86) surgeon, pathologist and pioneer in tropical medicine. (The Inns of Court in London continued to attract, as they had done over the centuries.) The distinguished Hebraist Evan John Evans (1827-91) had been at London, Scotland and Heidelberg; it was to Göttingen that the Congregationalist minister and historian Thomas Nicholas (1816-79) went. Among the most distinguished Welshmen of the day was Sir Henry Jones (1852-1922), educated at Bangor Normal College, at Glasgow, Oxford and Germany who became professor of Philosophy successively at Bangor, St. Andrews and Aberdeen. The list of these academic emigrants is a long one. But as already stated, the University College of Wales at Aberystwyth had opened in 1872; it had a principal, three professors and 26 students. Had it not been for the enormous efforts of Hugh Owen who collected money for its upkeep, the college would have closed. The dearth of students at the start is to be explained in part by the lack of facilities for pre-university training. (It is estimated that in the third quarter of the century only 4,000 boys were receiving higher education in Wales and for girls there were only Howells School Cardiff, Howells School Denbigh and Dr. Williams' School Dolgellau.) In 1880 Gladstone convened the Aberdare Committee to inquire into the provision of secondary and higher education in Wales. The Committee recommended two further university colleges—and as a result the college at Cardiff opened in 1883 and the one in Bangor in 1884. The three colleges originally prepared students for degrees of the University of London but in 1893 when the three were united in a federal structure, the University of Wales, the new university was empowered to grant its own degrees.

Lord Aberdare's Committee of 1880 realised how necessary it was to bridge the gap between elementary education and university and to this end it recommended that 'intermediate' schools should be established throughout Wales, supported in the main out of local rates and government subsidy. In consequence, the Welsh Intermediate and Technical Education Act was passed in 1889. The newly created County Councils and County Borough Councils were allowed to levy ½d. rate and the government agreed to share the expense of providing the schools. In a comparatively short time, intermediate schools (or county schools as they were often called) were built in most of the market towns of Wales; by 1895 there were 30 of them and by 1902, 95. Some of the old established grammar schools became county schools though others like Monmouth, Brecon and Llandovery remained independent.

The creation of these schools soon called for a uniform standard of competence and for this reason the Central Welsh Board was created in 1896. It had examining and inspecting responsibilities first in respect of the county schools established under the Act of 1889 and later in respect of most of the secondary schools which came into being as a result of the Act of 1902.

Wales, like the rest of the United Kingdom has shared in the *explosion scolaire* of the twentieth century and statistics show that Wales and Welshmen have taken more than a share of the provisions afforded. The *explosion* continues; for example, there was an increase of 4·9 per cent of under-fives in nursery schools during the year 1970-71 as compared with the previous year; during the same period there was a 2·2 per cent increase in the maintained primary and secondary school population and a 7 per cent increase in the number of full-time students at the University of Wales. There were over a thousand registered students in the Open University in Wales in 1971. Facilities, generally, have increased; new buildings have gone up, better equipment has been available, library resources have grown and the teacher-pupil ratio has improved (more so in Wales than in the rest of the country). Wales has shared in the education which improved communications have provided—the growth of the cinema, the success of the paper-back revolution, the popular press, radio, television (with specially devised schools broadcasts on radio from 1924 and on television from 1957);—these are common factors in the education of the Briton. Common too are the 'concerns' about education—the importance

165

of science teaching, sex-education, religious education, visual-aids, program-med learning, language-laboratories, in-service training for teachers, the eleven plus, intelligence tests, careers-guidance, pupil-guidance, Nuffield projects, student protests, the deprived, the handicapped . . .and many more.

Movements like Young Farmers' Clubs, Literary and Debating Societies, Chapel groups, the Red Cross, Cadets, Scouts, Guides have been popular in Wales and have afforded their own kinds of training. Pupils from Welsh schools have continued to go in substantial numbers to English universities and like the rest of the country the vogue for postgraduate education in the United States of America has caught on, too. Common with other countries is the growth of interest in the Social Sciences. The status of the teacher,—his freedom in approach to his subject, his conditions of service—is in line with the rest of the United Kingdom. So too is the philosophy adumbrated through the educational system; it inherits the same traditions as other western European systems and shares the thinking of Plato, Quintilian, Augustine, Comenius, Locke, Rousseau, Pestalozzi, Herbart, Froebel, Dewey, Montessori, Whitehead and so on; they are names on every student teacher's list.

The Acts of Parliament and the Reports—(Hadow, 1926, 1931, 1933; Spens 1938; McNair, 1944; Crowther, 1959; Albemarle, 1960; Beloe, 1960; Anderson, 1960; Newsom, 1963; Robbins, 1963; Plowden, 1967 (with its 'Welsh' version in Gittins, 1968); Dainton, 1968, to name some—which have emanated from Whitehall have had their effect on Wales as elsewhere. With the Education Act of 1902, the cornerstone of the State educational system in England and Wales, the powers of School Boards were handed over to the county councils and county boroughs—the local education authorities; board schools now became council schools and local authorities were granted powers to set up secondary schools and teacher-training colleges. (By the time the 1902 Act was passed, Wales had already taken the lead over England in the provision of secondary education because grammar schools had grown rapidly in consequence of the Welsh Intermediate Act of 1889.) In 1918, with the Fisher Act, the school-leaving age was raised to fourteen. The Act of 1944 was of major importance; education was to be divided into three stages, primary, secondary and further. There was to be secondary education for all. The age for school-leaving was to be raised to fifteen. There was to be compulsory religious education. Local education authorities were obliged to provide for the instruction of handicapped children. Education was to be provided for all children according to 'age, ability and aptitude'. (There have been other Acts during the century but most of them have modified provisions already made.) The tripartite system of grammar, technical and modern school, not a provision of the 1944 Act, seemed to grow side by side with it. In 1965 the Department of Education and Science issued instructions to all local authorities to prepare plans for reorganising their secondary education on comprehensive lines; the present Conservative government has relaxed the 'instruction'—but

166

'comprehensive' has been with us in theory for a long time and the first authority in the United Kingdom, officially, to go comprehensive was Anglesey in 1952.

So, in most respects, the education of the Welshman of the twentieth century is the same as the education of his neighbour. As such it is a rich, liberal and effective training. At times it has suffered from not having devised a philosophy of its own to match its own national needs, though the ideal of the average Welshman remains 'getting on in the world' and for such, the world is wider than Wales. In a penetrating study of the provisions of education available in a coastal village in South Cardiganshire, published in the early sixties, the author, David Jenkins, remarks:—

"The syllabus is one which might be found in any secondary school in Britain; it is unrelated to purely local or specifically Welsh needs . . . The result of such education is to add prestige to distant affairs and to alienate boys and girls from the local culture."

This has been the dilemma in the education of Welshmen—whether the allegiance to a wider empire makes a superior demand over an awareness of belonging to the local community. It is not to say that both are, of necessity, incompatible, but the dichotomy exists.

Whether it is to everybody's liking or not, Wales has a separate identity discernible in its history and manifest in its language, literature and traditions. It is a basic principle of educational provision that it should be geared to the fabric of the society which it serves and so it is not surprising to find that the Welsh scene has characteristics and provisions of its own. In 1907, a Welsh Department of the Board of Education was established with a permanent secretary at its head. In 1970, responsibility for education in Wales was transferred to the Welsh Office under the overall supervision of the Secretary of State for Wales. The Welsh Joint Education Committee, established in 1948, provides the machinery for securing cooperation and unity of action between all Welsh authorities, and as such is a body of major importance in the discussion and implementation of educational policy in Wales. (It also administers the G.C.E., C.S.E., and various technical examinations and sponsors Welsh language books for schools—to mention some of its functions.) The Central Advisory Council for Education and the Schools Council have their own Welsh committees; their publication of papers on various topics has made a significant contribution to educational studies. In 1967 the Central Advisory Council published its thorough report on *Primary Education in Wales* under the chairmanship of Professor Charles Gittins. It is a report of major importance; many of its findings were in harmony with its counterpart in England, the *Plowden Report*. It suggested a division of primary education between 'first schools' and 'middle schools'; it emphasised the importance of nursery education; it proposed the establishment of certain deprived areas as 'educational priority areas'. It recommended that education should be fully bilingual, with English-speaking children being taught in English and learning Welsh as a second language and vice versa. The attitude of parents in these matters was to be respected and authorities were to supervise and publish their language policies and try to ensure effective teaching of the second language. A subject that called for special notice was the production of Welsh books for children. The findings of the Gittins Report will colour thinking about primary education in Wales for a long time.

Meanwhile institutions in Wales had been growing. The University of Wales had greatly increased its numbers; in 1920 a new college had been established at Swansea and in 1967, the College of Advanced Technology at Cardiff joined the University as the University of Wales Institute of Science and Technology. In 1971 Saint David's College, Lampeter, was incorporated into the University. The Welsh National School of Medicine, another constituent institution of the University, moved in 1971 to one of the finest hospital complexes in Europe. In 1964, Gregynog Hall was opened by the University as a residential centre where selected students from the constituent institutions could follow short field and study courses arranged by departments or groups of departments. The Open University appointed a Regional Director for Wales in October 1969 and by 1971 there were main study centres at Bangor, Wrexham, Aberystwyth, Haverfordwest, Swansea, Pontypridd, Cardiff and Newport. The colleges of Education have increased their numbers; there are nine in all in Wales. Under the aegis of the University of Wales School of Education they now prepare selected students for the B.Ed. degree. (If the recommendations of the *James Report* of recent date are accepted, the shape and function of these colleges may alter considerably.) The Glamorgan Polytechnic is at Treforest and there are technical colleges, colleges of technology and colleges of further education. There are agricultural colleges and now a Welsh National College of Agriculture at Aberystwyth. There are colleges of Art at Swansea, Cardiff, Newport and Carmarthen. The Cardiff College of Music and Drama is now the Welsh College of Music and Drama. The Welsh College of Librarianship is at Aberystwyth. Coleg Harlech, unique in Wales, provides a liberal education for mature students and although its prime function is not to prepare for university entrance, quite a number of students proceed from there to the University of Wales. Only the theological colleges have dwindled; there is a Methodist college at Aberystwyth, Independent colleges at Swansea and Bangor and Baptist colleges at Bangor and Cardiff; the Church in Wales offers theological training at Burgess Hall, Lampeter and St. Michael's College, Llandaff.

The twentieth century has witnessed an extraordinary growth of national consciousness in Wales. The foundation of national institutions—the National

Library opened in 1910, the National Museum opened in 1922 (with its 'daughter institution', the Welsh Folk Museum at St. Fagan's in 1948) have made a significant contribution to the education of Welshmen. National feeling probably prevented the defederalisation of the University at one time proposed and such consciousness has caused concern among some about the expansion of constituent colleges with the influx of non-Welsh students. There have been efforts to establish a college where Welsh would be the medium of instruction. Indeed most of the educational debate of the century has been concerned with the language issue. After the publication of *Welsh in Education and Life,* the report of the Departmental Committee of the Board of Education in 1927, an inspector was appointed with special responsibility for the teaching of Welsh. A good deal of thought has been given to improve the quality of Welsh language teaching and a National Language Unit was opened in Treforest in 1968 to prepare audio-visual language courses for the learner. The Welsh League of Youth (Urdd Gobaith Cymru) has educated generations of young Welshmen. It was under its aegis that the first Welsh language school was established at Aberystwyth in 1939; it heralded a spate of Welsh and bilingual schools, primary and secondary—and provision for teaching through the medium of Welsh to a limited extent throughout the whole of the educational system. There is a National Union of the Teachers of Wales (U.C.A.C.), a Welsh Books Council with concern for the distribution of vernacular literature (produced by a small band of Welsh publishers some of whose Welsh language titles are helped by subsidy from a government grant and from the Welsh Arts Council). The B.B.C. and I.T.V. provide a certain amount of Welsh language programmes and programmes in English about Wales.

The chapels have ceased to be the force that they were and the literary and debating societies have lost some of their popularity. But the Workers' Educational Association and the University extension classes continue to attract substantial numbers of people. The workmen's institutes of the earlier part of the century and the workmen's libraries have lost a good deal of their educational importance, though the new, well-organised county libraries and travelling libraries give excellent educational service and the Adult Education Centres run by the local education authorities now provide courses in a variety of non-vocational courses. Local societies of all kinds (Naturalists, Music, Artists, Historical, Scientific etc.) are active and the Eisteddfod continues to be a cultural event of national importance. The Welsh National Opera Company, the B.B.C. Welsh Orchestra and the activities of the Welsh Arts Council in literature, music, drama and art, have added to the cultural provisions for Welshmen.

* * * * *

In September 1962 a new and major experiment in international education was launched when the first United World College (then known as Atlantic College) was established in a medieval castle at St. Donat's in the vale of Glamorgan; it stands a short distance away from Llantwit Major the site of that seminary of distinction in the sixth century which prepared missionaries to evangelise Wales and Europe. Wales in 1972 finds itself on the brink of a new era—the European age. In many respects, the richest periods in the cultural history of Wales were those when it was most in contact with Europe. Maybe the education of the new Welshman will be the education of the *homo Europaeus* whose service to Wales will be greater because he will have come into contact with that ground that gave him root long, long ago.

SELECT BIBLIOGRAPHY

There is no comprehensive study of the history of education in Wales written in English. There are however useful pamphlets published by Her Majesty's Stationery Office. For the Welsh reader, *Addysg i Gymru* edited by Jac L. Williams as the fourth in his series "Ysgrifau ar Addysg", published by the University of Wales Press, Cardiff 1966, is very good. Useful too, are the excerpts (many of them in English) to be found in the first two volumes of the series "Llygad y Ffynnon" edited by Hugh Thomas and published by the University of Wales Press, Cardiff 1972.

E. G. Bowen, *Saints, Seaways and Settlements* (University of Wales Press, Cardiff, 1969).

The Dictionary of Welsh Biography down to 1940 (Honourable Society of Cymmrodorion, London, 1959).

D. Emrys Evans, *The University of Wales* (University of Wales Press, Cardiff, 1953).

D. Simon Evans, Introduction to Doble's *Lives of the Welsh Saints* (University of Wales Press, Cardiff, 1971).

Leslie Wynne Evans, *Education in Industrial Wales* 1700-1900 (Avalon Books, Cardiff, 1971).

W. R. Jones, *Bilingualism in Welsh Education* (University of Wales Press, Cardiff, 1966).

Pioneers of Welsh Education (Faculty of Education, University College of Swansea).

A. J. Roderick, *Wales through the Ages*, Volumes I and II (Christopher Davies, Llandybie, 1959, 1960).

Primary Education in Wales (the Gittins Report) (H.M.S.O. London, 1967).

David Williams, *A History of Modern Wales* (John Murray, London, 1950).

Glanmor Williams, *The Welsh Church from Conquest to Reformation* (University of Wales Press, Cardiff, 1962).

THE LANGUAGE AND LITERATURE
OF WALES

D. ELLIS EVANS

ALTHOUGH the point would need proper qualification it could be argued that the Welsh language is the one feature beyond all others that gives to the people of Wales a distinctive character. Closely bound up with this is the artistic use of the language in literary forms in a continuous tradition attested from the very earliest period in its development. In this essay we can only touch briefly on a few selected topics. An attempt will be made (*a*) to indicate some of the advances made in the study of the Welsh language, (*b*) to draw attention to the main periods in its history and to some of the features of its structure, and (*c*) to outline the history and dominant features of the literary tradition. Special attention will be given to the present situation of language contact in Wales and to the condition and progress of Welsh literature in the revival of the twentieth century.

The influence of historical and comparative linguistics had made itself felt in Welsh linguistic studies well before the end of the nineteenth century, though less by the epoch-making *Grammatica Celtica* of Zeuss (1853) than by the pioneer *Lectures on Welsh Philology* of Sir John Rhŷs (1877). The figure who dominated the progress of Welsh grammatical analysis for much of the twentieth century was Sir John Morris Jones, who studied at Oxford under Rhŷs. His major study of Welsh grammar published in 1913 left its mark on a longish succession of minor studies (by and large descriptive and often prescriptive grammars). But there have been significant advances in the stricter application of the methods of historical and comparative analysis. The valuable work of continental scholars, culminating in the magisterial comparative grammar of the Celtic languages of Holger Pedersen (1909-13), also bore fruit in the study of Welsh and important works of painstaking scholarship have emerged, mainly in the spheres of phonological studies, etymology, lexicography and lexical borrowing. In most of this work pride of place has been given to the written records of the language as source material. Indeed the work of the grammarians usually proceeded hand in hand with the vital tasks of textual criticism and the editing and annotating of texts. Apart from compiling dialect glossaries and word-lists little attention was paid to the structure and systems of the spoken dialects in the nineteenth and early twentieth century. In fact, apart from a handful of dissertations submitted for higher degrees of the University of Wales, little headway was made until after the Second World War. Since then the activity in Welsh dialect studies and oral traditions has grown apace in a number of centres in Wales. There has been a full spate of important dissertations and it is now envisaged that versions of these will appear in printed form under the sponsorship of the Board of Celtic Studies of the University of Wales.

Linguistics has earned a place in its own right in the University and some of the latest topics and theories in linguistic studies have been applied to the description and analysis of Welsh. We have only one sizeable guide to the linguistic study of Welsh, concentrating on 'morphology'. This is T. Arwyn Watkins's *Ieithyddiaeth* (1961), understandably (but indiscreetly) criticised for attempting both too little and too much. We await the publication of a new study of word geography and the result of a research project on the distillation of a standard spoken (platform or public) mode of Welsh. However we still lack a wide-ranging and detailed description of contemporary Welsh embracing much more than the crystallised and traditional norm. But a great deal of potentially important work is in progress, especially in the field of bilingualism and applied linguistics, e.g. on the attitudes of children of different ages to the teaching and learning of Welsh (and of English) in Wales and their motivation for learning, on the preparation of suitable courses for the teaching of Welsh at various levels involving audio-visual aids, and on the constituent structure of the language. The bilingual situation we have in Wales is, of course, not static and motivation and attitudes can change fairly quickly and dramatically. But there is a great need for research into psycho-linguistics and socio-linguistics with an inter-disciplinary approach to the enquiries. Good work in these fields of study could dispel some of the ignorance and demolish some of the false theories bedevilling attempts at understanding the bilingual problem and the problem of language shift and erosion in Wales. Incidentally, serious and sensitive attention is at long last being given also to examining features of the English language in Wales.

The research work that has been done does enable us to understand a great deal of the history and development of the Welsh language. The question of origins, however, is still shrouded in a number of dark and insoluble problems. Scholars are now less dogmatic about the location of the cradle of the Celts and the position of the Celtic group of languages in relation to other members of the Indo-European family. There is a greater awareness of the need to establish the chronology of various correspondences and to take proper cognizance of typological considerations. Although it has not been totally demolished the old Italo-Celtic theory has taken some very hard knocks. Also some cautious, but attractive, suggestions have been made concerning correspondences between Celtic and Thracian, Phrygian and Iranian.

The Brittonic and Celtic and Indo-European ancestry of Welsh is certain. But the exact lines of cleavage and the chronology of divergence within Western Indo-European and within Celtic itself and the effect of pre-Celtic substrata on the systems of Celtic languages are all still subject to speculation. By the comparative and historical study of both Celtic and non-Celtic languages we are able to reconstruct to a limited extent the structure of the parent language Brittonic. The Latin intrusion in Brittonic reflects a stage of linguistic interference (by no means entirely lexical) commencing in the Roman period in Britain. It has received special attention because it is valuable for outlining the various changes which characterise the transformation of certain dialects of Brittonic into new languages. This transformation is now thought to have been more gradual, to have been less of a landslide, than some scholars used to imply. But by the second half of the sixth century the changes that had occurred were sufficiently fundamental and extensive as to result in the emergency of language systems for which we can justify the labels Early Welsh, Early Cornish and Early Breton. As the unity of the Brittonic speech communities was broken in the sixth and seventh centuries and thereafter the stream of changes caused a widening of local differences ultimately producing distinct and separate languages.

It is convenient to apply labels to particular periods in the history of the language although the dates suggested are fairly vague and not particularly illuminating. Thus Early or Primitive Welsh is the term used for the period from about the middle of the sixth century to the later eighth century. The dating of the transition from Early Welsh to Old Welsh coincides with that of the change from a period when extant records are exceedingly sparse (in inscriptions and Latin texts) to one in which texts written in Welsh become more abundant and more significant. Even then they are comparatively meagre. Although these have been studied in detail by a succession of eminent scholars their full significance will not emerge until manuscript sources are combed and scrutinised anew and the Old Welsh material is edited as a whole and analysed systematically. Incidentally, these sources reveal the use of Welsh to deal with fairly abstruse and technical matters such as weights and measures and calendrical computation.

The Middle Welsh period is rich in source material and may be said to extend from about the middle of the twelfth century to about the end of the fourteenth. It is a period of great variety in prose and verse, tales and romances, legal texts, historical (or quasi-historical) and religious and devotional works, medical tracts, grammars and metrical treatises, early poetry from the *hengerdd* period preserved in manuscripts from the Middle Welsh period, court poetry and the works of the early *cywyddwyr*. The beginning of the period was one of turmoil in which external influences flooded in, resulting eventually in a renaissance in Welsh literature and in an enrichment of the language. For Middle Welsh we have the well-ordered and thorough-going grammar of D. Simon Evans (published in Welsh in 1951 and in a valuable extended English version in 1964). But in this period too there is plenty of room for further study of the structure of the language, e.g. through analyses based on a stratification of sources, through the extracting of further information concerning dialectal traits and orthography and through a more systematic study of a topic such as semantics. The end of the Middle Welsh period is very ill-defined. The suggestion that it comes towards the end of the fourteenth century rests arbitrarily on a vague literary criterion; it is sometimes linked with the appearance of the poetry of Dafydd ap Gwilym. A divide based on internal linguistic change is so far difficult to establish although it has been suggested that orthographic changes seem to justify a later date about the middle of the fifteenth century. The Modern period is traditionally divided into Early Modern up to the sixteenth century (only the syntax and semantics of this period have been studied in any depth) and Late Modern dating roughly from the late sixteenth century to the present day. From the point of view of external history the late sixteenth century and early seventeenth was a fateful time for the language, a period of peril and dilemma and one that saw the growth of what has been termed a new 'belief in the vernacular'.

In outlining the characteristic features of Welsh we must recognise at once that it is basically Celtic, and that it and its sister languages Cornish and Breton resulted from the gradual splitting of the parent language Brittonic. Brittonic and Goidelic (the precursor of Irish, Scots Gaelic and Manx) were the two main varieties of Insular Celtic. The Celtic branch is fairly clearly differentiated from the other branches of Indo-European. One of the more interesting sound changes that had occurred by the Common Celtic period was the loss of Indo-European *p*. Thus Welsh has *edn* (also the related form *aderyn*) 'bird' and Irish has *én* beside Latin *penna* 'feather' (English *feather* is itself cognate, with *f-* from earlier *p-*). Welsh and the other Brittonic languages later recovered a consonant *p* from the development of an Indo-European labio-velar consonant (it also occurred in words adopted from other languages). Thus Welsh has *p-* in *pedwar* 'four' beside Latin *quattuor*. Irish here shows a velar *c-* (earlier *q*) in *cethir*. This is the origin of the old tags P and Q used to differentiate the two main branches of Insular Celtic. Welsh has cast off many of the morphological traits still present in other Indo-European languages. The neuter disappeared altogether. The old case endings were dropped leaving only very few traces in certain formations. This resulted from the weakening and loss of the old final syllables of Brittonic formations— the most important of all the changes involved in the transformation of the parent language. The Welsh verb, it is true, did retain many examples of old morphological processes, some of which have been adduced as uniquely important evidence for reconstructing the history of Indo-European. But by and large the verbal system has been transformed and has developed a system of periphrastic patterns in which a highly complex use is made of auxiliary verbs and of elements denoting various shades of verbal aspect. The general historical trend in the development of Welsh appears to be in the direction of a more isolating type of structure. But there are clear tendencies in other directions in some word-classes and categories.

The vocabulary is basically Celtic and ultimately Indo-European, as in *brawd* beside English *brother* and Latin *frater*, *tri* beside English *three* and Latin *tres*, *môr* 'sea' beside English *mere* and Latin *mare*, and *credu* 'believe' beside Latin *credo*. But, as is to be expected, Welsh does reflect the adoption of very many words from other languages with which it came into contact at various periods in its development. It borrowed from Latin and Irish and Norse and Norman French and, most of all, from English. The English element is nowadays becoming increasingly prominent and unassimilated, and therefore corrosive and injurious.

A characteristic feature that Welsh shares with all the other Insular Celtic languages is the mutation of initial consonants—in origin a series of systematic sound changes which had important results in the structure of these languages. Thus, according to one old theory which has been variously refined and qualified, Celtic had a system whereby consonants had a comparatively strong and a comparatively weak articulation depending on their environment. A weak single form in initial position following a preceding word ending in a vowel could undergo a systematic sound shift by the late Brittonic period. This meant that initial consonants could vary because their environment varied. Brittonic *pennos maros* resulted in *pen mawr* 'a big head' in Welsh whereas *inissi mara* gave *ynys fawr* 'a big island' with *fawr* instead of *mawr*. Gradually this type of mutation became productive in Welsh after the historical sound change had taken place. This so-called soft mutation acquired many functions, one of which was the marking of the feminine gender. The other types of consonantal mutations (nasal and spirant) also acquired grammatical status. Vowel alternation too is characteristic of Welsh. Although it is in some ways less common in present day Welsh (e.g. as a marker of number or of gender in *bardd* 'poet'/*beirdd* 'poets' and in *gwyn* (masc.)/*gwen* (fem.) 'white') than it was formerly it is still a prominent and complex feature attached to specific words and certain inflexional and derivational systems. Another curious construction that Welsh shares with the other Celtic languages is the fusing of personal pronouns with certain prepositions resulting in systematic conjugational paradigms (*gan* 'with': *gennyf* 'with me', *gennyt* 'with thee', etc.). A similar feature occurs in Semitic and is not unparalleled in Indo-European languages other than the Celtic ones.

Lastly, Welsh shows great complexity in sentence structure in regard to word order and rules of concord. There has been plenty of speculation on these matters. Firm conclusions have been properly drawn concerning some features; opinion concerning others (e.g. patterns such as *gwŷr a aeth* 'the men went' or *aeth gwŷr*) is still unstable. In fact we are only beginning to learn about the mechanisms and transformations that are attested in sentences of various types in Welsh.

However we must now turn to consider the present position of the language. A great deal of information concerning the recession of Welsh and the ascendancy of English in Wales during this century is available in the series of reports affecting the question of language that were presented to Parliament by various government departments. There are, of course, Census reports giving figures for Welsh speakers in Wales, commencing in 1891 (in 1911, 1951 and 1961 these figures were gathered together in separate volumes). Apart from these there have been at least five major government reports, the most important of which were perhaps the classic *Welsh in Education and Life* of 1927 and the defiant and buoyant Gittins Report on *Primary Education in Wales* of 1967 (a full list of references to other reports and many other studies will be found in Glanville Price's selective bibliography cited at the end of this essay).

So far no scholar has produced a comprehensive and detailed analysis of the external history and fortunes of Welsh. But we do know that over four hundred years of official proscription of the language and deprivation of the language of its prestige and authority eventually resulted in its decline and serious decay. And yet eighty years ago, if we are to rely on the Census figures for 1891, the majority of the population of Wales (54·4 per cent) were speakers of Welsh. The proportion of Welsh speakers had been more than halved (26 per cent) by the 1961 Census and the number of monoglot speakers was negligible (1 per cent). Many factors had contributed to the continuation of Welsh as a language known to the majority of the people of Wales until the end of the last century—not least the translation of the Scriptures into Welsh, the publishing of Welsh books, the Circulating Schools of the eighteenth century and the Sunday Schools of the heyday of Welsh Nonconformity. It has been cogently argued that industrialisation in the last century resulted in a redistribution of a growing population which kept people in Wales and spared the language from the major disaster that would have resulted from a mass rural exodus to England or overseas. Nevertheless industrialisation did undermine the language and culture of Wales in the second half of the century. If Welsh-speakers were kept in Wales there was also a great influx of people who did not speak Welsh into the industrial areas.

By 1901 only 15·1 per cent of the population are reported as monoglot Welsh-speakers. The continuing decline in what has been termed 'the hardcore who made it necessary for immigrants to learn Welsh' is an exceedingly bad omen for the revival of Welsh. An important factor here is the deliberate, though haphazard, attempt to prosecute the Department of Education's official policy of bilingualism, spelled out in 1953 in the report on *The Place of Welsh and English in the Schools of Wales*. Some purists and leading protagonists of the revival of Welsh have understandably predicted that this bilingual policy endangers the very life and foundation of the language. It is argued that the disappearance of monoglot speakers of Welsh will result in the final foundering of the language.

It must be remembered that Census figures concerning language are notoriously unreliable in regard to both the accuracy of the actual form-filling and the imprecise nature of the categories concerning which information is gathered in. There are various grades or degrees of bilingualism. Also there is a very wide range of variation in the amount of use made by individuals of Welsh or English and in the contact they make with the two languages. The quality of the language or languages transmitted by parents to their children can vary enormously. There is plenty of evidence of great impoverishment and a near collapse in quality in Welsh resulting from a reduction or restriction in the actual use of the language. English has penetrated and contaminated not only the vocabulary but also the basic patterns and idioms of Welsh. But this is certainly not as fateful and pervasive as some prophets of doom would have us believe.

The Gittins Report proposed that 'every child (in Wales) should be given sufficient opportunity to become reasonably bilingual by the end of the primary stage, i.e. between eleven and thirteen years'. How far its suggestions will be put into practice will depend very largely on the attitude of local education authorities and of teachers and parents. New attitudes and new methods and utter dedication and enthusiasm in teaching are vitally important. The compulsory implementation of a *thorough-going* bilingualism in the schools of Wales is, alas, neither practicable nor acceptable at present. The attempt to impose the minority language would probably not overcome the disinclination to learn it. The comparative success and steady growth of special Welsh-medium or bilingual schools (*Ysgolion Cymraeg*), both primary and secondary, to which parents send their children from choice, are the most hopeful signs on the educational front.

The demand for the recognition of Welsh as an official language of legal standing has in recent years been voiced most unequivocally by the Welsh Language Society established by young people in response to Saunders Lewis's challenging and aggressive 1962 radio lecture on 'The Fate of the Language'. Many leading Welshmen, firmly believing that the Welsh language is the supreme expression of the uniqueness of the Welsh as a people, gave the society support and guidance. Most notably the late Professor J. R. Jones, a philosopher of great integrity and incomparable passion, somehow summoned up that tremendous courage that is born of grim despair—the despair that can overwhelm a person confronted by the suffocating death of his mother tongue and of everything that is associated with it; this was movingly recorded in the writings of the last few years of his life. The challenging militancy, the irrepressible campaign to increase the prestige of Welsh and to extend the use of the language on mass media and in administration and before the law, the resort to public violence, must be viewed in the light of that sort of anguish, allied to an understandably impatient desire to get things done in order to try to reverse the tide of recession. The language issue has become a political matter. There are those who claim that political action must be taken to deal with all manner of social and economic factors that are thought to be causing a decline in the use of Welsh. Others realise that a greater measure of self-government would not wipe out the fear for the future of the language, would not necessarily lead to a greater measure of tolerance of differences in language. Militancy has already had the effect of sharpening and embittering the conflict in language loyalty in Wales.

The revival of Welsh must depend on the will of a sufficient number of people to retain it and use it and transmit it; this requires that the active use of Welsh in as many spheres of life as possible be shown to be and known to be an enjoyable and enriching and distinctively attractive normality. It has been rightly and poignantly emphasised anew that 'Welsh should not really be an end in itself; it should be the means of adding to one's enrichment of . . . life in a bilingual community'. The genuine and zestful desire among people of all ages to use Welsh naturally and freely is the only hope for the healthy survival and revival of the language. This is especially true now when language has become the plaything of an intolerant society in a disastrous game of pseudo-issues of language and of over-charging language alternatives with a new and imperfectly understood symbolic content.

Now we must begin our remarks concerning Welsh literature with a gloomy reference to the fact that the oldest sources that have survived have to be treated with extreme caution, not only because of the fragmentary and often abstruse nature of the records but also because we are all the while beset with unfamiliar concepts. All this makes the task of interpretation and appreciation quite arduous. Also we have to realise that the earliest Welsh literature continues Celtic traditions shared with Ireland and is part of the heritage that derives ultimately from the civilisation of the Celts at the peak of their brilliant artistic creativity in ancient Europe in the second half of the first millennium B.C. There are references in some of the comments of classical writers to the bards, the poets who sang 'to the accompaniment of instruments resembling lyres, sometimes a eulogy and sometimes a satire', who sang 'the valorous deeds of famous men composed in heroic verse'—poets who were entertainers and an important, influential and privileged professional class in time of war as well as in peace. But no work from the early Celtic period has been preserved simply because the early literature was related or sung and transmitted orally from one generation to the other. However the fact that the Celts were virtually illiterate until the Christian era does not mean that they were uneducated. An interesting passage in the work of Diodorus Siculus refers to the bombast of the Celts but also to the fact that they were 'quick of mind and with good natural ability for learning'. They needed little inducement to devote themselves to intellectual and artistic pursuits. Certainly their memory was unspoilt. They were well-accustomed and often thoroughly trained to retain lore and literature and all manner of traditional material. The amazing strength of oral tradition has been witnessed in Ireland right down to this twentieth century.

The earliest extant Welsh literature is in verse but in various ways the poetry itself often points to the existence of a wealth of early prose sagas, a body of literature that was much more extensive in range and quantity than we can now perceive. There are obvious and striking similarities to the earliest tradition in Ireland—in regard to recording native lore in triadic verse, in the production of certain forms of heroic literature, of poetry dealing with battle-exploits and other contests, poems of intercession, poems seeking reconciliation, request poems and bardic controversies, magnificent elegiac and celebratory and eulogistic verse, in regard to the emphasis laid on genealogy and the prominence given to catalogue poems, gnomic verse and nature poetry, riddles, mantic verse and poems of prophecy. Common features must derive in part from a common origin in an earlier age and in part result from contact and fusion in the community of the so-called Irish Sea province. The background is Celtic, although by the time of the earliest sources the literature has to be viewed in the context of Latin learning and ecclesiastic intrusion and disorientation. Therefore a richer understanding of our earliest literature is to be got by trying to understand more fully its cultural and social background and by comparison with the early Irish material (e.g. in regard to presentation and transmission, mythology and motifs, metrics and other embellishments). However, there is clearly a danger in making a fetish of comparison and of analysis of the background. But the archaism of the Welsh tradition should command attention and respect. The *Cynfeirdd* (early poets), the *cyfarwyddiaid* (tellers of tales) of Wales were in their profession and function in direct descent from the bards and entertainers of Celtic antiquity. This is part of the immense attraction of the earliest literature.

Here we shall touch on some of the highlights of the tradition in a manner which must, alas, be ruthlessly selective. We will try to concentrate on matters of consequence and give pride of place to the twentieth century renaissance and the standard and mood of fairly recent work.

The earliest extant literature survives in manuscripts dating from as late as the twelfth century onwards (with one or two minor exceptions). The precise dating, the manner of compilation and transmission and frequently even the meaning of the texts of a great deal of the work of the early poets are still occasioning a lot of uncertain theorising. For example, the celebratory stanzas of the Book of Aneirin may in some measure, directly or indirectly, reflect the work of a poet Aneirin using an early form of Welsh in the late sixth century in the land of the Gododdin between the Forth and Tyne in the Brittonic North. But there are accretions and interpolations in the text and it is exceedingly difficult to establish what is the genuine core of the work of a poet such as Aneirin or even to determine whether any of his work survives intact. The peculiar structure of the work attributed to Aneirin may not be primary; it seems to be the result of a longish process of compilation of songs, in part *perhaps* task or competitive poems imitating the earlier work of the sixth century poet. Be that as it may, like so much else in the early poetry these stanzas are both terse and tragic, both heroic and tender, the artistic and skilful work of professional poets who still had an important function in society. The poetry is richly adorned with a free but increasingly intricate and elaborate patterning of sound correspondences (this later evolved into a strict and stabilised system of alliteration and rhyme known as *cynghanedd*). There is no doubt that very much of the early poetry has been lost for ever. Sometimes we are left with only the bare names of some of the earliest poets; sometimes the authors of the scattered poems that have been preserved are unknown or uncertain.

The tradition of eulogy and elegy predominates in the court poetry of the princes in the eleventh and twelfth centuries although here too there are religious, nature and love poems. This work frequently reflects a great intellectual power and originality. Verbal ingenuity, allusiveness of style and archaism (including the conscious echoing of the work of earlier poets) are common. There is clear evidence of the social function of the poetry, of the duty of the poet to praise the leaders of society in his day. For various reasons we know all too little about the bardic order itself, its grades and hierarchy, the intricate rules of the bard's craft, his legal and social status and privileges, his long training and the methods employed in his instruction.

The medieval Welsh prose that is extant, some of it probably written at least as early as the eleventh century, has a wide range in quality and character. There is, for instance, a wealth of legal texts in Welsh, prose of a very high order in which are expressed precise descriptions and definitions and complex distinctions. In the internationally famous collection of saga literature known as *The Mabinogion* the most remarkable of the tales are probably *The Four Branches of the Mabinogi* and *Culhwch and Olwen*. These are chock-full of the tantalising debris of old mythological themes and motifs. They reveal in different ways a most effective mastery of style, less consciously ornate and baneful than some other tales and later rhetorical exercises and parodies. The sophisticated romances *Owein and Luned, Geraint and Enid* and *Peredur* show more abundant evidence of Norman influence. The precise relationship between these well-known Welsh texts and French counterparts is still not clear, but hardly anyone would now deny a native Welsh origin in an earlier tradition. Recently it has been demonstrated that the thirteenth and fourteenth centuries saw the production of an important and substantial body of prose literature, especially translations (mostly from Latin and French) of various technical manuals, chronicles, tales and legends and a welter of theological and religious works. This reflects in no small measure the opening of the flood-gates to admit the wider learning and culture of Western Europe into the mainstream of Welsh literature; it shows the importance of the learned, ecclesiastical, monastic context in which this literature blossomed. The comparative poverty of the native tradition may have impeded the creation of a prose as virile and rich as that of the later Renaissance period.

Wales produced much of its greatest poetry from the fourteenth century onwards, especially in the golden age of the *cywydd* from the middle of the fourteenth to the middle of the fifteenth century. The *cywydd* is a verse form that dominated the output of the so-called poets of the aristocracy of the later

Middle Ages and the Early Modern period, a rich and varied genre with its own special modes and conventions. Eulogy and elegy are still prominent themes, but there is also high seriousness of thought and austere instruction and commentary on life's tribulations and purpose, and there are supplications, petitions, contentions and prophecies and a good deal of poetic jesting. The poetry of the *cywyddwyr* is renowned for its artistry and verbal skill, its syntactic breaks and side-steps, its sparkling epigrams and its constant love of subtle counterpoint. Of the *cywyddwyr* Dafydd ap Gwilym (*c.* 1325-80) was the most inspired and truly imaginative and playful genius, a brilliant master of the new idiom and a great influence on his contemporaries and on many of his successors. He was indeed one of the greatest poets of medieval Europe.

With the Reformation and the Renaissance the need for a more adequate medium of expression resulted in the cultivation of a new prose to express the ideas and thoughts of the age. And this coincided with the first appearance of printed books in Welsh towards the middle of the sixteenth century. It is only a slight oversimplification to claim that the production of the New Testament (1567), the Book of Common Prayer (1567) and the Bible (1588) in Welsh gave Wales a standard vernacular. The translation of the Bible was undoubtedly the supreme contribution of the age to Welsh literature. From then on Welsh prose books (mostly translations) appeared without break in defence of the principles of Protestantism; Catholic exiles also produced publications to counteract the Protestant propaganda; both Protestants and Catholics were imbued with the ideas and ideals of the Renaissance. The Welsh Language was rescued from inferiority and further degradation; it was greatly enriched and stabilised to reveal fresh vigour in the majesty and beauty of humanistic prose. The Puritan writer, Morgan Llwyd, produced a major prose classic, rhetorical and eloquent, in his *Llyfr y Tri Aderyn* (1653). Later writers produced further outstanding prose work the most notable of which was probably Ellis Wynne's *Gweledigaetheu y Bardd Cwsc* (1703).

The seventeenth and eighteenth centuries saw the emergence of free metre popular poetry, less professional and reflecting English influence. There was a vogue for carols, folk-poetry and ballads and the popular versified drama known as interludes (*anterliwdiau*). From the middle of the eighteenth century there was a fruitful poetic revival associated in particular with the Morris brothers of Anglesey and Goronwy Owen—poets well versed in both the classics of the ancient world and in the native tradition and also well aware of the Augustan classicist models of their day in England. In contrast to this activity stands the hymn-writing that resulted from the religious revivals of that century. William Williams of Pantycelyn (1717-91) was the greatest interpreter of the Methodist Revival. His many memorable writings are the fruit of spasms of profound inspiration which produced a passionately personal and deeply spiritual literature that is still slightly mysterious in its fervour and intensity.

The vast and varied literary output of the nineteenth century is at long last being eyed with a healthier measure of respect and appreciation. Here we can only mention three outstanding figures. Islwyn (1832-78) was a great pensive poet. For all the difficulty and alleged confusion of his work he has fairly consistently attracted the appreciative attention of the ablest of our literary critics down to this very day. Secondly, Daniel Owen (1836-95), Wales's only novelist of great genius, stands out as one critic put it 'like a great mountain on wide plains'; his work is particularly strong in characterisation and dialogue; his great feat was to mirror and interpret the mood of change in Victorian Wales with artistry, vitality and imagination; an air of almost truculent pessimism pervades his work, relieved by frequent and brilliant flashes of a more benign humour. Then thirdly Emrys ap Iwan (1851-1906), a man of great critical intelligence, came heavily under the influence of continental ideas and writers and challenged his contemporaries in pamphlets and critical essays and sermons. Although his main purpose was to restore self-respect and confidence to his own people, his work is important in the development of modern Welsh prose. His style is modelled on that of earlier humanistic prose classics, incisive, clear, refined and carefully structured.

The Welsh language was destined yet again to be a brilliant tool in the hands of the writers of a new and amazing literary reawakening. Towards the end of the nineteenth century and during the first half of the twentieth Wales was blessed with a succession of literary giants of imaginative creativeness. Many of these were in various ways connected with the University of Wales, founded in 1872. We have mentioned Sir John Morris Jones (1864-1929) already—the grammarian and dogmatic critic who propagated his ideas about purism and rigid standards in diction and usage and about what he considered to be aesthetically proper. Another was T. Gwynn Jones (1871-1949) who dominated the literary scene in Wales in the early part of this century as scholar, critic, translator and above all as a poet intensely concerned about his craft. He experimented with the strict metres and transformed them to convey his own emotions delicately and fluently; he returned idealistically and sensitively to early Welsh and Celtic history and legends for inspiration; he had a fine sense of rhythm and a marvellous gift for the evocation of a mood. Several other writers played a major role in the revival and in the widening of horizons: R. Williams Parry (1884-1956) was pre-eminent among nature poets and developed from an early sensuous, well-nigh magical romanticism to an attitude that was more fearful and grim and to a more biting and intense social consciousness; W. J. Gruffydd (1881-1954) was a writer of varied gifts and of violently conflicting tendencies and contradictions, including, for example, both a rebellion against narrow Victorian standards and a kindly nostalgia for the society of his youth—he was poet and essayist and story writer, scholar and critic, biographer and autobiographer, but he probably exerted most influence as the lively and critical editor from 1922 to 1951 of the literary periodical *Y Llenor*, a quarterly of very high standing indeed; Sir Thomas Parry-Williams (b. 1887) is a very distinguished scholar, a poet and pre-eminently an essayist, metaphysical, introspective, cynical, even despairing, exploring the reality of human experience and the mystery of the universe in a style that is terse, polished, unaffected and really powerful.

In the third and fourth decades of the century Welsh writers strike new notes of patriotism and political nationalism, of social unrest and Christian commitment. Chief among them were Saunders Lewis (b. 1893), with his European outlook, his fervent nationalism and immense respect for the native tradition, and the well-beloved poet and scholar D. Gwenallt Jones (1899-1968). Gwenallt's views evolved from a leftist socialism that was hostile to religion to an ardent patriotism and deep religious conviction. His poetry has been popular and influential not only because of its challenging concepts and deep sincerity but also because a lot of it is celebrated for its fine phrasing and subtle cadency.

So far we have limited our references in the main to some of the leading poets of the revival up to the time of the Second World War. But important advances were made too in prose writing, in works of scholarship (especially in historiography), in essays and criticism, in prose fiction, biography and autobiography, in literature of travel and in translations of literary classics from other languages. But fewer writers of prose established themselves as figures of great distinction. Here we will mention only one or two authors who have been in the forefront as short-story writers and novelists. Kate Roberts (b. 1891) has written sensitively and vividly in her short-stories and novels of the struggle of characters, mainly women, from the rural society in which she was brought up, a struggle against poverty and adversity and all manner of pressures and affliction. There is a sad stoicism and pathos in her work and an awesome respect for life. She has also responded with splendid resilience and versatility to contemporary problems. D. J. Williams (1885-1970) too was at his best in his writing about the home of his youth. His work is lively, humorous and kindly, but also at times bitingly satirical and unashamedly propagandist. A strong flavour of his native Carmarthenshire dialect enriches his sprightly prose and all his work reflects his relish for colourful and interesting characters and personalities.

The forties and fifties saw the maturing of other important authors. The best novels of T. Rowland Hughes (1903-49), subtly nostalgic and benevolent, humorous and often impassioned, again centred on a local community; they placed him in the position that most nearly approached that of Daniel Owen's genius. Then J. Gwilym Jones (b. 1903) wrote musing psychological essays and resourceful and sensitive plays analysing social problems. Playwrights of distinction writing in Welsh are rare. Saunders Lewis is probably the noblest, the most powerful and versatile of Welsh dramatists. His earliest play, in verse, *Blodeuwedd* (completed in 1947), is a singularly beautiful and delicate poetic re-creation of an ageless theme taken from the fourth branch of the Mabinogi—a theme of love and hate and of the mystery both of human fellowship and otherworldly forces. Waldo Williams (1904-71) was certainly one of the century's finest poets, mystic and ascetic, deeply religious and introspective and sorrowfully concerned with contemporary problems; he had a most remarkable vision of both the universal and the particular, of the cross-weave of human society and of the mystery of self-identity.

It now becomes increasingly difficult to name names and to estimate what contemporary work will stand the test of time. This is not made easier by the recent deceptive increase in the number of literary or quasi-literary books published in Welsh and the tendency towards greater diversity in content and often artless widening of horizons. The comparative abundance of material stems very largely from a more liberal monetary patronage of publishers and authors alike from governmental funds, an artificial prompting or shoring up that is not without its dangers. This type of increase in output *can* coincide with a lowering of standards, a diminution of creative power and a temporary cultural or quasi-cultural frenzy when the medium of expression is critically impaired or imperilled. Nevertheless those who have turned to Welsh writing for the pleasure and satisfaction that great literature can give will not have been disappointed by some of the poetry of the late fifties and sixties, especially the work of Euros Bowen, Bobi Jones and Gwyn Thomas and other younger poets. The most notable contributions in prose in this period have come, with a few exceptions, from an older generation of authors such as Kate Roberts, D. J. Williams, Tegla Davies and Caradog Pritchard.

Sweeping generalisations concerning features thought to be peculiar to the Welsh literary tradition have little or no value. One could argue, for instance, that there is a constant awareness of tradition and an impulse to preserve that tradition in Welsh literature; that there is always a more or less clear note of nationalism; that there is nostalgia and by and large a strong religious tone and a sensitivity to another world; that there is always the sustaining of a myth of deliverance and heroic triumph; that there is an appreciation of the music and magic of words, a love of a richly expressive and ornamented form, a fondness for an epigrammatic turn of phrase. But the vital point after all is the tenaciousness, the resilience, the flexibility of the literary tradition. It has been a permanent tradition despite many violent jolts and many phases of innovation; it has amazingly survived the very severe damage to the structure of Welsh society in this twentieth century, through two destructive wars and periods of depopulation and depression and erosion of the vernacular.

Moreover it is not easy for us to assess aright the restless mood and disturbed awareness displayed by present-day writers of literature in Welsh. But we must note that there does appear to be a new orientation, an air of serious and vital concern that is by no means despairing or vengeful, a contemplation, a meditation that is mercifully tinged with hope and confidence as well as dismay. There are still diverse authors of great distinction writing in Welsh who in their literary creation earnestly strive to understand and express permanent human values and qualities in a world that is full of sorrow and wrath and contention.

185

SELECT BIBLIOGRAPHY

Sam Adams and Gwilym Rees Hughes, eds., *Triskel One: Essays on Welsh and Anglo-Welsh Literature* (Christopher Davies, Swansea and Llandybïe, 1971).

Joseph P. Clancy, *Medieval Welsh Lyrics* (Macmillan, London, 1965).

Joseph P. Clancy, *The Earliest Welsh Poetry* (Macmillan, London, 1970).

Anthony Conran, *The Penguin Book of Welsh Verse* (Penguin Books, Harmondsworth, 1967).

Elwyn Davies, ed., *Celtic Studies in Wales: a Survey* (University of Wales Press, Cardiff, 1963).

D. Simon Evans, *A Grammar of Middle Welsh* (The Dublin Institute for Advanced Studies, Dublin, 1964).

Kenneth Jackson, *Language and History in Early Britain* (Edinburgh University Press, Edinburgh, 1953).

R. Brinley Jones, *The Old British Tongue* (Avalon Books, Cardiff, 1970).

W. R. Jones, *Bilingualism in Welsh Education* (University of Wales Press, Cardiff, 1966).

Henry Lewis and Holger Pedersen, *A Concise Comparative Celtic Grammar* (Vandenhoeck u. Ruprecht, Göttingen, 1961).

Proinsias MacCana, *Celtic Mythology* (Hamlyn, London, 1970).

Gerald Morgan, *The Dragon's Tongue: the fortunes of the Welsh Language* (The Triskel Press, Cardiff, 1966).

Thomas Parry, *A History of Welsh Literature*, translated from the Welsh by H. Idris Bell (Clarendon Press, Oxford, 1955).

Thomas Parry, ed., *The Oxford Book of Welsh Verse* (Clarendon Press, Oxford, 1962).

Glanville Price, *The Present Position of Minority Languages in Western Europe: a Selective Bibliography* (University of Wales Press, Cardiff, 1969).

Ned Thomas, *The Welsh Extremist: a Culture in Crisis* (Gollancz, London, 1971).

J. E. Caerwyn Williams, ed., *Literature in Celtic Countries* (University of Wales Press, Cardiff, 1971).

THIN SPRING AND TRIBUTARY
WELSHMEN WRITING IN ENGLISH

ROLAND MATHIAS

IN a Wales where three-quarters of the population have no tongue but English, Anglo-Welsh writing—that is, writing in the English language by men or women of Welsh birth, descent or association—is an entrenched reality, indeed an inevitability, even if there exists no worthwhile Anglo-Welsh literary culture amongst the English-speakers of Wales to match it. Without such a culture the bilingual Wales that many envisage will prove rather a territory sadly and unsympathetically divided. Yet the remarkable twentieth century achievement of the Anglo-Welsh, especially in poetry, is either ignored by readers who have had an education orientated exclusively towards the peaks of a purely *English* culture or treated at the level of an individualised and dylanesque myth about the Welsh, of sociological rather than literary significance. That this situation has some of the dimensions of tragedy cannot be doubted, and the time for altering it may be very limited. The future identity of Wales may conceivably depend more upon the achievement of such an alteration than upon any other single factor.

But this is to run before the horse to market. It is first of importance to establish the manner in which the English language grafted itself upon Wales and to discern in those who came to use it, willingly or unwillingly, the vocational or cultural motivation for writing in it. This in turn may throw some light on the nature and scale of the achievement of such writers before the twentieth century and point the changes both in intention and quality as the language became in Wales a majority tongue rather than the vehicle of small and clearly defined classes.

The first settlement of English in the territorial area of Wales began in 1109, when Flemings whose homes had been inundated in the floods of 1106-7 and who had first been 'planted' along the Tweed were given lands about the upper reaches of the Cleddau in Dyfed, probably to prevent any recurrence of that night raid on Pembroke Castle the previous Christmas in which Owain ap Cadwgan had carried off the Princess Nest. Historians have been bland and assumptive about this event rather than analytical: Camden applied his now well-thumbed phrase *Anglia Transwallina* only to the hundred of Rhos, in which the Flemings were actually settled, not to all the hundreds south of the Landsker in which English has been the dominant, perhaps the only, language since the middle of the twelfth century. George Owen of Henllys surmised that far more Englishmen than Flemings were planted, and the extent to which clearance and colonisation took place up to a language line which Southall's map of 1892 shows as remarkably valid even then has never been sufficiently examined. In the most southerly parts of this cleared zone the burr in the speech of villagers suggests settlement from Somerset and Devon, probably as the result of cross-channel trade. This last factor, mentioned with a vagueness complementary to that noticeable in the discussion of Little England beyond Wales, is supposed also to have anglicised the peninsula of Gower, at a time uncertain but probably before the fifteenth century.

These two clearances of Welsh speakers were confirmed and stabilised by constant contact with Bristol, Bridgwater, Barnstaple and other English ports, in much the same way as Pembroke Dock, with its naval tradition, was in the first half of the twentieth century sustained by its vocational and family connections with Portsmouth, Devonport and Chatham. It should be plain, therefore, that Anglo-Welsh poets like Sir Roger Lorte of Stackpole (1608-1664), George Stepney of Prendergast (1663-1707) and Sir John Scourfield of Williamston (1808-76) were as much the product of their home environment as of their Oxford or Cambridge education, and that Anna Williams of Rosemarket (1706-83), however much she may have owed to Dr. Johnson, likewise had no option but to write in English. Amongst poets writing now, Peter Preece of Stackpole and Gower-born Harri Webb began from the same position.

The establishment of royal burghs, chiefly in North Wales, occasioned the planting of a few more Englishmen, while the punitive laws which forbade Welshmen to become burgesses strengthened the anglicising effects of the commerce on which towns were based. But in terms of numbers this was a minor development, ultimately little more important than the fact that the few Welsh chapmen and travelling entertainers became acquainted with English. Of greater significance was the need for Welsh students to attend university in England or abroad, at Paris, Padua or Seville. Long before Jesus College was founded at Oxford in 1571 Oriel had been a gathering-ground for Welsh students, who had earned an identity and a posset of wounds in street battles with English town as well as gown. Fortuitously, perhaps, it was out of this background that the first ascertainable Anglo-Welsh poem emerged—Ieuan ap Hywel Swrdwal's 'Hymn to the Virgin', which he wrote about 1470 as a species of *Welsh boast* (using English words and syntax but spelling largely in Welsh).

This was an isolated precursor of the troop that followed when English was compelled upon certain classes of Welshmen by the Acts of Union of 1536 and 1542. Henry VIII's intention, broadly, was to sell the Union with England, to the Welsh gentry in particular, with the bait of opportunity to hold office, and to offer to Welshmen in general, whom he regarded with 'a singuler love and favour', equality with his English subjects provided they attained to 'perfect . . . knowledge' of his laws and accepted his determination 'utterly to extirpe alle and singuler the sinister usages and customes differing from the same'. The most immediate effect of this on Welshmen who remained poor and in Wales was in the law courts. The Act of 1536 laid down that 'all justices . . . shall proclaim and keep . . . all . . . courts in the English tongue; . . . no person or persons that use the Welsh speech or language shall have . . . any office . . .

189

within this realm of England, Wales or other the king's Dominion . . . unless he or they exercise the English speech or language'. For the gentry the new dispensation was far more compelling. It became necessary almost immediately for those who had not followed Henry Tudor to London and made their minor fortunes there to equip themselves in English: there was a rush for enrolment at the Inns of Court (whose courses were briefer and much less demanding than those of Universities) so that the aspiring sons of landed families might, with a minimum of legal knowledge, qualify to hold office as escheator, sheriff or justice of the peace, the first two of which positions in particular offered splendid opportunies for oppression and the robbery of local enemies. The extreme effects of this were temporary, but English was firmly established as the language of opportunity.

By a time very little later schools equivalent to those established in England by the young Edward VI had appeared—at Brecon, Abergavenny, Carmarthen and Ruthin, for example—and although the education there received was almost entirely through the medium of the classics, it proved, in the end, an anglicising influence, not merely because some schoolmasters in Wales were Englishmen but much more fundamentally because contact with fellow-students at University afterwards was bound to persuade a potential writer that his educated audience, his sympathetic audience, lay in that infinitely wider segment of the classically educated produced by schools in England. This was true even for a bilingual and privately-educated Welshman like Henry Vaughan (1621-95), whose stay at Oxford led him to celebrate his beloved Usk for the benefit of his English friends and contemporaries. Newly-rich gentry such as the Wynns of Gwydir, two of whose heirs about 1600 were educated at Bedford and Eton respectively, were even more aware of the inevitability of an English audience.

Men of property in Wales, then, either because of their own knowledge of the metropolis or because of relationships with office-holders at the Tudor court could not avoid this extra dimension: they knew that employment at home, whether in the Church or in the law, was bound up with a skill in the use of English. By the late seventeenth century Cors-y-gedol, Nannau and Penybenglog, the last households to support a resident Welsh bard, had abandoned the practice. Even those who contrived to save themselves from such a desertion of the Welsh language, whose lives were devoted to fighting such desertion, could not, as they rose in social status, prevent their descendants from deserting it. The Welsh poet and patriot Lewis Morris, one of the three brothers of Llanfihangel-Tre'r-Beirdd, became Deputy-Steward of the Crown manors in Cardiganshire in 1746; his fourth son, William, married the heiress of Blaen-Nant in Pencelli, Breconshire, and was counted indubitably a gentleman; *his* son Lewis became a solicitor in Carmarthen and his grandson Sir Lewis, though born in 1833 in that sufficiently Welsh town, was sent to finish his education at Sherborne and Oxford. It was almost inevitable that he should have been an *Anglo-Welsh* poet.

That process took three generations. With the Stradlings it happened earlier and more quickly. Sir Edward Stradling of St. Donats (1529-1609), the patron of Dr. John David Rhys and his Welsh grammar and named by Thomas Wiliems of Trefriw in 1632 as one of the two great defenders and users of the Welsh language, had for heir a distant and English-educated kinsman in Sir John Stradling (1563-1637), who founded Cowbridge Grammar School and wrote *Beata Pacifici* (1623) and *Divine Poems* (1625) in English. Whether they were educational or professional or lineal, the pressures of these centuries on the gentry of Wales seemed irresistible.

By the middle of the eighteenth century the Welsh language was widely regarded as no better than a patois, a peasant tongue fit only for the ignorant. A pamphlet of 1682 had referred to it as:—

". . . native gibberish . . . usually prattled throughout the whole of Taphydom except in market towns, whose inhabitants being a little raised begin to despise it . . . and it is usually cashiered out of gentlemen's houses."

Breconshire, studded with gentry more thickly than were most shires, and Radnorshire, perhaps affected by the proselytising of Dissent (which had its essentially English origins at Brampton Bryan, Llanfair Waterdine and Beguildy), were plainly those areas (apart from South Pembrokeshire) where John Wesley had least difficulty in making himself understood. His visits to Maesmynys, near Builth, from 1743 onwards, for instance, drew crowds who had no need of an interpreter. It is not surprising, then, that Richard Hall (1817-66), the Brecon shopkeeper, or William Churchey, his fellow-townsman, who published a volume entitled *Poems and Imitations of the British Poets* in 1789, or D. Rice Jones, another Breconian whose poem *Isolda* appeared in 1851, or Thomas Jeffery Llewelyn Prichard of Trallong (better known as the author of *The Adventures of Twm Shôn Catti*) who published *Welsh Minstrelsy* in 1824, should have written in English—even less so that John Lloyd, the old Etonian who built the mansion of Dinas and whose *Poems* were published in 1847, should, like his fellow-scholars Sir Charles Hanbury-Williams of Pontypool (1708-59) and George Powell of Nanteos (1842-82), have done the same.

Meanwhile, the settlement of Englishmen in Flintshire, Denbighshire and Montgomeryshire in the late sixteenth and early seventeenth centuries had induced some Welsh-speaking Welshmen to come to terms with the English language. The motive for this was plainly evangelical. Morgan Llwyd, a native of Merioneth, served the Parliament during the Civil War and then, influenced no doubt by his own training at Brampton Bryan and Llanfair Waterdine, settled as pastor of the 'gathered church' at Wrexham, where much English was already spoken. Amongst his numerous poems are thirty-one in English. This same desire to evangelise was also plainly the genesis of the English writing of the preaching giants of the eighteenth century, William

191

Williams, Pantycelyn, and Peter Williams of Carmarthen, as it had been of that of John Penry of Cefnbrith, the early Puritan martyr. Penry wrote from England: the other two had English Pembrokeshire and Breconshire contiguous. Iolo Morganwg (1747-1826), another bilingual Welshman, was dissimilar only in that he had a more national and secular propaganda in mind and was at least a little concerned to show that he, a self-educated stonemason, had mastered the English measures as well.

Implicit in this theme of evangelisation (from about 1740 onwards) is a very singular linguistic reversal. The original Puritan impulse that came in by way of Llanfaches, Brampton Bryan and Wrexham had been alien, English. It was transformed, first by the Circulating Schools of Gruffydd Jones and their successors in North Wales organised by Thomas Charles of Bala, then by the Nonconformist all-age Sunday Schools of the late eighteenth and early nineteenth century, into nothing less than a society speaking the Welsh language which acknowledged ideals radically different from any to be found in England except amongst progressive minority groups. Within this Welsh society were to be found some eighty per cent of the population of the original Welsh-speaking areas: outside it were the anglicised squirearchy, if resident, the Church of England, and those unfortunates like schoolmasters, church-wardens and gardeners whose living depended on either. In the new industrial areas (after 1820) managers, under-managers and perhaps foremen had to stand with their English masters outside the Welsh cocoon. This radical development had been materially assisted by the behaviour and practice of a Church which could refuse all preferment to Ieuan Fardd (1731-88), the best Welsh scholar of his time, practise pluralism, neglect the duties of preaching and treat its Welsh bishoprics too often as mere stepping-stones to the real hierarchy of the Church *in* England. Amongst anglicising influences, from the seventeenth to the nineteenth century, the Church must take a prominent place, the efforts of individuals to alter this notwithstanding. It is no surprise, therefore, to find amongst Anglo-Welsh writers a substantial number of clergymen—Charles Symmons (1749-1826), David Lloyd (1752-1838), Eliezer Williams (1754-1820), Edward Davies (1756-1831), Thomas Marsden (1802-49) and David and Thomas Hughes of Ruthin, father and son, the latter of whom in his poem 'Snowdon' (published in 1864) penned these lines:—

> "Soon, shall 'Dim Saesneg' be a sound gone by,
> And, like the echoes of the breezes, die.
> 'Tis well t'were so! the people now are one,
> Need but one tongue to work in unison."

Henry VIII could have wished for no better proselyte—a veritable Arthur Kelton of the Railway Age. Evan Lloyd (1734-76) escaped from both the mediocrity and the attitudes of orthodoxy by being a much worse Churchman and one frequently invisible in London.

Thus far it is plain enough that Anglo-Welsh writers—with the possible exception of a few politically committed individuals like Ebenezer Jones (1820-60), the Chartist poet resident in London, and Robert Holland Price, who celebrated the Chirk Volunteers in his poem 'The Horrors of Invasion' (1804)—can be described either as the products of English-speaking areas of Wales or as stamped with the orthodoxies of their class or vocation. They were gentlemen, clergymen or professional men who had had a classical education at school, if not at university. The reservoir from which they were drawn never held more than ten per cent of the population of Wales, and probably held much less. Not surprisingly, genius, even high talent, was rare, and when it was found—as with Henry Vaughan, George Herbert (who, though born at Montgomery Castle, spent almost all his short life in England) and John Dyer—those who possessed it were excepted from the generality either in vocation or residence.

Nor was there any significant cross-fertilisation between writing in English and writing in Welsh. Lewis Morris (Llewelyn Ddu o Fôn) demonstrated, in his poem, 'The Fishing Lass of Hakin', an excellent feel for English words and rhythms, and others, notably perhaps Pantycelyn and Iolo Morganwg, could use the English modes entirely correctly and passably well. But at no time were they concerned to try the effect of, say, the rules of Welsh *cynghanedd* in an English poem. Anglo-Welsh writers, as one might largely expect from their social status, showed no sign of desiring to learn from the Welsh until outsiders—notably the undeflatable George Borrow and Gerard Manley Hopkins during his stay at St. Beuno's—gave them a lead. But this was a late, in its effects a twentieth century, development. The earlier 'friends of Wales', from Churchyard and Drayton to the devotees of the Grand Tour (mini-version)—whether they were aesthetic theorists like Gilpin, informed observers like Benjamin Heath Malkin or those like Wordsworth who felt 'something far more deeply interfused'—had all concentrated on the natural scene and its emanations. Ecstatics like Luke Booker or an esotericist like the author of *Aylwin* did not extend the range much further. Only Thomas Gray in the eighteenth century, and Thomas Love Peacock and Matthew Arnold in the nineteenth, had picked at the language as an extension of the antiquarianism of Thomas Pennant and his like, and their largely historical emphasis has had no modern fulfilment of quality except the late novels of Oliver Onions.

Meanwhile, economic exigencies had driven many Welsh families to England, and out of the bosom of these arose writers, only a few of whom may reasonably be set within a viable canon of Anglo-Welshness, who nevertheless looked back occasionally to their origins. Gerard Manley Hopkins has already been mentioned. There may be added John Donne, John Hoskyns (once of Llanwarne), John Aubrey, Thomas Traherne, Christopher Smart, William Morris, George Meredith, and perhaps even that Mary Ann Evans who preferred the name George Eliot.

The nineteenth century, however, closed the categories of writer so far mentioned. Within Wales both the education available and the balance of population were drastically altered. The British and National Schools which fulfilled the function of all-age primaries, although they taught in English, had comparatively little effect in anglicising the population of genuinely Welsh areas, though they certainly increased the numbers of those able to use the English language. Where the environment was strong enough—the 'Welsh Not' notwithstanding—Welsh remained the language of the playground and home. And occasional upsets like the Treachery of the Blue Books of 1847 even gave it impetus. But the foundation of the County Schools from 1895 onwards was a different matter. A Secondary School conducts a pupil into and through that period of adolescence when a genuine approach is made to literature. Glyn Jones, in *The Dragon has Two Tongues*, has emphasised that it is the language in which the imagination is released at this time, the language in which a mastery of words and syntax is achieved and an appreciation of word-values and connotations begun, that must be the language in which that pupil afterwards sets any writing of his that he wishes to be excellent rather than merely competent. In that sense the education in and through English to which all Welsh boys and girls, and most of all those of academic and literary potential, were subjected by the new County School system was crucial.

It was, nevertheless, the population change in South-East Wales which hastened the educational process so remarkably that what the early decades of the twentieth century saw may fairly be dubbed a revolution. The industrial klondyke of Merthyr and the adjacent coal-bearing areas of Monmouthshire and East Glamorgan attracted in the first instance a predominance of Welshmen from Breconshire, Cardiganshire, Pembrokeshire and Carmarthenshire, so that there was a point—about, say, 1870—when an immigrant industrial society using the Welsh language had been created. But the later decades of the nineteenth century were to see this rudimentary creation overrun by immigrants from England. The 1851 Census showed that 14,189 of the inhabitants of Merthyr, over twenty years of age, came from the four Welsh counties mentioned: these, with the 9,120 who were born in the town and the additional 4,146 who were born in the neighbouring areas of Glamorgan would, no doubt, have assimilated the 2,330 Irishmen and the assorted 5,308 who came from counties mainly in England. But a later set of statistics from the newer mining areas of Glamorgan reveals the dimensions of the change. In the decade 1871-81 37 per cent of the immigrants came from the counties of Gloucestershire, Somerset, Devon and Cornwall, as against 38 per cent from neighbouring counties of South Wales. The balance came from further afield still. The cycle of slump and boom in the coal and steel industries not merely increased the proportion of English immigrants up to 1911: it also caused 35,000 natives of Glamorgan to leave the country in the nineties, many of them women going to London to help their families by entering domestic service. An ultimate proportion of English-speaking incomers which may be set, without exaggeration, at 40 per cent—a figure possibly far too small for some areas—could

194

not be absorbed by an insufficiently established Welsh society. Despite the efforts of the numerous chapels, English, the language of the masters, remained also the language of the large un-assimilated groups. It was inevitable that it should become the *lingua franca*. In playground and street even a child who heard Welsh in the home would hear only English and, since Glamorgan and Monmouthshire between them accounted for more than half the population of Wales, the drop in the number of Welsh-speakers in the years between 1900 and 1950 was far more disastrous than any that had happened before or than has happened since. 200,000 of them were lost between 1931 and 1951, a period during which a schooling in English and the pressure of an English-only majority took their full toll.

So overpowering was this development on those who lived in the industrial areas of South-East Wales, as well as on the inhabitants of Cardiff, Swansea and other larger towns, that parents who themselves spoke Welsh were utterly convinced of the futility of teaching Welsh to their children, whose future was to lie, if not in a more fortunate England, in a Wales in which commercial and industrial progress depended on English. Thus writers-to-be like Glyn Jones, Dylan Thomas, Vernon Watkins, Idris Davies and Alun Lewis grew up unversed in Welsh, in varying degrees and from attitudes by no means identical, but nevertheless very close to speakers of the language and within the culture which it had handed on. Out of this break and the sadness born of it came the specific quality of Anglo-Welshness which this generation of writers possessed. They knew, if only by the observation of the child, what Welshness was, and were capable either of exploiting it or, in the end, achieving a poignant evaluation of what they had lost.

What Gwyn Thomas has revealed of his childhood provides perhaps the most exact example available in Anglo-Welsh literary history. Born at Porth in the Rhondda in 1913, the youngest of twelve children, he records that his elder brothers and sisters all spoke Welsh to their parents, but that by the time he reached the age of muttering the language of street and playground was so exclusively English that no attempt was made to speak to him except in that tongue. The great 'shift' in Porth, then, had already taken place by 1916. In *A Welsh Eye* Gwyn Thomas adds a further comment on this:—

> "We were not, in terms of nationality, a homogeneous people. Into the valleys had poured as many Englishmen as indigenous Welsh. The only binding things were indignity and deprivation. The Welsh language stood in the way of our fuller union and we made ruthless haste to destroy it. We nearly did."

Those bonds of mongrel indignity and deprivation were the basis for the Cynlais Moores, the Penry Murdochs and the Shadrach Simses of Meadow Prospect, and Gwyn Thomas has never moved from the loyalty he first felt to that downtrodden English-Welsh community towards any later evaluation, in better times, of what he owed to the initial Welshness of his inheritance. In

195

that respect he stands almost alone amongst contemporary Anglo-Welsh writers.

It is—to go back to the language-change in its general aspect—sufficiently obvious why the supply of Welshmen who could write only in English broadened so markedly in the twentieth century. Nor was this simply a matter of numbers. It was also the release of the talent, in English, of a whole new social class, and one with an experience of life in conditions (whether as to deprivation, indignity, eccentricity or undammable eloquence) which an English readership might well find uniquely attractive. The upper-class, clerical and professional origins of Anglo-Welsh writing—thin stream that it had always been—were lost in the new flood. Nonconformity at last came into its own. The children of families who could never have been sent to the older grammar schools (which were rarely, in any case, in or near industrial areas) were admitted to the new County Schools. Glyn Jones has pointed out (in *The Dragon has Two Tongues*) that up to this time Welsh-speaking radical Nonconformity had provided the 'talent belt' in Wales, the nearest thing to the 'creative, enlightened, literature-producing middle class in England', and that an Anglo-Welsh writer appeared—or might well have appeared—whenever such a radical, Nonconformist, Welsh-speaking family began to speak English. Of that first wave of Anglo-Welsh writers, presently to be treated in detail, perhaps only Geraint Goodwin and Emlyn Williams escape this definition by belonging to geographical areas where Welsh weakened earlier or later and to backgrounds that were not industrial.

So much may be agreed without difficulty. What is a little puzzling, however, is that it took Anglo-Welsh writers such a relatively long time to appear in any considerable numbers. It was 1937, with the appearance of Keidrych Rhys's first issue of *Wales*, before there was any general awareness of Anglo-Welsh poetic and histrionic talent waiting in the wings, scarcely able to contain itself. Of possible reasons for this three come to mind. The first is the smallness of the County Schools when first established: many of them had fewer than a hundred children on roll until well after the First World War. It is conceivable that between, say, 1900 and 1920 there were many potentially creative children (who not infrequently fail to appear in the highest academic bracket at an early age) who never received the new secondary education possible. Idris Davies, for example, was one of these: it cost him some years of adult life to recover from an adolescence in the pit and from the lack of the education he needed to launch his poetry. Jack Jones would have been another but for having been born a couple of years too early for Merthyr's first secondary school.

A second reason, however, is more fundamental. It lay in the nature of the education offered by the new Secondary Schools. In English as it was, it nevertheless partook very fully (because of the teachers who transmitted it) of the virtues and vices of that education in Welsh which had evolved from the Circulating Schools to the all-age Sunday Schools and from there into the

196

British and National Schools of the later nineteenth century. All the education of the first two had been in the Bible, and excellence in that education had been measured, particularly from the day of Thomas Charles, by examination, sometimes written but more often oral. This system put a heavy premium on memorisation and accuracy rather than analysis and interpretation, and through all the changes of syllabus and emphasis that followed teachers continued to stress these elements because it had been by these means that they themselves had been taught. Sir Owen M. Edwards, with his Oxford training, found it necessary to criticise this emphasis in his 1909 Report as Chief Inspector. He suggested that:—

> "the Central Welsh Board should now consider to what extent their rigid examination system may be the cause of the wooden and unintelligent type of mind of which their Examiners complain."

But this was a chicken and egg situation, a cycle remarkably difficult to break. This predilection for caution and accuracy, for memorisation as the key to success in examinations, brought back into the system teachers—they had to be teachers for lack, economically, of other opportunity—who had themselves succeeded by means of it and wished for nothing more than the similar success of those whom they taught. It scarcely needs saying that creativity and independence of mind were undervalued in such an educational structure. To be successful academically it was necessary to remain in a stage of arrested development. This, more than the chapel pieties and trade union conformities that writers have tended to stress, was the really constricting element in the environment of an Anglo-Welsh writer born since 1890. Not merely did it produce a host of late developers—Dylan Thomas was an obvious exception because he 'bucked' the system from the beginning, and Alun Lewis another because he was at Cowbridge Grammar School, a school of the English mould, where he was taught English by an Englishman; it may also have been a contributary reason why Idris Davies, alone of Anglo-Welsh poets, was able to tackle the bitter realities of the General Strike of 1926 and the years of deprivation in the Valleys directly. Many of his fellows, though not radically different in origin, had been cautioned by academicism into a silence they could break only by what Gwyn Thomas has called 'a sidling malicious obliquity' or by escape into rural values their education has blessed.

There is one more reason to offer for the delay in the damburst, one connected, in some of its aspects, with what has been said already. Anglo-Welsh writing lacked a platform, had no journal in which to express itself until the arrival of *Wales* in 1937. More important still, it lacked leadership, direction and a successful example. The writing of Arthur Machen and W. H. Davies, chronologically a bridge, had little to say to the young writer of 1920-30. Machen, an unlikely product of the tradition previous (having been educated at Hereford Cathedral School), worked out his Europeanised fascination with the occult against a background either of his native Gwent or

197

of a partially-disguised West Wales. Like W. H. Davies, he was a 'sport' off the old stock. And Davies himself, even more accidental and unusual because devoid of any secondary education, had become, in his Nailsworth home, the better-supported John Clare of a resolutely English poetic tradition. Edward Thomas, to whom Davies had cause to be grateful, was, despite his fortuitous connection with Owen M. Edwards at Oxford, in contact with few in Wales except Gwili (John Jenkins) and relatives at Pontarddulais. Recognition after 1950 of his stature as a poet and his very general inclusion in the list of Anglo-Welsh poets cannot make of him a formative influence on Anglo-Welsh writing before that date.

It was in these circumstances that leadership devolved on a personality unlikely in a different way, the bilingual Caradoc Evans (1878-1945). Whether or not Caradoc was one of the most notable grudge-bearers of all time (which seems an eminent possibility), his quick dark cameos of hypocritical, callous, miserly and lecherous Cardi peasants might well have been accepted as the work of a *petit-maître* of fiction but for his insistence, not merely to his publisher but subsequently and interminably to the public, that everything he wrote was *true*, a chapter-by-chapter *exposé* of a squalid and degraded society spreading from Rhydlewis southwards to Teifi. *My People* (1915)—together with the books immediately following, *Capel Sion* (1916), *My Neighbours* (1919) and his play *Taffy* (first performed in 1923)—may be seen, in one aspect, as the first and most successful exploitation of Wales for English eyes. Whatever the emotive sources of such writing, that it was an exercise in sales-calculation need not be doubted. Caradoc was always his own best publicity man.

His work, which at its best (for all its limitations of mood and subject-matter) is rivetingly economical and direct, is additionally important in the present context because it gave direction to subsequent Anglo-Welsh writing. Of the two elements in it, the exploitation of Wales unknown and the seeming hatred of the indigenous, Nonconformist-dominated rural society of Welsh Wales, the first was more generally copied. Rhys Davies and Glyn Jones, Caradoc's most immediate successors in the short story, transmuted his hatred into a delight in eccentricity (in the first, of character, situation and society itself, in the second, of physical characteristics)—Glyn Jones contributing too a lyricism of boyhood and life and landscape entirely foreign to Caradoc—but the rift which Caradoc had created was for the time unbridgeable. Welsh-speaking Welshmen thought of Anglo-Welsh writing as destructive of the Welsh way of life and, over a period of three decades, there is little doubt that they were right. A kind of jocosity about it added speed to the disappearance of the Welsh language. The fact that Anglo-Welsh writers did not see their work in this light is one aspect of their education exclusively in *English* literature (Glyn Jones and Geraint Goodwin, for instance, appear to have been influenced by D. H. Lawrence) and of their preoccupation with the London market, in which Caradoc Evans had been conspicuously the most successful of them all. Caradoc, indeed, was the example which enabled many of them to

198

break out of the strait-jacket both of academicism and of Welsh conformities. It pointed in the direction of defiance, one that the ego-compass of the writer responds to well.

For all that, there was something of an interval of silence after the impact of *My People* and its satellites. A. G. Prys-Jones edited in 1917 a volume called *Welsh Poets*, the first anthology of Anglo-Welsh poetry, but apart from W. H. Davies, Ernest Rhys and the editor himself few of the contributors deserve to be named in the Anglo-Welsh succession. Rhys Davies began, after 1920, to make a reputation for himself: Glyn Jones had his first poems published in *The Dublin Magazine*; Richard Hughes, unrecognised as an Anglo-Welsh writer because of his public school education, had his burst of precocity and fell silent; and Robert Herring found room in *Life and Letters*, as the thirties wore on, for contributions from Welshmen writing in English. But it was a quiet time just the same.

When, therefore, the first number of *Wales* appeared, carrying the work of Dylan Thomas, Glyn Jones, Nigel Heseltine, Ken Etheridge, Idris Davies, Ll. Wyn Griffith and Keidrych Rhys, the sheer verbosity, virtuosity and histrionic talent of most of its contributors made London critics conscious of a Welsh *wave* likely to carry as far as their safe seats and further. There was an element of overshoot about this, the head of water built up behind the dam, unlikely to be fully replenished. There was also the particular quality of genuine Anglo-Welshness, that absorption with and mastery of words which came at least partly out of the *feel* of Welsh life (with its emphasis on eloquence, its amused and amusing verbal rebellion against authority, conformity and deprivation). And there was, above all, the consciousness that Wales was *new* subject-matter, unworked and potentially profitable.

Anthony Conran, in a recent article on Brenda Chamberlain, describes the characteristics of the writers of this first wave:—

"It was a bravely cosmopolitan, rather exotic generation, the first Welsh-born writers to take advantage of the English market. Not since the buccaneers and gentlemen of fortune of Elizabeth's reign had Welshness seemed so colourful and exportable a commodity. They were the expansionist Free Trade generation, as opposed to our present Protectionist days, drably making hay behind the tariff of the Arts Council grant. Most of them . . . had something of the mountebank about them: a glitter of phrase, a perhaps too eager gift of the gab, a sense that bards and mountains and colliers were hot news, to be rushed into print before anyone else got there first."

This mountebank air as much enveloped the successfully sentimental novels of Richard Llewellyn and Richard Vaughan as it had done the dastardly gloom of Caradoc Evans's stories. Whether it was Welshness that was being exported may perhaps be doubted. It was certainly a wordy and often brilliant exhibition of differentness.

199

In the forefront of the new push were genuine poets like Dylan Thomas, Vernon Watkins and Glyn Jones. Keidrych Rhys, whose enterprise provided them with their platform, was himself dedicated to bringing Wales up to date, eliminating the provincial, organising emancipation. Despite a genuflection in his second editorial to 'the small shopkeepers, the blacksmiths, the non-conformist ministers, . . . the miners, the quarrymen and the railwaymen' by whom literature was carried on in Wales, his real purpose was to out-Auden Auden, delete the harmoniums and the eisteddfodau and, in his staccato fashion, to offer an 'advanced' commentary on the conservative eccentricities of the Wales of the late thirties. Most of the poets and writers of the second rank who found a place in *Wales* followed him in this, including Idris Davies, some of whose poems of beauty and emancipation, written at this time, ring with a falsity that he later and sadly recognised. It would be fair to add that a decade later many of these writers, like Idris, had begun to retrace their steps.

But the direction of the poets was, in any case, different. Vernon Watkins, already emancipated by his education at Repton and his reading in French and German from any sense of confinement in Welshness, achieved the approval and support of T. S. Eliot and a kind of unexamined and unread recognition by London critics. His esotericisms were those of intellectualised myth, not of the deployment of words, and his progress was individual, without influence on the Welsh echelon that was developing. Dylan Thomas, on the other hand —and Glyn Jones too, in a manner less echoing—were devoted to words for their own sake. What Dylan achieved, without specifically intending it, was an anti-Auden revolution, a poetry of sound which, particularly in wartime and for long afterwards, struck a note of romantic self-regard, of escape into obfuscation, to which English society, undergoing for much of this period a peculiar stress, responded whole-heartedly. It is important here to state plainly that Dylan Thomas was a poet *à l'anglaise*, not so much because he had been deprived of Welshness by his upbringing as because—at bottom—he had drunk the pure milk of *English* poetry in an anglicised environment from his infant literacy, because he saw himself as a twentieth century John Keats, professionally and exclusively devoted to poetry and dying early, because London, initially, encompassed his whole desire as a poet, and because the essential romanticism of his apparent metaphysic of bodily symbols was not merely a graft on the English tradition but was unconsciously recognised as such by the English response (even though the elements of novelty in his work were automatically associated with Welshness). That the metropolitan emphasis proved temporary did not affect the other elements, least of all those that were romantic and egocentric. It is a paradox that the Auden School whose dominance he ended had been concerned with that 'speaking to the people' which, though very occasional in the English tradition, was integral to the Welsh conception of the poet's function.

Whether the overwhelming success and reputation of Dylan Thomas, still the only Anglo-Welsh poet known even to the *literati* in the United States and countries overseas, bears a just relation to his ultimate status as a poet only time will tell. But that he changed the direction of *English* poetry for almost two decades is undoubted. In literary history his place is assured.

Behind the first wave, however, a second and more varied one was preparing. In February 1939 appeared the first number of *The Welsh Review*, more academic than *Wales*, more interested in literary standards and less in a specific direction. Its editor was Gwyn Jones, a short story writer and novelist of distinction and subsequently the first historian and assessor of the Anglo-Welsh movement. Even earlier—in 1937 (for the writers who crested this wave were in few cases younger than those on the other)—was published the *In Parenthesis* of David Jones, a work of words about the First World War in which the Welsh and Cockney heritages, united in Jones himself, were accorded their 'valid signs' against the extreme of human chaos confronting the soldier. It had taken him nine years to write. During the Second War Gwyn Williams, immured in Cyrenaica, began to translate Welsh poetry, an enterprise which emerged first in *The Rent That's Due to Love* (1950) and then in *Presenting Welsh Poetry* (1959). In their way a contrast, however unintentionally, to the frenetic quality of Keidrych Rhys's misleadingly titled *Modern Welsh Poetry* (1944)—in fact, the second anthology of *Anglo-Welsh* poetry—these volumes heralded the even more extensive translations from the Welsh by Anthony Conran and the American Joseph Clancy.

In 1946 appeared *After Every Green Thing*, the first volume of poetry by Dannie Abse who, if he sought emancipation, sought it from his Jewish heritage rather than the vaguer confines of the Cardiff where he was brought up. Residence in London and his own poetic development made of him a writer (of novels and plays as well as of poetry) whose nostalgic backward glances rarely disturbed his attention to the world scene.

In Carmarthen in the same year Keidrych Rhys published R. S. Thomas's first book, *The Stones of the Field*. Another six years were to pass before *The Critics* acclaimed *An Acre of Land*, a book which R. S. Thomas had had to publish at his own expense. It was a slow emergence, characteristic of a swimmer against the tide.

Of the second wave, indeed, only Gwyn Thomas, a late developer like the rest, was making in the same general direction as those of the first. The others, even where they were turning back to the Welsh heritage, were doing so individually and in isolation. It is clear, in retrospect, that one of the reasons for their non-recognition by the public initially was that they did not conform to the image of Anglo-Welshness, already sociologised into a rabelaisian and verbose myth born of the 'instant Dylan' of the pubs. Each of these individual writers brought to poetry deep preparation and considerable learning. The poetry of David Jones, though recognised by Eliot as outstanding from the beginning, is only now—in the seventies—beginning to be widely appreciated for its peculiar compound of archaic naming, modern colloquialism and seemingly loose yet intensely calculated structure, and seen as talismanic, both

201

traditional and vital, against the quakes and collapses of *terra informis*. R. S. Thomas, as dominant since 1960 as Dylan Thomas was before it (and over a more intellectual readership), has moved from the contemplation of Manafon Man against his starved pastures, through a bitter Nationalism (which of all his themes has attracted the most attention), back to deeper and more demanding religious themes. Alone for long, he was the harbinger of the many Nationalist poets to come.

The several directions of this second wave, its different dorsal shapings, prevented, then, any general recognition of change. R. S. Thomas, however widely acclaimed, remained an individual whose success in London was the basis on which he was able to hold the stage. It was not till Raymond Garlick, editor of *Dock Leaves* since 1949 and collector and provider of three parts of what is known about Anglo-Welsh writers before 1900, made the healing of the breach with Welsh feeling and Welsh writers an explicit aim, both editorially and personally, that there was some small recognition that the criteria of Anglo-Welshness were changing. Even then feeling was slow to mature. By 1960 Raymond Garlick's olive branch, all the more efficacious because English-grown, was drooping sadly, and at the end of the year he gave up the editorial chair of what had become *The Anglo-Welsh Review* and took a post in the Netherlands. The fifties had indeed proved a dispiriting decade, full of the dead ends of Dylanism and virtually empty of new writers. The growing reputation of the novelist Emyr Humphreys, whose fourth book, *Hear and Forgive* (1952), together with a broadcast talk he gave about that time on 'the Protestant novel', were other signs of a new direction, it is true; but, like R. S. Thomas, he was appreciated as an individual writer without there being any noticeable change in the general climate in which Anglo-Welsh writing operated. In the eyes both of Welsh writers and the Welsh-speaking public the Anglo-Welsh remained subject to the charge that they had sold a heritage for a mess of pottage.

In 1963 and the years immediately following the ability of the newly-formed Welsh Arts Council (previously only a Welsh Committee of The Arts Council of Great Britain and unwilling to make any financial grants to literature) to support Anglo-Welsh writing—whether in periodicals or books—altered the dimensions of the scene materially. But the opinion change, which came a little later, arrived independently. When Meic Stephens founded *Poetry Wales* in 1965 it was in answer, not merely to his own beliefs, but to the pressure of an increasing number of writers of Nationalist sympathies who had felt stifled in the previous dispensation. In part this followed the lead of the Guild of Welsh Writers, formed in London about 1963 by Bryn Griffiths. London-based poets like John Tripp, Sally Roberts and Tom Earley, who were members of the Guild, were reinforced by those like Harri Webb who, though no longer young, began to write when they felt they had a public to write for. Indeed, a feature of the new dispensation and not in essence a Nationalist one, was the reappearance of poets like Leslie Norris and John Ormond who had last been seen as irresolute toe-dippers in the already broken wave of romantic verbosity and who had fallen silent, as for their differing reasons, they recognised a false start. Whether it was the appearance of patronage, as in Harri Webb's satiric 'Cywydd o Fawl', that re-peopled the stage at this juncture may be doubted. The sociological background to changes in literary fashion—as to the supply of writers—is complex and perhaps ultimately indecipherable.

In 1968 Yr Academi Gymreig (Welsh writers of status in conclave) accepted a request from a deputation of Anglo-Welsh writers that an English section of the Academi should be formed. Even at this stage there was considerable suspicion of the prodigals who declared their return, and it required an overwhelmingly generous speech from the veteran Welsh writer D. J. Williams to secure their admission. Perhaps from this moment may be dated the 'protectionist' era referred to by Anthony Conran. Of the London-based writers only David Jones (who has never lived anywhere else), Dannie Abse, Tom Earley, Goronwy Rees and Richard Jones have not returned to Wales: Welsh Arts Council money is subsidising Welsh publishers and only a few writers now look to London for recognition. Physically and spiritually most Anglo-Welsh writers are *home* and like it. The present is 'drab' only in the sense that problems of distribution and bookshop sales, the relative absence of a reading public for books published in Wales (not unconnected with the exclusively *English* education referred to previously), colour the scene more darkly than hope would wish. But that there is a literary *renaissance* of a size comparable with the first birth of 1937 may reasonably be claimed.

Since about 1965 poets and writers of Nationalist sympathies have been dominant. Raymond Garlick (who returned to Wales in 1968), Meic Stephens, Harri Webb, John Tripp, Gwyn Williams, Emyr Humphreys and Peter Gruffydd constitute the largest single group, with Ned Thomas's *Planet* (founded at the end of 1969) as an additional orb in their day-sky. R. S. Thomas is of them and not of them, admired and regretted as was Achilles glooming in his tent. Other poets like John Stuart Williams, Leslie Norris, John Ormond, Herbert Williams, Alison Bielski, Tom Earley, Robert Morgan, Gillian Clarke and Alan Perry are much less politically cohesive, but with few exceptions (of which Peter Finch and the youngest age-group are the most significant) they demonstrate an allegiance to the Wales of the past which would have been most uncommon in 1937. This change of attitude is exemplified nowhere so well as in *The Dragon has Two Tongues* (1968) of Glyn Jones: it was the first sympathetic examination in depth of the springs of Anglo-Welsh writing.

The effect of the changes since 1960 is remarkable. Through the poetry anthologies *Welsh Voices* and *The Lilting House* and perhaps even more noticeably in the annual collections *Poems '69*, *Poems '70* and *Poems '71* (though all of these had different editors) there is a singular unanimity. J. P. Ward, an Englishman resident for some years now in Swansea, identifies this, in part, in a review of *Poems '71*. The conventions governing Anglo-Welsh poetry at present are, he writes, those of 'remembering' (the personal past or the mythic or the historical past), the emphasis on 'the domestic, the familiar or the neighbouring', a predilection for the rural or semi-rural (with the life of the individual held in balance against it) and the 'colloquial tone', modest, unextravagant, gentle. There are, he notes, few metaphysical or tightly worked intellectual poems, no *erotica* or *exotica*, and few, if any, excursions into the future. He might have added that there are more than a few bitter political poems. The commitment to Wales is undoubted. One of the weaknesses of this phase, as hostile critics have not been slow to point out, is that Anglo-Welsh writers feel much less free to tackle non-Welsh subjects, probably because they feel that their credentials as Welshmen are still in doubt.

It ought to be added that poetry is still the dominant mode. Despite the eminence of Emyr Humphreys (also, be it noted, a poet), the experience and reputation of Rhys Davies, the past novels of Gwyn and Glyn and Jack Jones, Henry Treece and George Ewart Evans, the more recent ones of Richard Hughes, Raymond Williams, Ron Berry and Alexander Cordell (to name a thoroughly dissonant quartet), and the emergence of a new novelist in Aberystwyth-born Richard Jones, the novel is still not a firm part of the Welsh-man's repertoire. The enormous vogue for short stories disappeared with the English market for Welsh eccentricities. Drama has flickered gustily, from the early days of J. O. Francis and Richard Hughes, through Emlyn Williams's capture of the West End, to the television plays of Alun Owen and Alun Richards and the serials of Elwyn Jones and Elaine Morgan. Whether it is true that the Welshman is, as traditional wisdom would have it, 'short of puff' or whether the current emphasis is an inseparable part of the persistence, in Anglo-Welsh writing, of a *Welsh* view of the writer's duty to the community is arguable. Certainly the modern Anglo-Welsh poet disclaims his English fellow's wish to be bohemian and different, an ego-centre fumbling for relationships in a fragmented society: he is above the salt, perhaps, as the bards were, but devoted to the public interest rather than to his own romantic self-satisfaction. This view depends in part on his being, or having been, something other than a poet—a miner, a schoolmaster, a shepherd, a university lecturer, a minister of religion—and on his desire to strike a balance between society's good and the freedom needed to record, remind, comment, guide, even lead. It is a part-timer's standpoint rather than a professional's, a fact which brings its own limitations as well as a peculiar wholesomeness. The wheel has turned a long way since Dylan Thomas's time.

David Jones, never physically part of this scene, who came at Wales by inheritance and books, nevertheless presides in spirit over this epoch of writing. 'We are', he writes in his Preface to *The Anathemata*, 'in our society today, very far removed from those culture-phases where the poet was explicitly and by profession the custodian, rememberer, embodier and voice of the mythus . . .', but poetry is still politically dangerous 'because it evokes and recalls, is a kind of *anamnesis* of, i.e. is an effective recalling of, something loved'. 'There must', he

204

adds, 'be no mugging-up, no "ought to know" or "try to feel"; for only what is actually loved and known can be seen *sub specie aeternitatis'*. There can be little doubt of the loving and knowing, either in the main body of Anglo-Welsh poetry today or in novels like those of Emyr Humphreys. Wales is still, for many, a reactor energising and making available the 'valid signs' and understandings the writer needs.

It is a pity that the English-speaking public of Wales has so far neither sufficiently recognised the undoubted achievement of Anglo-Welsh writing nor understood from its recent attitude that a reorientation of interest towards Wales, indeed a veritable cultivation of knowledge of and about Wales, are urgent necessities for the future health of a community speaking two languages but claiming to be one people. Universities and schools in Wales have in this respect a special responsibility that they have so far not seriously tried to meet.

SELECT BIBLIOGRAPHY

Is there an Anglo-Welsh Literature? by Saunders Lewis (Cardiff, 1939).

The First Forty Years by Gwyn Jones (Cardiff, 1957). Reprinted in *Triskel One*, edited by Sam Adams and Gwilym Rees Hughes (Llandybie, 1971).

The Dragon has Two Tongues by Glyn Jones (London, 1968).

An Introduction to Anglo-Welsh Literature by Raymond Garlick (Cardiff, 1970).

PERIODICALS

Wales, edited by Keidrych Rhys. First series, 1937-9; second series, 1943-9; third series, 1958-9.

The Welsh Review, edited by Gwyn Jones. First series, 1939; second series, 1944-8.

Dock Leaves, edited by Raymond Garlick, 1949-57. In 1957 the magazine became *The Anglo-Welsh Review* and was edited till 1960 by Raymond Garlick. Since that date the Editor has been Roland Mathias.

Poetry Wales, edited by Meic Stephens, 1965- . Two numbers were edited by Gerald Morgan (1968).

Planet, edited by Ned Thomas, 1969- .

205

ANTHOLOGIES

Welsh Poets, edited by A. G. Prys-Jones (London, 1917).

Modern Welsh Poetry, edited by Keidrych Rhys (London, 1944).

Presenting Welsh Poetry, edited by Gwyn Williams (London, 1959).

Welsh Voices, edited by Bryn Griffiths (London, 1967).

This World of Wales, edited by Gerald Morgan (Cardiff, 1968).

The Lilting House, edited by John Stuart Williams and Meic Stephens (London and Llandybie, 1969).

Welsh Short Stories (London, 1937).

Welsh Short Stories, edited by Gwyn Jones (London, 1940).

Welsh Short Stories, compiled by Gwyn Jones (London, 1956).

Welsh Short Stories, edited by George Ewart Evans (London, 1959).

The Shining Pyramid, edited by Sam Adams and Roland Mathias (Llandysul, 1970).

Twenty-Five Welsh Short Stories, selected by Gwyn Jones and Islwyn Ffowc Elis (London, 1971).

MUSIC IN WALES

OWAIN T. EDWARDS

XI

IT would be more ambitious than realistic in a chapter of this length to hope to cover every important aspect of music in Wales and so, a word of introduction might be found helpful outlining the scope of this account. Since my own interest has been in the music of the eighteenth century onwards, I have not attempted to interpret the sources available much before that, which are mostly literary, but have paid attention to the various forms music has taken in Wales in comparatively recent times. I have not tried to interpret that well-known description of music in Wales at the end of the twelfth century, found in the writings of Giraldus Cambrensis; neither have I tried to assess whether the nation has been a *particularly* musical one since that time. The music discussed comes after the period in which a robust bardic tradition, with music considered an integral element of it, had flourished in Wales. Starting in the sixteenth century, with the effects of the Dissolution of the Monasteries and the Act of Union discernible on the course of music, I shall be describing in this chapter how there emerged in Wales two streams of music: that of the educated gentry and the music of the population in general, the *werin*, two streams which from the eighteenth century are gradually brought together with the rise of congregational singing. I shall be emphasising in this connexion the importance of the Methodist Revival and the Sunday School movement, and in particular the benefit gained by the adoption of the tonic sol-fa system of musical notation. Folk music in its different forms and the musical instruments traditionally associated with it in Wales will be briefly introduced, and to bring this account up to date I shall be indicating some trends in Welsh music at the present.

The Welsh way of life in the Middle Ages being completely rural centred on the monasteries and manor houses, and music was associated with both. But with the gradual anglicization of the Welsh landed classes following the accession of the Tudors, and decisively after Henry VIII's Dissolution of the Monasteries in 1536 when these, the traditional forces of greatest influence and support in cultural life had been removed, Welsh music had a setback. Let us look at the effect of both these factors, taking the Dissolution of the Monasteries first.

Although its immediate impact on the people as far as music was concerned would not have been great, the dissolution of the monasteries extinguished almost completely the practice of liturgical music in Wales. An outpost at which it survived was the cathedral at St. David's, but with this exception it meant the end of an indigenous tradition of liturgical music in Wales; this was to have an enervating effect on Welsh music. Biographical details of Welsh

208

musicians of this period are very sparse, particularly the interesting evidence of where they were brought up and who trained them before the ones whose names we remember rose to prominence in London. But since there was no other training ground for church musicians, it may be assumed that the Welsh monastic establishments and larger churches played an active part, judging by the number of Welshmen holding musical posts in London in the sixteenth century. Amongst these were John Lloyd and Robert Jones, Gentlemen of the Chapel Royal in the early part of the century. Another, Philip ap Rhys, was organist at St. Mary-at-Hill in 1547 and also of St. Paul's Cathedral. His *organ mass*, a kind of composition fairly commonly met with on the continent from the fifteenth to the seventeenth century, is the only one extant by a British composer. His colleague, as Master of the Choristers at St. Mary-at-Hill was another Welshman, Richard Williams. Slightly later, in 1563 Richard Edwards, poet and musician, was Master of the Chapel Royal. His celebrated, 'In going to my naked bed', in the *Mulliner Book*, is a precursor to the elaborate vocal style of the English madrigal.

The most harmful consequence which the Dissolution of the Monasteries had on Welsh music was that it stifled the means of providing future generations with a training at home in the music of the church. That the only surviving British *organ mass* was written by a Welsh composer could indicate that the ecclesiastical establishments in Wales were in closer contact with their counterparts on the continent than similar establishments in other regions of the British Isles—the great Cistercian Abbeys of Valle Crucis and Strata Florida, for example, with the order's houses in France. Alternatively, Philip ap Rhys might have had practical experience of the *organ mass* while working abroad. It would not have been difficult in the early sixteenth century for a musician to have taken part in the music of any service. Throughout Europe the same services were conducted in Latin, and the changes which distinguished the Anglican Service from the traditional services of the Roman Catholic church were not to be brought about until the middle of the century.

Although Henry VIII's declaring himself Head of the Church in England in 1534 had been an unprecedented and radical step which had immediate effect, the provision of an acceptable order of service for his new Church of England took rather longer. The outcome of fierce conflict between the Catholic and the Protestant factions was that it was not until the very end of his reign and into that of Edward VI that the changes were eventually introduced, and during this period both factions succeeded in getting laws passed in their favour. In 1539, for example, while the confiscation of the lands and wealth of over a thousand monasteries was continuing, Cranmer's Bible was issued in English, based on the authorised translation of Miles Coverdale. Yet, the same year saw an affirmation of Catholic doctrine in the Statute of Six Articles.

Like Martin Luther, Henry VIII was an accomplished musician, and he had intended preserving in the new form of service the Catholic sung liturgy. But at that time any kind of polyphony smelt too strongly of 'Popish' music for the extreme Protestants, who advocated having the service said in the vernacular, considering even organ music 'a foolish vanitie'. The king's musical discretion may be seen in the compromise he was forced to accept. In his re-organisation of the cathedrals in 1542, it was made clear, with regard to those of the New Foundation, that the duties of the organist should be undertaken by a professional musician not one of the minor clergy who happened to have some musical competence. Despite his personal liking for polyphonic music he had to listen to Cranmer's case for the simplification of church music, 'as near as may be for every syllable a note so that it may be sung distinctly and devoutly'. After the accession of Edward VI the first stage of the reformation of the service was completed. When the publication and use of the first *Book of Common Prayer* had been ratified by the Act of Uniformity, John Merbeck's *Book of Common Praier noted* was published in 1550. Merbeck's settings are still sung today, and anyone who has heard or sung them will probably not find it difficult to appreciate why musical establishments in the 1550s had little sympathy for the austerity of such unison singing.

Polyphony was once again favoured with the reversal to Catholicism during the five years of Mary Tudor's reign, but the publication of Merbeck's settings and of a number of metrical psalters and compositions in simple four-part style which appeared about the same time, had established the prototype of a particular style of chant and hymn tune which, when once again there had been a reversal to Protestantism, was to become a distinctive feature of *congregational* church worship. The injunction in the Act of Union (1536) that Wales should be 'incorporated, united and annexed' to England, supported by appropriate legislation abolishing Welsh laws and outlawing the Welsh language, meant that when the church changed from conducting its services in Latin to the vernacular, no provision had been made for translating the services into the vernacular of the people of Wales. And though the translation of the Bible into Welsh was authorized by Elizabeth I *as an aid to Welsh people learning English*, there was nothing in Welsh to teach the new, simplified musical style of the Anglican church.

Such instruction was obviously called for since previously the sung service of the Catholic church, in the more substantial ecclesiastical establishments, had been performed by trained musicians often singing elaborate polyphonic settings of the Mass, the congregation being silent observers, whereas now in Elizabeth's Anglican church not only the choir but the whole congregation were requested to participate in chanting the psalms. Church music was in a very poor condition in Wales at the end of the sixteenth century: it was a decided disadvantage that both the style of the music and the language of the service were unfamiliar to most of the people in the congregations. Attention was naturally paid first to the psalms. Various metrical translations of selected psalms were published in Welsh from 1603, all without music. The earliest to appear with tunes included, *Llyfr y Psalmau, wedi eu cyfieithu, a'i cyfansoddi ar fesur cerdd, yn Gymraeg* (London, 1621), by Edmund Prys,

210

Archdeacon of Merioneth, has an introduction from which it may be gathered that both the simple style of the tunes and the practice of congregational singing were new to the church in Wales. Contrary to the expectation one might get from the title, that these were a literal translation of the psalms to be sung rather as in the manner *now* customary in the Anglican service, the Welsh translation is cast in verse and was to be sung with a note of the melody to each syllable, simply like a hymn. Of the twelve tunes Edmund Prys gives (ten of which had appeared elsewhere before) one at least is familiar today as the *Old Hundredth*.

To return to the second of the factors contributing to the setback suffered by Welsh music in the sixteenth century: the gradual anglicization of the Welsh landed classes following the accession of the Tudors. Landed families were either leaving Wales or assuming English manners and the English way of life, and speaking English at home. It was not a caprice of fashion that brought this about, a fad for speaking the Welsh king's foreign language, but the provision already referred to in passing, made in the Act of Union to outlaw Welsh as an official language. Members of such families as would have been eligible to have held offices under the Crown but who would have been disqualified had they not spoken English, adopted English as an every-day language, thus gradually becoming further removed from the general peasant population than wealth and possessions naturally tended to make them. From then on there were two currents of Welsh secular music: the one practised by the gentry, which was new, following the main stream of English music, and the other by the *werin* continuing in the folk tradition while the bardic tradition declined.

An impression had been made in the English court circle by the harpers retained in the households of Welsh aristocratic families attending the court of Henry VII. The position of harper to a noble family had traditionally been a highly coveted one, often hereditary, and harpers had been subjected to a long training with strict examinations to test their competence. By the middle of the sixteenth century, however, the musicians who had qualified in the traditional way were being troubled by the rising incidence of players who had not joined the profession 'legally' and apparently were bringing it into disrepute. Representation was made to the Crown for protection against this encroachment of their rights and Queen Elizabeth, through the Council of Wales and the Marches, commissioned a Welsh gentleman, William Mostyn, of Flintshire to sort the dispute out by conducting an examination to eliminate the charlatans:—

> "Vagrants and idle persons naming themselves minstrels, rhymers and bards are lately grown into such an intolerable multitude within the principality of north Wales that not only gentlemen and other by their shameless disorders are oftentimes disquieted in their habitations but also the expert minstrels and musicians in tongue and cunning thereby much discouraged to travail in the exercise and practice of their knowledges."

211

Amongst the musicians who succeeded at the Eisteddfod at Caerwys in 1567, graduating as *Pencerdd* (the highest degree) and qualifying to teach the harp, was William Penllyn who is noteworthy as the composer or collector of the earliest Welsh harp music extant. This is preserved in a manuscript copy made by (and named after) Robert ap Huw 'in Charles I's time' which is now in the British Museum.

During the seventeenth century Welsh music continued with little change along the lines described: in the traditional manner of folk music for the *werin*, the harp music also being displayed as an occasional diversion in gentlemanly households; the kind of music that was fashionable in England was fostered by the landed classes; and, with little enthusiasm or ability being shown by either sector, some congregational music in the church services for both in the chanting of the psalms. Taking these lines of development separately, I do not think that the music fashionable in England, and played by the anglicized gentry in Wales made any noticeable impression on the other kinds of Welsh music until the late nineteenth century. And Welsh music and composers made little impression either on English music during this period.

Further research might establish whether some musicians with Welsh names whose work was played in England were in fact Welsh, such as John Humphries and 'Mr. Edwards' whose concertos were published in the mid-eighteenth century, and whether William Evance, a slightly later keyboard composer, was the anglicized Welshman one might suspect. A John Jones, the singing of one of whose chants is said to have moved Haydn deeply, was organist of St. Paul's Cathedral from 1775 to 1796. However, it was not as a composer but as a performer that he made his mark, the mark by which Welsh musicians were usually known.

A few Welsh harpists had continued from the sixteenth century onwards to find employment with aristocratic households in England. One named Powell even went to settle in Jamaica when his patron the Duke of Portland was appointed governor there. His son, a friend of Handel's in London, was the player for whom the harp obbligato in 'Tune your harps to cheerful strains' in the oratorio *Esther* was written. Through the harpists traditional Welsh music encroached onto the music of England, even becoming fashionable towards the end of the eighteenth century.

It could be held that the isolation of the cultural life of the *werin* up to the closing years of the eighteenth century was not without the advantages of giving time for a healthy folk music tradition to get established in place of the bardic tradition which had been predominant in Wales up to the sixteenth century. The music of the *werin* had its vocal and instrumental forms, and dancing was popular notwithstanding attempts made, though by no means successfully, to suppress it during the Methodist revival. Musical source material is almost entirely absent before the seventeenth century and present-day study relies heavily on the early printed editions of harp-airs (in particular the collections by the blind harpist, John Parry of Ruabon: the first with Evan

Williams, published 1742, *Antient British Music; or, a Collection of Tunes, Never before Published, Which are retained by the Cambro-Britons,* other collections by John Parry alone following *c.* 1761 and 1781; and Edward Jones' *Musical and Poetical Relicks of the Welsh Bards,* 1784, again followed by the same author's *The Bardic Museum, of Primitive British Literature . . . with great pains now rescued from oblivion . . .,* 1802), and the first collections of folk songs made by Maria Jane Williams, *Ancient National Airs of Gwent and Morganwg,* 1844, and John Thomas (Ieuan Ddu) *Y Caniedydd Cymreig. The Cambrian Minstrel,* 1845.

With the foundation in 1906 of the Welsh Folk-Song Society, and the publication of its Journal from 1909, the danger of losing completely the body of Welsh folk song was averted. The number of people singing these songs unselfconsciously was declining rapidly, and it has since. But certainly the sympathetic and scholarly attention paid by members of this society to folk material has been a vital factor in keeping the tradition alive, and the means of making known what a rich tradition it is.

The characteristic distinction between the instrumental and the vocal folk music is that the latter, including Love songs, Spring and Christmas carols, Work songs, Lullabies, Nonsense songs, Solo and Chorus songs, and Ballads are essentially melodic while the harp-airs, in the contour of their melodies as well as in their generally clear feeling of key, are harmonic. Some of the folk songs proper would not have been accompanied, such as the ones basically in the Dorian or Aeolian mode, which early folk-song collectors report using intervals other than those which could be accommodated on the harp, the most popular Welsh instrument. Contrasting with these short, often intense pieces of small vocal compass the ballads were diatonic, they might have a wider compass and were certainly much longer, running to as many as twenty or thirty stanzas. These could have been accompanied by an instrument or simply by the singer tapping a repetitive rhythm on the ground. But while these folk songs and ballads have a particular appeal to Welsh-speaking people— understanding the language is important, as the shape of the line and its rhythm are so closely wedded to the natural lilt and accentuation of the words—it is the Welsh art of singing *penillion* which attracts wider attention. This unique form of singing possibly originated in the middle ages. There are literary references to the art but no musical evidence of the actual intricacies of how it was done until described by Edward Jones (Bardd y Brenin) in his *Musical and Poetical Relicks of the Welsh Bards,* 1784. While the ballad was always in the first place sung by the ballad monger, and the folk song proper arose naturally out of the *werin* themselves, singing *penillion* was a specialist art in the bardic rather than the folk tradition.

The style of doing so varied in different parts of Wales; what was called the South Wales style described nothing more than singing the *penillion* ('stanzas') of a ballad, or any other kind of folk song, to instrumental accompaniment, singing the words to the tune. The distinctive style, that of North Wales, was

213

a kind of free chanting, a melodic declamation of a poem cast in one of the strict bardic metres while a harp air was being played. It is a paradox of the art that whilst it is a form of solo singing the soloist would not be said to be singing a song: the soloist traditionally *improvised* his own melodic line, which aimed at being good, clean counterpoint in accompaniment to a harp air with which everybody was familiar already. Once started, the familiar tune is taken for granted and attention is fixed on the soloist who, besides improvising an interesting and melodic part and attempting to convey the changing moods and tone of the poem appropriately, has to observe certain conventions with regard to when he should join in after the harpist has started and ensuring that he has sung all the words of the *pennill* so that he can finish exactly with the harp. It is a fascinating and difficult fusion of poetic and musical art, still very much alive today although singers' confidence to *improvise* the counterpoint, rather than learn someone else's setting, seems to have waned.

The majority of Welshmen today would probably have little sympathy for the harp-air, yet this was the form of Welsh music which first became generally known in England through the publications mentioned, by blind Parry and Edward Jones, in the late eighteenth century. It was a period when 'people of quality' were beginning to take a fashionable interest in the remoter parts of the British Isles. Superseding the aristocratic Grand Tour of the early eighteenth century, and far cheaper and more convenient, travel in Wales, Scotland and Ireland provided a stock of experiences which could be recounted for a life-time. As an example of the public interest in travel and exploration, Captain Cook's *Journey around the World* which appeared in London in the autumn of 1784, was first published in a handsome edition of 2,000 copies; all of them, at £3 14s. each, were sold within two days. And the spate of travel books describing journeys through Wales from the 1770s onwards, following Thomas Pennant's pioneer accounts, and particularly marked in the 1790s, numbered more than fifty by the 1830s.

Reminiscences of their visit to Wales in the form of harp-airs, which could be played on the new piano-forte, were a saleable commodity and some publishers had hopes for anglicized Welsh songs as well. George Thomson of Edinburgh is noteworthy in that he aimed high and commissioned leading European composers to provide accompaniments to the melodies he gave them, and actually succeeded in getting Welsh song arrangements for voice with instrumental accompaniment from Haydn, who made forty-one and Beethoven, despite his objection that he was not being paid enough, who did twenty-six. But though graced by the names of masters of this calibre they do not sound like Welsh music. And as such stilted arrangements were readily available in print, they may even have had a weakening influence on the living tradition of Welsh folk music during the century.

Before considering the third line of development, congregational music and the rise of choral singing, briefly a word about the musical instruments

214

traditionally associated with Wales. The three mainly involved were the harp, the crwth and the pibgorn. Precisely why one instrument should be considered most appropriate in expressing the characteristic temperament of one nation and not of another, and what it was that made some people respond to its appeal while others did not, is a matter of interesting speculation. Of course opinions about the kind of tonal characteristics people consider to be most attractive or appropriate, and which characteristics of an instrument ought to be exploited, change from generation to generation and the instruments enjoying some popularity in one period may well have been superseded

Figure 1.

The Mostyn Silver Harp

by new favourites a century later. But, although we are astonishingly fickle in the kind of music we like listening to, and our forbears in European society obviously had the same failing judging by the profusion of musical instruments created from earliest times to satisfy some widely differing tastes in instrumental sound, the harp has been held in particular regard for about eight centuries in Wales.

Its form and tone have changed through the years from the small, heart-shaped Celtic harp originally strung in Wales with plaited horsehair but from the fourteenth century with gut strings (despite the conservative opposition eloquently put by Iolo Goch in his *Ode to the gut harp*), the larger, yet still

215

easily portable triple harp, introduced from Italy and commonly played in Wales from the end of the seventeenth century, to the pedal harp with which we are all familiar as an instrument in the modern symphony orchestra. The technique of playing also changed of course and the early practice of plucking the strings with the finger nails would appear to have been superseded by the current technique, using the fleshy tip of the fingers instead, about the end of the eighteenth century. Harp making was an indigenous craft in Wales, Llanrwst and Cardiff being particularly associated with it, and it is interesing to note that Welsh harp makers and consequently the Welsh players (or,

Figure 2.
A Triple Harp

equally, *vice versa* . . .) adhered to the principle of the pre-renaissance harp, up to the early part of the present century. This was that the harp rested against the left shoulder and the top strings of highest pitch were played mostly by the left hand while the right took the bass. On the continent, however, the practice was influenced by the keyboard arrangement by which the right hand played the highest part and the left the bass, so changing over, the harp was then played resting against the right shoulder, which is still the current practice.

That the medieval practice continued in Wales until the triple harp went out of common use at the end of the nineteenth century does, I think, indicate the strength of the bardic tradition and as part of this the very high esteem a master harpist was held in. One can certainly believe, particularly up to the sixteenth century: 'Tri dyn ydynt ogyfuwch, sef brenin, telynor, ac esgob.' (Three men are of equal prestige, a king, a harpist and a bishop.) Although musicians had kept the secrets of their profession to themselves, when the profession as such had more or less disappeared by the seventeenth century after the anglicization of the Welsh landed classes, amateur harpists clung to as much as they had of traditional performing practice. Though emotionally not the symbol of cultural identity which the heart-shaped Celtic harp is to the Irish, the harp has a secure place in Wales today, and amongst the finest performers on the instrument the Welsh musicians Osian Ellis and Ann Griffiths are virtuosos of international repute.

An impression of the early Celtic harp may be had from the drawing of the little silver model awarded to master harpists by the Mostyn family in the sixteenth century. This is shown on Figure 1. The three parallel rows of strings of the triple harp (the outside pair were tuned in unison to a diatonic scale, the inner row provided the accidentals and duplicated two of the degrees of the scale already in the outer rows) may be seen in the drawing of a triple harp seen in Figure 2.

Figure 3.   *Pibgorn*

The crwth and the pibgorn became obsolete about the beginning of the nineteenth century, and specimens of these instruments are now extremely rare. Examples are shown in Figures 3 and 4.

The pibgorn is a single-reed instrument with a tone something like an oboe. The two cow horns, mounted on either end of the cylindrical pipe, point in opposite directions: the instrument being held more or less vertically when played, the lower horn flaring outward serves as a bell to amplify the sound and the upper horn, opening only wide enough to cover the player's mouth, conceals the reed which is contained within the cavity of the horn out of reach of the player's lips. As a melodic instrument it may have been used in combination with either the harp or crwth, but this is conjecture. There is no music composed specifically for the pibgorn extant, and it is more probable that the pibgorn was usually played alone to avoid the necessity of the stringed instruments, in the absence of any standardization in pitch, having to tune to

217

it. (That Robert Griffiths, a nineteenth-century writer on Welsh music, refers to the fact that Ann Edwards, once proprietor of the Hand Hotel, Llangollen, was *good* at tuning the triple harp, would suggest that the task of getting this formidable instrument's ninety-odd strings in tune within itself was more than enough for most harpists, let alone possibly having to alter the pitch of the whole instrument for the sake of playing a dance or two with a pibgorn.)

As for the crwth, this is in many respects the most fascinating of the three instruments, being a *bowed* harp. Unlike its closest surviving relative on one side of the family, the Finnish *talharpa*, it has a neck and fingerboard, while like another now deceased, the sixteenth-century *lira da braccio*, it has a pair of strings lying off the fingerboard which can be either bowed or plucked by the left thumb. But unlike both it has an entirely distinctive bridge stopping the six strings not normally, but at an oblique angle: one foot of the bridge rests on the belly the other passes through one of the two circular sound holes and rests on the back, serving thereby as a sound post to transmit the vibrations of the strings from the belly to the back. As strings are perishable, and once they have all snapped the bridge falls off and gets lost, and as only six genuine specimens of the instrument are known to have survived, all without their bridges, the amount of arching in the bridge and the question of whether the 'long' leg of bridge should pass through the right or the left sound hole, have not yet been satisfactorily decided. The opinion that the arching of the bridge was only very slight indeed—as suggested by the rigid abstinence from any tendency in the sides to narrow opposite the bridge as in the violin to allow the bow to be tilted in order to isolate one string at a time—has been borne out from the practical experience of trying to play my crwth with different bridges. And it would seem most reasonable to me that the 'long' leg of the bridge should pass through the right sound hole (on looking towards the instrument) so that the sound post should function as in the violin under the strings of highest pitch and greatest tension.

The crwth's strings were tuned, according to eighteenth-century writers, to the following intervals.

As in the case of the pibgorn it is uncertain what kind of music the crwth played, but most historians would agree that it was probably used both alone and in accompaniment to the harp, in song and dance.

Although his main intention had been to put the Welsh Bible into his countrymen's hands as an instrument of conversion, perhaps the most effective outcome of Griffith Jones, Llanddowror's system of circulating schools was that it had brought literacy to a high proportion of the population of Wales.

One estimate put the figure at *c*. 160,000 by the time of his death. When the Methodist Revival broke out in Wales in 1736, with the preaching of Howell Harris and Daniel Rowland, the response was made by a people who if not already literate took measures to become so, and who turned with earnest devotion to their Bible and, shortly, their hymn books. Since the leaders of the Welsh Methodist movement were from 1739 closely associated with Whitefield and Wesley, they were not slow to learn about the power of the hymn, and for a nation with as yet no tradition for choral singing the hymn was the means of discovering another dimension of emotional experience.

Figure 4.

Crwth

The drawback in the first years of the revival was that there were few Welsh hymns and far fewer hymn tunes that fitted them. And people had yet to learn to sing together acceptably. The use of musical instruments to lead and support the singing was not encouraged. Even the revival's most prolific hymn-writer, William Williams, Pantycelyn, was against it. Congregational singing, introduced in 1744 towards the end of the first wave of the revival, was to become the most characteristic feature of the second.

During the foregoing twelve years William Williams had been publishing his latest collections of hymns, fitting them to English tunes he liked (for example, the lively tune 'Easter Hymn' or 'Salisbury', best known to the words 'Jesus Christ is risen today'), or in very few cases he adapted Welsh secular tunes. With these publications the music was never included: the people learned the tunes from one another and in these early stages would have sung (as near as possible) in unison, not in harmony. But the publication in 1762 of Pantycelyn's *Caniadau y rhai sydd ar y Môr o Wydr* coincided with a second revival in which the convincing force was not, as before, the preaching, but the congregational singing. People in small rural communities walked miles, singing jubilantly all the way, to hold fellowship meetings in hymn-singing in neighbouring villages and the practice of congregational singing became widespread throughout the whole of Wales. Though William Williams, Pantycelyn, was the most prolific hymn-writer of the period, the hymns of other people were also sung of course, and it has been suggested that those of one of the others, Morgan Rhys, were probably the most frequently sung of all.

In actually learning how to sing, the nonconformist congregations gained from the teaching of itinerant musicians working within the Anglican church to improve on the low standard of psalm chanting. Particularly influential in this sphere were Evan Williams of Llangybi and London (composer also of eight of the twenty-four tunes contained in *Llyfr Gweddi Gyffredin* (The Book of Common Prayer) 1770, for use with Edmund Prys's psalms, the first Welsh publication in which both the tune and the bass line were printed), and John Williams, Dolgellau. And, later in the century as nonconformist teachers of congregational singing, were Dafydd Siencyn Morgan, Llangrannog, and Henry Mills, Llanidloes, head of a musical family which was to exert a continuing influence on Welsh congregational music throughout the greater part of the nineteenth century. People were taught how to produce their voices more acceptably and were given experience in class singing, but at this time, at the end of the eighteenth century, the singing was still in unison and the tunes which they sang were all committed to memory since very few musicians, even amongst the itinerant singing teachers, could read a note of music.

Instruction of *some* kind in Welsh was offered with increasing persistence from the turn of the century onward until every respectable hymn book included, at the very least, an introductory discourse on the importance of appropriate and correct singing as a medium for worship, as well as, possibly, a scriptural justification for it. But although preceded by John Williams's (Siôn Singer's) *Cyfaill mewn llogell* (1797), the hymns of which are introduced by a discussion on theoretical aspects of music, the first practical music rudiments book in Welsh did not appear until 1838. This was John Mills', *Gramadeg Cerddoriaeth* (Grammar of Music) a thoroughly good book which ran to a number of editions.

As more and more Welshmen tried their hands at composing hymn tunes the controversy arose as to whether hymns ought to be sung in unison to the melody alone, or in harmony. In the 1820s and 30s even this was not a straight forward decision for the advocates of harmony; the question was hotly contested whether they should sing in three- or four-part harmony. It is clear, however, that while people had obviously been experimenting, by singing hymn tunes in harmony, it was *not* the general practice by the middle of the century. Richard and John Mills affirm, in the foreword to *Y Cerddor Eglwysig* (1847), that *the tune* was the most important vehicle for the hymn. But, only on the premise that every single person in the congregation had to sing in order to partake of the worship, and out of consideration for the usual assortment of high and low voices, they advocate singing in harmony as the solution, to give everyone something they could manage. Harking back to the sixteenth-century practice of according greatest responsibility to the tenor parts, and unlike the arrangement of parts we are more familiar with, in which the sopranos sing the tune in the top, they printed the score in four parts with the tune in the line above the bass and suggest:—

> "Teach the *tune* to the body of the congregation. Then if there are enough singers, put a number of the men with the strongest voices to sing the *bass*; young men whose voices are breaking sing the *middle part* (or failing this, you might choose men with supple and high-pitched voices); and boys whose voices have not started breaking take the *top part* . . . We think this is the most natural arrangement, and the only one which gets the whole congregation singing, and so involved in the worship."

So wrote Richard and John Mills in the mid nineteenth century. Congregational singing had, however, deteriorated and certainly lost its general appeal since the 1762 revival. The concern of a few musicians, like the Mills brothers, for encouraging a better understanding of music and the controversies about singing in unison or in harmony, and whether or not a harmonium might be permitted in chapel, are indicative perhaps of resuscitative efforts. By the 1860s, nevertheless, Wales had entered a phase of congregational singing such as it had never seen before. Indeed, it was the beginning of the *choral* tradition. With the publication of Thomas Williams's (Hafrenydd's) *Ceinion Cerddoriaeth* in 1852, a collection of choruses by Handel, Haydn, Mozart, Mendelssohn and others to which Welsh texts had been adapted, and of John Roberts's (Ieuan Gwyllt's) *Llyfr Tonau* in 1859 which, besides being a masterly selection of 459 hymn tunes, contains chants and twenty-five anthems, more good music was generally available with Welsh words to it than there ever had been previously.

In 1859 another revival broke out. In three years 17,000 copies of Ieuan Gwyllt's *Llyfr Tonau* were sold. He had insisted in the preface to his hymn book on the vital need for holding properly conducted rehearsals, at which the whole congregation should be present, to learn the tunes and words of the hymns they sang in their services. This exhortation was taken seriously, and at a time when prayer meetings and other services occupied people almost every night of the week the singing rehearsal was considered an essential feature of a chapel's programme of events. People were enthusiastic; they wanted to learn, and the strenuous leadership in particular of Ieuan Gwyllt, John Ambrose Lloyd and Edward Stephan (Tanymarian) was rewarded by the growth of a sound choral tradition. But it is doubtful whether choral singing would have become the national preoccupation it did, had it not been for the successful introduction of Curwen's tonic sol-fa system of music notation at precisely the period when people were once again taking up their hymn books in a religious revival.

Convinced by John Curwen's exposition of his system in Liverpool in 1860, and with his permission to publish an explanation of tonic sol-fa in Welsh, Eleazer Roberts and John Edwards soon demonstrated the value of the system to their sceptical fellow musicians in the Welsh nonconformist churches by inviting them to test children who had learned tonic sol-fa in sight reading. To follow up the publication in Welsh of Curwen's tonic sol-fa handbook, and of his hymn book in sol-fa (both in 1861), sol-fa classes were established at Sunday Schools throughout the country. It is interesting to note, incidentally, that those who took the important first step of learning sol-fa in Wales and then teaching it to others, were almost without exception ministers of religion.

The nonconformist church as a whole was given a strong lead in adopting the sol-fa system by its most influential members. Ieuan Gwyllt, for instance, was entirely in support of it: his hymn book was published in sol-fa notation in 1863, and for a period of four years (1869-73) he was editor of the journal *Cerddor y Tonic Solffa* (The Tonic sol-fa Musician) which, besides publishing new music, carried information about the latest singing festivals and news from sol-fa classes, including the names of successful candidates for the examinations of the Tonic Sol-fa College, London. This college was regarded widely in Wales as 'the poor man's university'. Its highly successful system of training in general musicianship led to the award of Licentiate and Fellowship diplomas. But while these were for the few, the *Advanced Certificate* was an objective many were proud to achieve. Someone who had taken his '*A.C.*' was recognized socially as having a musical standing, only a step from going on to take the *Gorsedd* examinations and assuming a bardic title.

The advantages of tonic sol-fa were, mainly:

(1) that it was a very cheap form of music notation;

(2) within limits it was effective and easily learned;

(3) it instilled what was most valuable in a singer: a sense of accurate time and a sense of accurate *relative pitch*, which equipped him to be a useful singer of any music, not merely set pieces learned parrot-fashion.

And results of the tonic sol-fa movement were many. First was the rise of good four-part congregational singing in Wales and, in an effort to extend the usual repertoire of known hymn tunes which could be used in services, the establishing of annual singing festivals, known by various names, but most generally by the name *Cymanfa Ganu*. All the chapels in the district would learn about forty selected hymns and meet usually for two services under the direction of a competent musician. The *Cymanfa Ganu* conductor became a popular figure and achieving eminence in this role was, along with that of eisteddfod adjudicator, the accepted indication of a musician's national status.

Choral societies were also set up throughout the country. At the beginning they were based in the chapels, which came to compete with each other at the local as well as the national eisteddfod level—thus giving impetus to the eisteddfod. These choirs became acquainted with the range of oratorios and shorter pieces that were issued in cheap tonic sol-fa editions. The '59 revival had been the means of bringing people into chapel where they had felt the warmth of the singing and through learning to read sol-fa they were enabled to make music themselves. Living in a milieu in which music was practically everybody's concern was obviously stimulating. This is evinced by the number of composers and singers who contributed to Welsh musical life from then on into the first decades of the present century. Welsh choral singing won a reputation in England, particularly after the victory of the massed South Wales choirs—'Caradoc's Choir'—at the Crystal Palace in 1872 and 73. Despite the back-biting (that all they had was lung-power, one Welshman being worth three London singers), an immediate outcome of their first visit was that Boosey & Co. thought it worthwhile commercially to publish *The Songs of Wales* (1873), edited by the most eminent London-Welsh musician, one of the leading Eisteddfod adjudicators and a professor at the Royal Academy, Brinley Richards.

Welsh choirs performed frequently in London, including in their programmes pieces by Welsh composers. The most prolific of these, and for a period the musician whose influence was greatest in Wales was Joseph Parry, whose rise to prominence as the first Professor of Music (1874) at the newly-founded University College of Wales, Aberystwyth, from being a pit boy at Merthyr working for half-a-crown a week at the age of nine, became something of a national legend. It was not only his ability which made him influential, but the fact that he had had a professional training. While at the Academy he had taken the external Cambridge D.Mus., and from the time he started his musical career was fully occupied in it. Unlike the musically-gifted ministers of religion and the legion of other good amateurs in Wales, he was one of the very few professionals.

One notes with regret, in considering this late nineteenth- and early twentieth-century period of Welsh music, how poverty and the lack of a place for a professional musician in Welsh society prevented so many gifted composers for many years from leaving the mine or the shop for a full-time career in music. Some never escaped. There was an extraordinary concentration of musical talent in the Welshmen born during the second half of the nineteenth century, the potential of which was never fully realized. W. T. Rees, John Price, J. T. Rees and Tom Price, for example, were miners, D. Emlyn Evans was a tailor, John Owen Jones a grocer's assistant, J. H. Roberts a quarryman—men who were writing songs of real poetic beauty, as well as oratorios and other large-scale works, whose only chance of ever hearing them performed was to win first prize at the National Eisteddfod.

The music composed was almost entirely vocal; the eisteddfod was a standing influence in this direction, a consumer requiring all kinds of solo and choral pieces for the range of competitions held. As yet little competence had been shown in the writing of chamber music or purely orchestral pieces. There was seldom an opportunity in Wales to hear an orchestra before the First World War, and few people played orchestral instruments. Joseph Parry's orchestral writing, even, is drab and elementary, which is suprising since he admired the music of Verdi and was familiar with that of his contemporaries. In piano accompaniment writing, on the other hand, some composers showed a natural flare, like R. S. Hughes and John Owen Jones one of the finest organists in Wales in the twenties and thirties. At the University Colleges at Cardiff and Aberystwyth and at the various private music schools, students could learn about instrumental music but rarely heard orchestral instruments apart from the harp and the violin and if there were a local band, the brass as well. To remedy the situation, when Walford Davies began as Professor of Music at the University College of Wales, Aberystwyth in 1919, professional instrumentalists were employed to give regular series of concerts and to teach their instruments, establishing thus an arrangement which has since been widely adopted throughout the world.

With the marked rise of interest in instrumental music between the wars opportunities for playing were offered by the orchestral societies which were formed in most towns, and—though hardly a particularly Welsh feature— playing at the 'silent pictures'.

The preoccupation with choral music had meant that Welsh people tended to have distinctive perimeters to their musical experience. True, those who sang the principal oratorios participated in music which was common to European culture and experience. But the majority of eisteddfod pieces, anthems and denominational hymn-tunes remained 'Welsh' and made little impact on the European scene. With increasing attention being paid to instrumental music in the twenties and thirties and to some extent though not proportionate, the decline in choral singing, Welsh musical taste began to align itself with the mainstream of European music. At the same time, as more Welsh students pursued studies in music, their professional knowledge— coming to bear on the classes they taught, the eisteddfod committees they sat on, the choirs, the *cymanfaoedd canu*, the orchestras they conducted—gradually influenced the traditional idea of what music was, with a recognition of wider perimeters, even a different set of values. And the folklore belief, that the amateur performance is somehow more genuine and therefore preferable to a professional one, would appear at last to have given way to a less inhibiting view.

Recent developments emphasize how musicians in Wales are now participating in the whole of the European musical culture and the parochialism which circumstances had forced upon them formerly is seldom now in evidence. The organization of the National Youth Orchestra of Wales by Irwin Walters in 1945 provided an impetus for musical school children *to aim* at a professional standard, and it is no coincidence that practically all the present generation of younger Welsh performers and teachers of music have passed through the national or their regional youth orchestra. And it is particularly valuable, in gaining the wider perspective, for members of these youth orchestras to be able to see for themselves the stature of the Welsh composers whose music they perform in a context of the best of European music. The first Welsh composers to show an understanding of the orchestra and to use it imaginatively were a group born about the time of the First World War: Daniel Jones, David Wynne, Mansel Thomas, Grace Williams and Arwel Hughes. In keeping with the modern tendency to write works for smaller forces, it is noticeable that these composers, and possibly to an even greater extent the following generation, Alun Hoddinott, David Harries and William Matthias, have produced a great deal of chamber music. Although Daniel Jones was an innovator on the European scene in composing music with a progressive metrical framework, the lead towards *avant garde* music in Wales came mostly from English composers who were, or still are, resident in the country: Reginald Smith Brindle and Bernard Rands at the University College of North Wales, Bangor, and Ian Parrott, Professor of Music at Aberystwyth. Finally, the most recent new departure of interest has been the setting up of electronic music studios at the University Colleges at Cardiff and Bangor.

While on the one hand efforts have been made to promote an appreciation of the traditional Welsh folk music and dance, steps have also been taken to encourage new music for the future. With the foundation of the Llangollen International Musical Eisteddfod in 1947 under the musical direction of the music publisher and authority on Welsh folk music, W. S. Gwynn Williams, aspects of the Welsh tradition have been seen within the context of a European folk culture as beautiful and interesting, worth practising rather than preserving lifeless. Also looking ahead, the Guild for the Promotion of Welsh Music, founded in 1954, and the B.B.C. in Wales sponsor composition through commissioning new works while the Welsh Arts Council is active in supporting all kinds of musical performances, from amateur opera to music club concerts.

In the nineteenth century the availability of music with Welsh words had been a decisive factor in the rise of choral singing. Now, as then, the fact that it has a Welsh text *may* make a piece of music acceptable whereas otherwise it might not have been regarded worthy of 'performance'. Even so, it is a healthy development that a new kind of Welsh folk music is arising. Akin

225

musically to the international 'protest pop' it is *Welsh* emotionally, expressing particular sentiments in the Welsh language. A conclusion one comes to, considering this as with earlier Welsh music is that the music of this nation has always been intimately associated with the language.

ACKNOWLEDGEMENTS

As footnote references to sources have not been used in this book I wish to make grateful acknowledgements here to the following sources for material used in this chapter, and to express my indebtedness to the authors in question.

J. Curwen and Sons Ltd. for W. S. Gwynn Williams, *Welsh National Music and Dance* (London, 1932); University of Wales Press for R. D. Griffith, *Hanes Canu Cynulleidfaol Cymru* (Cardiff, 1948), Gwyn Thomas, *Eisteddfodau Caerwys* (Cardiff, 1968), Hether Kay (ed.), *The Land of the Welsh Dragon* (Cardiff, 1969); Hinrichsen Edition Ltd. for Peter Crossley-Holland (ed.), *Music in Wales* (London, 1948); The Gwynn Publishing Co. for W. S. Gwynn Williams (ed.), *Caneuon Traddodiadol y Cymry* (Llangollen, 1961 and 1963); Ernest Benn Ltd. for Percy M. Young, *A History of British Music* (London, 1967); B. T. Batsford Ltd. for Anthony Baines, *European and American Musical Instruments* (London, 1966). And in the following journals: *Ulster Folk Life* (Vols. 15-16), Essays presented to Estyn Evans, 1970, I. C. Peate, 'Crwth a Thelyn'; *Llên Cymru*, 1960-61, Vol. VI, A. O. H. Jarman, 'Telyn a Chrwth'; *MAN*, 1947, 17, I. C. Peate, 'Welsh Musical Instruments'.

"FOR WALES — SEE ENGLAND"
THE ARTIST IN WALES

ROGER WEBSTER

XII

THE only attempt at a comprehensive survey of the visual arts in Wales is that of the late David Bell, *The Artist in Wales* (1957). It is a rather diffident, apologetic book. Initially Bell took as his model *Cent Chefs d'Oeuvre de l'Art Français,* but quickly realised that his 'masterpieces' would look 'rather thin when dressed up in Welsh flannel'. He had to reconcile himself to the fact that 'the fine arts have played a negligible part in Welsh life, the applied arts only a rudimentary one'. That this should be so should cause neither surprise nor shame. Bell would after all have been hard put to it to list a hundred English, Irish or Scottish masterpieces or, for that matter, a hundred works of major significance from Scandinavia or Russia. The visual arts have had their greatest expression in the wealthy mercantile communities of Italy, France, Spain and the Netherlands. Wales, in common with the rest of Britain, has always been on the periphery of European art.

Unfortunately, even in the Dark Ages, when the visual arts flourished along Europe's western seaboard, Wales was still peripheral to a movement which had its most sophisticated expression in Ireland and Scandinavia. There is nothing in Wales to compare with the Book of Kells or early Irish Christian monuments, and when more complex stone carving reached Wales in the eighth and ninth centuries the end products were, in general, little more than inferior imitations of Irish and occasionally Scandinavian work.

The Norman conquest of Wales established a bridgehead to Europe, as Anglo-Norman castles, cathedrals and abbeys all bear witness. Wales may have been on the edge of Europe, but no one standing, for example, in remote St. Davids, flanked on one side by the cathedral and on the other by Bishop Gower's palace, could doubt that it was not an integral and significant part of European culture. As there was no national art in the modern sense in the middle ages, it is difficult to differentiate between the work of foreign crafts-men and that produced by Welshmen. The cathedrals at St. Davids and Llandaff have stylistically so much in common with the late twelfth century parts of Hereford cathedral and other churches and abbeys in the Marches and West Country, as to suggest a regional style and even possibly that the same band of masons travelled throughout the area. Bishop Gower employed 'foreign' masons to build his palace at St. Davids but the same architectural features were copied by local craftsmen in the Bishop's more humble residence at Lamphey. Dr. Colin Gresham has shown the way in which local stone carvers in North Wales, although initially imitating English work, ultimately developed their own idiom. Thus in the middle ages stylistic innovation came from the outside. Welsh artists either copied or adapted new

228

SLEEPING JESSE.   Oak, length 120 in. (detail)
St. Mary's Parish Church, Abergavenny

styles. This was true even of wood carving, the most developed artistic activity of the period.

The widespread building and renovation of churches in Wales in the latter part of the fifteenth century was an expression of the English perpendicular style which was itself an aspect of the late Gothic movement in Northern Europe. The perpendicular towers at St. John's Church, Cardiff, and at Wrexham and Gresford parish churches, the distinctive roof, the misericords and other wood carvings at St. David's Cathedral, and the fan-vaulted screen at Conway parish church, are all manifestations of a style that had its richest expression in East Anglia and other of the more affluent parts of England. The most astonishing wood carving of this period—the Abergavenny Jesse— shows Flemish inspiration, its fluidity and naturalness betray a sophisticated humanism that one would never have expected to find in Wales at this time.

If 'nationality' had little meaning in the medieval period, neither had the term 'art' in its modern usage. In the middle ages art was functional and educative; there was no distinction between artist and craftsman. In medieval Wales the wood carver had the same status as the bard, and both were patronised by the *uchelwyr* (nobility). The main patron of the mason and wood and stone carvers was, however, the Church. When Henry VIII broke with Rome and ordered the dissolution of the monasteries, he forced an abrupt severance with the middle ages and prevented England and Wales from being involved in the continuing tradition of religious art in Catholic Europe. The Baroque and Rococo had little direct influence on England, on Wales they had none at all. Even so, the political integration of Wales with England in the Tudor period inevitably led to her artistic domination by her wealthier neighbour. The much quoted *Encyclopaedia Britannica* direction 'For Wales— See England' is painfully accurate as far as the visual arts are concerned. At the very time when national schools of art were being established in Europe it was impossible for Wales to nurture an artistic tradition of her own. Not that the English tradition was much to emulate. From the Tudor period onwards the development of the visual arts in both England and Wales was fitful: there were brilliant individuals (both foreign and native artists) but little artistic continuity. A dedicated Anglophobe like Sir Nikolaus Pevsner has to use all his subtlety to trace the tenuous links in an English tradition. It is only with the development of Romantic painting at the end of the eighteenth century, foretold by Wilson and culminating in the work of Turner, that England and Wales made a coherent and significant contribution to European art.

The tendency in the sixteenth century for patronage to move from the Church to the aristocracy was greater in England and Wales than even in the rest of Protestant Europe. It was the gentry and wealthy merchants, building new houses and commissioning portraits to hang on their walls, who patronised architects and artists. Even the Puritans, who so violently objected to visual representations of God, were happy to have their own portraits painted. The essentially 'provincial' status of the visual arts in England and Wales is shown

230

by their dependence on visiting artists from Europe who became the fashionable portrait painters of their time: Holbein in the court of Henry VIII, Van Dyke in that of Charles I, Lely during the Restoration, and Kneller who was continuously active during five reigns from that of Charles II to that of George I. 'Fine art' thus became a fashionable and esoteric activity centred on the court and supported by the mercantile wealth of the metropolis. Monastic and other centres of artistic activity outside London declined; only local craftsmen remained. The Welsh gentry, increasingly anglicised by the Act of Union flocked to the capital. If they could not afford to do so they had to make do with Dublin where they could have their portraits painted by fashionable artists like Robert Hunter and Robert Home, or even Chester where there was always a minor portraitist like Thomas Leigh who was active in the mid-seventeenth century. All that remained in Wales were local craftsmen—carpenters, masons, potters and weavers—meeting the essential needs of isolated peasant communities and perpetuating traditional skills that were little affected by changing fashions.

The occasional Welshman who, despite his environmental disadvantages, showed artistic ability had, like his counterparts in the English provinces, to leave for London or for the continent in order to find an outlet for his talents. The most outstanding of all Welsh artists, Richard Wilson (1713/14-1782) studied and worked in London and spent extensive periods in Venice and Rome. He only returned to Wales to die. Thomas Jones (1742-1803), Wilson's pupil, whose paintings have been increasingly appreciated in recent years, had a career that almost exactly followed that of his teacher: study and work in London interspersed with an extensive visit from 1776 to 1783 to Rome and Naples, and followed in 1787 by retirement to his native Radnorshire.

Wilson began his career as a portraitist but, on his visit to Italy, his interest changed to painting landscapes. He concentrated on this for the rest of his life, achieving a simplicity of design and an evocation of light and space that was unparalleled in Britain at that time. Following the example of Claude and Poussin, Wilson's early landscapes were of mythological figures in idealised settings. This was a response to the contemporary taste for the neoclassical and the 'sublime'. Often enough, however, the classical figures in Wilson's landscapes, and the titles he gave his pictures, seem to be an afterthought: his real interest was the landscape itself. This earned him Reynolds's well known stricture that he 'introduced gods and godesses, ideal beings into scenes which were by no means prepared to receive such personages. His landscapes were in reality too near common nature to admit supernatural objects'. Inevitably, Wilson became increasingly interested in 'pure landscape', and the pictures in this vein which he based on Welsh subjects are amongst his most notable achievements. It was with these pictures that Ruskin considered that 'the history of sincere landscape art founded on the meditative love of nature begins in England'.

In a sense Wilson's 'meditative love of nature' foretold a change in the late

231

RICHARD WILSON. VALLEY OF THE MAWDDACH (c. 1770) 35½ in. x 41½ in.
By permission of the City Art Gallery, Manchester

Market Day at Aberistwith

Thomas Rowlandson. MARKET DAY AT ABERYSTWYTH (1792).
Pen and Water stained with colour
By permission of the National Library of Wales

eighteenth century from the 'classical', the 'ideal' and the 'sublime' to the 'picturesque': to landscapes which, although not overpowering and awesome, appealed because of their irregularity and strongly marked, if transient, contrasts in light and shade which highlighted ruins, twisted trees and other symbolic objects. The picturesque, perhaps, found its most characteristic expression in the English garden which did not consist of formal patterns as on the continent, or even attempt to recreate the ideal landscapes of Claude, but rather emphasised the naturalness of the scenery with winding paths, serpentine lakes and a visual surprise around every corner. Thomas Johnes, with the help of two of the greatest authorities on the picturesque, Richard Payne Knight and Uvedale Price, created such a landscape at Hafod in Cardiganshire. This he completed by inviting Thomas Baldwin the Bath architect, to build a mansion in an elaborate Gothic style. Hafod became an inspiration for a generation of students of the picturesque. Sir John Summerson for example has suggested that the most important result of John Nash's sojourn in Carmarthen between 1783 to 1795, was not that he built Palladian villas for the local squirearchy, but that, through his association with Thomas Johnes and his circle, he became initiated into the mysteries of the picturesque.

The ruin, either real or simulated, was an essential element in the picturesque landscape, and amongst the most frequent visitors to Wales in the late eighteenth century were the antiquaries, collecting material which they later gathered together in accounts of their 'Welsh Tour'. These antiquaries were often accompanied by a topographical artist to provide them with illustrations, and it was in this way that in the eighteenth century a number of English artists were introduced to Wales. Henry Wigstead's *Tour of North and South Wales* (1800) was, for example, illustrated by Thomas Rowlandson, whose sensitive and delicately coloured pen and wash studies record with great sympathy the more domestic and intimate aspects of Welsh life. Rowlandson was on holiday and he left the more biting and satirical side of his nature behind in London.

Moses Griffith (1747-1819) the self-taught artist from Lleyn was the only Welshman who had any significance as a topographical artist. He was employed to illustrate Thomas Pennant's *Tour* and his understanding of the picturesque can be seen in his watercolour *Pulpud Huw Llwyd o Gynfal* (1806). When, however, this picture is compared with J. C. Ibbetson's striking view *Phaeton in the Storm* painted eight years earlier, it is possible to discern the extent to which the Yorkshire artist had advanced from the 'picturesque' to the 'romantic'. Elements in a picturesque landscape inevitably became symbols of man's desires, doubts, sorrows and fears—an interest in the picturesque implied a romantic attitude. However, once a picture becomes primarily an expression of an artist's feelings it ceases to be about a particular place. Ibbetson's picture could be of a mountain setting anywhere; there is little significance in its being located in Wales.

The most romantic of artists, however, needs some initial inspiration from the world about him, and Welsh castles (especially that at Conway) were at the turn of the century considered to be particularly appropriate subjects. It was at Conway where, in 1800, J. S. Cotman, in the company of a group of young artists brought together by Sir George Beaumont (that most influential of nineteenth century patrons) was first introduced to the picturesque. Indeed, every significant landscape painter in Britain, with the exception of Constable, at some time or other made a visit to Wales; the romantic possibilities of the Welsh landscape being most fully exploited by Cotman, Girtin and Cox and pre-eminently so by Turner, whose turbulent and atmospheric pictures lie at the heart of the romantic movement.

At the very time that English artists were making their incursions into 'Wild Wales', Wales was itself undergoing a profound economic and social change. Between Turner's first visit to Wales in 1793 and his last in 1799 the iron industry had spread from Merthyr and Dowlais along the north eastern rim of the South Wales coalfield. Within fifty years both the North and South Wales coalfields were being fully exploited, and by 1870 the whole of Wales was served by a network of railways. Although there was during these years a dramatic movement of population from countryside to coalfield, the fundamental cleavage in the social structure remained. The English industrial 'colonists', emulating the airs and graces of the rural gentry, bought estates and built vast houses. Their taste was, however, not for the fanciful gothic favoured by Thomas Johnes, but rather for the more solid 'neo-Romanesque'. They were, after all, the industrial barons. William Crawshay, commissioned Robert Lugar, who had popularised the neo-baronial style, to build Cyfarthfa Castle. His example was followed by Walter Wilkins, who, having made his fortune in India, bought an estate at Maesllwch in Radnorshire, and employed Lugar to build a castle in medieval style. Wilkin's son completed the project and, in order to feel more at home in his new residence, changed his name to De Winton. Most dramatic of all, Thomas Hopper rebuilt Penrhyn Castle for the slate magnate George Dawkins-Pennant, and created a vast neo-Norman residence whose grandeur is matched only by its lack of comfort. Penrhyn Castle can perhaps only be rivalled by the reconstructions made by William Burges in the eighteen seventies of Cardiff Castle and Castell Coch for the third Marquess of Bute and financed by the profits from Rhondda coal. Despite Burges's reputation as a medieval scholar, and his pre-Raphaelite eye for detail, his world was that of Victorian fantasy. How otherwise can one explain the fairy tale towers at Castell Coch and the presence of an oriental harem in Cardiff Castle?

The creators of the new Welsh transport system were also in sympathy with the new aesthetic. Thomas Telford combined engineering skill with a passion for medieval castles. The mock medieval towers he created to support the chains of his suspension bridge at Conway inevitably look bogus when silhouetted against the real thing. However, his bridge over the Menai, and

235

JULIUS CAESAR IBBETSON.   PHAETON IN A STORM (1798).   Oil on canvas $26\frac{1}{4}$ in. x $36\frac{1}{4}$ in.
By permission of the City Art Gallery and Temple Newsam House, Leeds

Moses Griffith. PULPUD HUW LLWYD O GYNFAL (1806).
Watercolour 11¼ in. x 15½ in.
By permission of the National Library of Wales

his aqueducts on the Ellesmere canal at Pontcysyllte and Chirk are far more successful embellishments to the landscape. The arch-romantic Sir Walter Scott considered the Pontcysyllte aqueduct 'the most impressive work of art he had ever seen' while shortly after the opening of the aqueduct at Chirk J. S. Cotman was painting it as though it were a ruin in the Roman Campagna.

The emergence of the pre-Raphaelite narrative painting in the second quarter of the nineteenth century, and the resultant decline of romanticism, for a time isolated Wales from the main stream of English art. The Welsh gentry and the new entrepreneurs, continued to collect works of art and some like the Crawshays, Pennants and Boothbys, bought some notable pictures, although it was not until the present century, when the two remarkable sisters Gwendoline and Margaret Davies filled their home at Gregynog with French Impressionist paintings, that a really significant art collection was gathered together in Wales.

This activity scarcely touched the mass of the Welsh people. There is no parallel in the visual arts to the development of literature, or even of music, in Wales in the nineteenth century. A predominantly nonconformist population retained a puritan objection to painting and sculpture. Even so, the multitude of chapels built during the century were the most significant expression of popular art of the period. As the majority of these chapels were designed by local builders with ideas culled from architects' pattern books, their style is an eclectic and bizarre mixture. The nineteenth century Welsh chapel is in reality an expression of the folk-picturesque. The gentry had their gothic and neo-baronial halls, the people their Bethesdas, Salems and Zions.

In the latter part of the nineteenth century some incursions were made into Welsh prejudice against the visual arts, and art competitions and exhibitions were even introduced into the National Eisteddfod. These, however, soon displayed all those characteristics that we have come to associate with art at the Eisteddfod: complaints or, what were perhaps worse, condescending comments about low standards by the predominantly English adjudicators and selectors, tension between the professional and amateur artists, and the general impression that the visual arts were very much a fringe activity. One of the most frequent causes of comment was the lack of interest taken in the Eisteddfod by the Royal Cambrian Academy. This lack of concern was, however, to be expected. The Academy was largely a by-product of the English preoccupation with the picturesque and, as though to emphasise the fact, in 1881 it established itself in its permanent headquarters at Plas Mawr, Conway. The Academy's membership, even today, comes largely from Lancashire and Cheshire and its influence on Wales has been slight.

English manufacturers, on seeing the achievements of their continental rivals at the Great Exhibition of 1851, were spurred to an interest in design. Unfortunately, the only consumer industry of any significance in Wales, fine Swansea and Pontypool porcelain, had long since gone into decline, and there was little interest in design in the heavy industries. There was thus not a great interest in Wales in art and design education, although classes in drawing, financed by the Science and Art Department of South Kensington, were held in Wales as elsewhere. It was Science and Art Department sponsorship that led to the establishment of art schools at Cardiff, Newport, Swansea, Llanelli, Carmarthen, and Wrexham and for a time at Caernarvon. The staffs of those schools (with the notable exception of W. Grant Murray, Principal of the Swansea school from 1910 to 1943) had little influence on art in Wales. The art schools are strangely isolated from the rest of the Welsh educational system and they are never mentioned in any of the histories of Welsh education. Although the Welsh intermediate schools, founded in the eighteen nineties, included 'drawing' in their curricula, this was almost always an optional minor activity taught as a second or third subject by teachers qualified in other fields. The late Ceri Richards, who was a pupil at Gowerton Intermediate School during the first world war, was so exasperated by the lack of art teaching in his school that he joined private evening classes in Swansea where, with a group of ladies, he learnt to copy reproductions.

In the constituent colleges of the University of Wales art was taught only in the teacher training departments. A proposal by the University Court in the nineteen twenties to establish a National Chair of Architecture and Applied Art was rejected, as was a more modest suggestion that a University lectureship in art be established. Welsh educationalists have, in general, regarded art as a somewhat frivolous 'extra' with little educational or economic value: a pupil only learnt to use his hands after manifestly failing to use his head. The only major educationalist to hold a different view was Sir Owen M. Edwards who, under the influence of Ruskin and Morris, advocated the inclusion of both art and handicraft in the curricula of all Welsh schools. Through articles in his journal *Cymru*, he attempted to give his fellow-Welshmen an understanding of the history of European art, and, by including numerous illustrations, to improve their visual sensibility. He achieved, however, only a modest success. The only Welsh artist in the early part of the century to have any impact on Wales was Christopher Williams whose huge allegorical paintings had an enormous popularity. This was especially true of his picture 'Deffroad Cymru' where Wales is symbolised as a female figure emerging topless out of a stormy sea!

Wales's major artists, during the first half of this century, were still forced to train and to work outside the Principality. Augustus and Gwen John and J. D. Innes were all students at the Slade and spent most of their working life in London or on the continent. For brief periods from 1911 to Innes's death in 1914, he and Augustus John made the ultimate picturesque gesture by following bands of gypsies around Wales. Innes was influenced by early nineteenth century English artists, (especially Cotman) and both he and John, through their association with the Camden Town Group, came into contact, albeit indirectly, with French Post-Impressionist painting. It is this that accounts for their adventurous, almost *Fauve*, use of colour and the boldness

239

Augustus John. ROMANY FOLK (*c.* 1907). Oil 13½ in. x 10½ in.
By permission of the National Museum of Wales

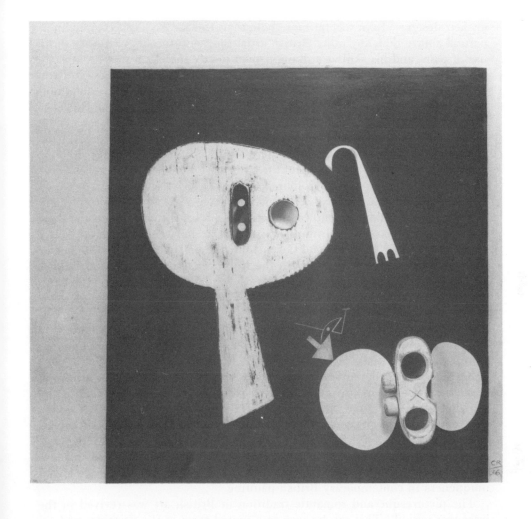

CERI RICHARDS   WHITE AND DARK (1936)   Construction 21¼ in. x 19¾ in.
By permission of the National Museum of Wales

of their designs. John was far more bold than Innes. He had, possibly, more natural ability than any other British artist this century: his virtuosity in the use of paint and his skill as a draughtsman justify the claim that he was 'the last of the old masters'. His sister Gwen studied at Whistler's school in Paris, and for the latter part of her life she lived at Meudon, a semi-recluse confining her painting to portraits of women and children all in simple poses. However, with these pictures of modest scale and quiet tones, Gwen John created, as Sir John Rothenstein, has suggested, 'an impression of extraordinary grandeur'.

The same comment might be made of the work of David Jones, another Catholic convert who has also spent the latter part of his life in severe isolation. David Jones's luminous watercolours, as might be expected of an artist who is as distinguished as a writer as he is a painter, have a strong literary and poetic quality. The freedom he shows in organising his paintings betrays at least indirect influence of Post Impressionism. It is, however, as true of David Jones, as it was of Augustus and Gwen John and of Innes, that he remains an isolated figure on the fringe of both the European movement and of English art. Expatriot Welsh artists would seem to be doomed to remain 'outsiders'. This was equally true of Ceri Richards, Wales's most distinguished artist in the post war period. English critics have found it impossible to 'place' him. After a period of study at Swansea College of Art, Richards moved in 1924 to the Royal College in London where he was first introduced to Post-Impressionist painting. His work was influenced by Matisse, but later he came under the spell of the Surrealists and especially of Max Ernst's experiments with the free association of ideas. Richards had a bewildering number of starting off points for his 'visual metaphors': the finery of London costermongers, the poetry of Dylan Thomas and numerous musical themes, pre-eminent amongst which is Debussy's prelude *La Cathedrale Engloutie*. In each of these series of paintings he showed great technical brilliance—a command of vibrant colour and of sinuous line that is of signal uniqueness in contemporary British painting.

The picturesque and romantic tradition in British art was revived in the inter-war period. This can be seen in a muted form in the paintings of Ceri Richards, but is more directly discernible in the work of those artists who are primarily landscapists. For the most pre-eminent of these artists, Graham Sutherland, Wales played its traditional inspirational role. When Sutherland turned from engraving to painting in the early 'thirties he was too dependant on the quiet domestic 'home counties' tradition of Samuel Palmer. His work was a failure amd most of it he destroyed. In 1934, however, Sutherland made the first of many visits to Pembrokeshire, and it was here in an entirely new environment that he learnt to 'paraphrase' the landscape and discover his mature style.

Other English artists, like Nash and Piper, followed Sutherland in a search for inspiration amongst the hills and romantic ruins of Wales. There is, however, only one major artist who has found his subject matter amongst Welsh

242

industry,—the Polish painter Joseph Herman,—and his work thus has a peculiar significance. Herman left Poland in 1936 and for a time lived in Belgium. At the outbreak of the war he came to Britain, and in 1944 he made a chance visit to Ystradgynlais where he immediately decided to stay. For Herman the miner and the industrial landscape expressed 'the dignity of human labour' and his paintings, with their abstract and monumental forms and rich glowing colours, were 'secular altarpieces'. During the time Herman spent in Wales he also showed that the most depressing industrial landscape can have visual excitements. 'Violet roofs at the foot of green hills. Pyramids of black tips surrounded by cloud like trees the colour of dark bottle'. It was thus that Herman saw Ystradgynlais.

By today Herman's pictures have much the same historical value as eighteenth century topographical drawings. His miners are likely to be working in a plastics factory. In the quarter century since the end of the war Wales has undergone an economic and social transformation. Although the coal industry has declined, the country as a whole has shared in the unparalleled prosperity of the British Isles. The development of secondary and further education and the establishment of large comprehensive schools has resulted in a growing demand for specialist teachers of art, and this in turn has resulted in the growth of art and of art departments in colleges of education. These developments have encouraged a number of English artists to settle in Wales and even for the occasional Welsh artist of ability to continue to live here. The reorganisation of art schools following the publication in 1960 of the Coldstream Report, has resulted in courses at two art colleges in Wales, at Newport and Cardiff, being recognised as leading to the Diploma in Art and Design. This has had the effect of concentrating the majority of artists in Wales in the South East. It is because they are teachers at Newport College of Art that John Selway and Jack Crabtree came to live in Wales, and that Ernest Zabole, the Rhondda painter, and Peter Nicholas, the Monmouthshire sculptor, continue to live here. The Cardiff College of Art has attracted Mervyn Baldwyn, Tom Hudson, Eric Malthouse, Terry Setch and David Tinker to Wales. The latter in more recent years has been head of the revived art department at the University College of Wales at Aberystwyth, which now organises undergraduate courses in fine art. Robert Hunter, the Liverpool artist, has taught at Trinity College, Carmarthen, for over twenty years and has completely identified himself with West Wales. Selwyn Jones, by becoming head of the art department at Bangor Normal College, has been enabled to return to his native Caernarvonshire.

Since the war, therefore, professional artists have come to work in schools and colleges all over Wales. In the 'fifties these artists had little opportunity to exhibit or sell their work. It is true that from 1950 onwards the National Eisteddfod attempted to attract the more professional artists by replacing competitions by an open exhibition. Even so, the visual arts have never really had a satisfactory place at the Eisteddfod: few works are sold and over

243

JOSEPH HERMAN.   THREE MINERS (1955).   Oil 18 in. x 10 in.
From the collection of Mrs. C. Thompson

the years selectors have made some eccentric decisions, tending always to favour the primitive rather than the professional. The Contemporary Art Society for Wales, founded in 1938, has played a much more significant role than the Eisteddfod in encouraging the professional artist. The other main show place for Welsh painters and sculpture in the 'fifties was the open exhibitions organised by the Welsh Committee of the Arts Council. All open exhibitions, however, have to have selectors and many of the more radical artists came to the conclusion that their work was constantly being misunderstood and undervalued. In 1956 a group of these artists formed themselves into the 56 Group, in order to provide opportunities to show their work, each member having an unquestioned right to space at the Group's exhibitions. The 56 Group has been markedly successful in drawing attention to the work of the most original artists working in Wales. As time went on their task became easier. Indeed by the mid-'sixties it seemed as though something of a revolution was taking place in the Welsh attitude to the visual arts. Exhibitions and the work of individual artists was being given extensive coverage by television, and the *Western Mail* for the first time found it worth while to employ a regular art critic. Abstract art ceased to be the subject of astonished incredulity. Some people were even prepared to buy contemporary paintings. During this period commercial art galleries sprang up in many places in Wales, and two of them, the Howard Roberts Gallery at Cardiff and the Dillwyn Gallery at Swansea, had adventurous policies and showed the most original work that was being done in Wales at that time. Unfortunately, however, Wales has just not got a sufficient number of sympathetic and affluent patrons to give lasting support to such ventures, and both galleries were ultimately forced to close. The best Welsh artists now look to the booming London art market as an outlet for their work. Thus Wales once again has become a distant province of the London art world, and within Wales the momentum of the 'sixties seems to have been lost. Even the impact of the 56 Group has diminished, and the National Eisteddfod Exhibition at Bangor in 1971, if it had not included Kyffin Williams's striking record of his visit to Patagonia, would have been the weakest since the early 'fifties. One is forced to the conclusion that the visual arts remain a minor activity in Wales, hardly impinging upon the consciousness of the nation.

It is difficult to explain this recurring apathy. There are today more opportunities to see original works of art than ever before. The art department of the National Musuem of Wales has as exciting a collection of pictures as can be seen anywhere in Britain outside London. The Welsh Arts Council has, over the years, organised exhibitions throughout Wales. (In 1968 the Council achieved a record number of thirty four exhibitions at forty one different centres resulting in one hundred and fifteen showings in all.) These exhibitions have often been of major historical importance. For example, the exhibition of *British Art and the Modern Movement* at the National Museum in 1962 brought together for the first time a number of the most significant works of the 'thirties, and *Art in Wales* at the Glynn Vivian Gallery at Swansea in 1964 surveyed four thousand years of art in Wales to A.D. 1850.

All this activity, however, has only reached a tiny fraction of the population. There was in any case during the latter part of the 'sixties a growing disenchantment amongst artists about the meaningfulness of the 'art object',— easel paintings or isolated pieces of sculpture. The colleges of art (including those in Wales) were in the vanguard of the new pop culture. This new view suggested that art must be taken out of the studio and into the world in order to create 'an environment activated by art'. The Welsh Arts Council responded to this new aesthetic and, spurred by the lack of suitable galleries in many parts of Wales, in 1967 initiated a 'poster project' whereby a group of artists were commissioned to design large posters that were hung on 250 regular advertisement sites all over Wales. Although this scheme received world wide notice, in retrospect, it seems an odd idea. It was after all rather pointless to hang what were essentially 'studio paintings' in the open air, especially as the artists who were commissioned turned out work that looked insipid side by side with the advertisements for beer and detergents created by experienced commercial artists.

This experience, however, convinced the Welsh Arts Council of the deficiencies of the traditional exhibition and, as a result, it developed a new policy which, not only recognised a variety of media including film, photography and television, but was also concerned with the use made of art and design by society. For example, the exhibition of toys *Play Orbit* organised in 1970 jointly by the Welsh Arts Council and the Institute of Contemporary Arts was, according to its creator Jasia Reichardt, 'an attempt to narrow the gap between objects as "works of art" and those other things which fill our environment, fulfil our spiritual needs, and which, often jor arbitrary reasons, don't have such elevated titles'. In order to explore further the art of the commonplace, the Council has organised a series of highly original and significant exhibitions on the themes of War, Work and Worship. These multi-media exhibitions include a wide variety of material ranging from well known examples of high art to picture postcards.

All this is, of course, in the well worn tradition of Ruskin and Morris that Owen M. Edwards so admired. It has a particular attraction for us in Wales, lacking as we do anything but the most tenuous tradition of high art. Even so one inevitably has the nagging fear that we may be fooling ourselves—rather like the contemporary pretence that the Beatles have the same value as Bach. We have to recognise that the heightening of a nation's visual sensibility can only be achieved after patient education over many generations. Here the signs are not very propitious. The University of Wales which, because it is a national institution, plays a uniquely significant role in the nation's life, has never been very aware of the visual arts and the University's constituent colleges have, in the post-war period, had development plans which display greater visual insensitivity than perhaps any university in Britain. The creation of

246

the University of Wales Institute of Science and Technology has, however, at last given the University a department of architecture. It is also true that the reformed colleges of art are beginning to have an impact on Welsh life, and there are certainly a greater number of well qualified teachers of art in Welsh schools than ever before. Even so, there is little evidence of experimentation in art teaching. The Welsh Committee of the Schools Council has not yet been presented with a single development project in the teaching of the visual arts. This is all the more sad as a massive and coordinated educational effort is needed at all stages of education if by the year 2000 the fine arts are to begin to play more than a negligible part in Welsh life, and the applied arts more than a rudimentary one. If we do not make this effort the direction 'For Wales—see England' will continue to apply to the visual arts.

SELECT BIBLIOGRAPHY

David Bell, *The Artist in Wales* (London, 1957).

T. S. R. Boase, *English Art 1800-1870* (Oxford, 1959).

W. G. Constable, *Richard Wilson* (London, 1953).

Colin A. Gresham, *Medieval Stone Carving in North Wales* (Cardiff, 1968).

Edward Mullins, *Joseph Herman* (London, 1967).

John Rothenstein, *Modern English Painters* Vol. 1 (1952), Vol. 2 (1956).

David Thompson, *Ceri Richards* (London, 1963).

J. R. Webster, *Ceri Richards* (Cardiff, 1961).

J. R. Webster, *Joseph Herman* (Cardiff, 1962).

Welsh Arts Council, *Art in Wales: a survey of 4000 years to A.D. 1850* (Cardiff, 1961).

INDEX